MW01602382

The Washington Compromise

Joseph Churba

University Press of America, Inc.
Lanham • New York • London

Library of Congress Cataloging-in-Publication Data

Churba, Joseph
The Washington compromise / by Dr. Joseph Churba.
p.   cm.
1. United States--Foreign relations--1945-1989. 2. United States--
Foreign relations--1989   I. Title.
E840.C497   1995   327.73'009'045--dc20   95-32019   CIP

ISBN 0-7618-0087-5 (cloth: alk: ppr.)

⊖™The paper used in this publication meets the minimum
requirements of American National Standard for Information
Sciences—Permanence of Paper for Printed Library Materials,
ANSI Z39.48—1984

*Dedicated to the memory of
Major General George J. Keegan (USAF)
for his scholarship, integrity, and courage.*

TABLE OF CONTENTS

Prologue.. i

1 A Crime of Principle 1

2 The University Years, Vietnam, and Meir Kahane 11

3 The Air Force Years: The Shock of "Intelligence".................. 19

4 The Yom Kippur War:
   Warning, Disaster, and the Kissinger Doctrine........................ 29

5 The General Brown Affair.. 41

6 Israel and the American Jewish Establishment........................ 47

7 The Reagan Campaign: Revolution to Betrayal, Act I........... 59

8 The Reagan Campaign: Revolution to Betrayal, Act II 73

9 Arms Control and Ferdinand Marcos 87

10 Lebanon Quagmire.. 93

11 The International Security Council 109

12 Trouble in America's Hemispheric Backyard........................ 117

13 Libya's Qaddafi: Confrontation and Dialogue 127

14 Highway (and By Roads) to China.. 145

15 China Meets China.. 157

16 Campaign 1988: The Affirmative Strategy 167

17 Grappling with the Big Bear 179

18 Wooing the Lion of Damascus 197

19 Iraq: The Key That Did Not Turn... 213

20 Poking the Pariah of the Pacific.. 223

21 A "Jerusalem" Compromise.. 243

22 An Intense Dialogue with the Russians 259

23 The End of the Cold War: A Final Accounting 283

24 A Longer Geostrategic View... 293

Conclusion.. 309

Index.. 315

PREFACE

As a chronicle of events spanning a quarter century and my interpretation of them, this political memoir is by its nature intensely subjective. For this I do not apologize, since by definition that is the nature of history.

Suffice it to say, that even when conforming to the accepted rules of historiography, such an enterprise is always hazardous. But for the exceptional few who also participate in the making of history even at its margin, evaluating developments is far more daunting because of the time factor. The temptation to revise and update developments is at least as great as the need to see their portent for the future. Even so, the emphasis has to be on the chronicle of events themselves. Accordingly, the challenge is to accentuate relevance by shading the more blatantly dated material and bringing out the more enduring. Equally important, conclusions must be broadened in an attempt to make them less contemporary and thereby less vulnerable to the next bow-waves.

In the preparation of this work, I owe a particular debt to two colleagues: to Walter Hahn for his discerning and judicious final editing; and to Sol W. Sanders whose patience and skill reduced a complex manuscript to structure and clarity. I wish to thank others, too, who were generous of their time, effort, and advice: Joel Carmichael for his rigorous scrutiny in editing the initial draft; Professor William Van Cleave for his sensitive political insights and unfailing encouragement; Robert Morton who has given ungrudgingly to the research and accuracy of my data; and Joel Gilbert and Carolyn Long for both their editing review and unstinting support in bringing this work to light. And for helping me with many of the tedious chores in preparing the manuscript for publication, I wish to thank my talented and loyal assistant, Mary Frye.

Joseph Churba
Washington, D. C.
May 1995

PROLOGUE

Several days after the inauguration of the first Reagan Administration, in January 1981, with echoes of celebration still in the air, I had my first encounter with the Washington Compromise.

At first blush the term Washington Compromise may come across as pedestrian, even redundant. Compromise, after all, is supposed to be the lifeblood –or is it the lubricant?– of democracy. Is not, therefore, Washington also the capital of political compromise?

True—if compromise is viewed as a fundamentally above-board process of political conversion toward decision-making. However, I have a different form of transaction in mind. The Washington Compromise, in my definition, denotes the surrender of principle in return for "capital currency." I refer, in other words, to a corruption of the democratic process.

What do I mean by "currency"? One can take the narrow definition of the word: Heaven knows there have been enough (indeed, ever more frequent) scandals in Washington involving financial corruption. One does not have to be an economic determinist, moreover, to acknowledge that many motives ultimately lead back to the economic one. As I will bring out later, an economic motive certainly was conspicuous behind the forces that ostracized me in the first Reagan Administration in 1981.

But my term embraces more: it entails principle surrendered in return for political advantage, bureaucratic edge, personal job security and advancement—in short, principle sold for the coinage that is subsumed under "power" as the main currency in the nation's capital.

"Principle" may be a controversial concept to some. Cynics suggest that, like beauty, principle is in the eyes of the beholder. They are contradicted by the legacy of centuries of theologians and moral philosophers who have given us a rather solid sense of what principle is all about—in other words, have taught us to distinguish right from wrong.

In the field of foreign policy, there is a more specific application of principle—call it the common, societal good, or the "national interest." A broader definition of the Washington Compromise then comes into focus: it involves forfeiture (deliberate or not) of the national interest for the sake of political and/or personal advantage.

Interestingly, in retrospect, there was a fairly widespread recognition of the equation of principle and national interest in the earlier years of America's immersion into world politics after World War II. It was reflected in the oft-repeated phrase that "politics stops at the water's edge"— that, in other words, there is a line of national security interests beyond which the process of compromising cannot proceed. It is significant that one no longer hears that phrase.

In its essence, the Washington Compromise also describes a process of appeasement—a process that works at several levels. At the level of policy-formulation in Washington, appeasement takes place on the bureaucratic and party-political battlegrounds. What often emerges from those battlefields is a foreign or defense policy that already represents, in effect, a "preemptive sacrifice" of national interest—i.e., appeasement—in dealings with adversaries at the international level.

A telling example of this process, which will also be touched on in the chapters that follow, relates to the U.S.-USSR negotiations on strategic nuclear arms during the "Kissinger years" (1969-1976). Henry Kissinger, came to Washington as an historian imbued with a Spenglerian view of history—i.e. a view of the relentless decline of the West— which he had expressed in numerous writings. This view was reinforced in the perception of Kissinger, the statesman.

As he revealed in interviews, he saw the harbingers of a U.S. retreat on the world stage—a U.S. "weariness to carry the burden"—in the reactions of the American populace to the Vietnam War. He viewed as his principal task as statesman, beyond extricating the United States from Vietnam, that of accomplishing as graceful an American accommodation as possible to the shifting tides of power in favor of the Soviet Union and other "power centers."

The Strategic Arms Limitation Talks (SALT) were conceived by Kissinger as the principal vehicle of such "graceful accommodation." They were designed essentially to apply a brake to an otherwise relentless Soviet thrust toward strategic nuclear superiority (even though Kissinger, in a famous expostulation, tried to minimize the significance of such superiority). In order to apply that brake, the U.S. was willing to render a whole host of concessions which, over time and in their totality, in effect amounted to acceptance of most of the Soviet terms in the negotiations.

Kissinger's predilections found a strong echo in large parts of the U.S. foreign policy establishment—the so-called "arms control constituency." Members of this "constituency," in and out of government, were distinguished by a disposition to look upon arms negotiations not from the vantage point of vital U.S. national interests threatened by an adversary, but in terms of a "global problem" to be solved in concert with the Soviet Union.

What thus emerged in SALT were U.S. policies of outright appeasement. And what may have applied the brakes to the Soviet thrust toward categorical and nuclear supremacy—and the emphasis is on "may"—was not Henry Kissinger or the (ultimately discredited) SALT treaties, but rather the collapse of the Soviet Union. It is doubly ironic, given his earlier policy assumptions, that Kissinger in his eulogy at former President Nixon's graveside in 1994 listed the collapse of the Soviet Union among the Nixon Administration's accomplishments.

The Washington Compromise also manifests itself in the disparity between political rhetoric and actual policy. The wider the margin of electoral victory, the greater the disparity. As mentioned, political pundits invoke the rationale that compromise is an integral part of the democratic process and, therefore, necessary. Here a distinction must be made between legitimate compromise and the cynical rationale for betraying the platform upon which political leaders are elected. Insofar as this practice is bipartisan, acceptance of this dual standard inevitably leads to wide swings in voter behavior, and the kind of popular revulsion we are now witnessing by the electorate. Indeed, as both major political parties are moving in the same direction, voter contempt for the democratic system itself is growing as our leadership redefines statesmanship. In reality, the advocates of Washington Compromise are the promoters of honest hypocrisy. However, in the end, democracy will not survive such "honesty."

In the case of President Ronald Reagan, whose electoral victory was based in large part on a broad consensus on national security imperatives that transcended partisan lines, his Washington Compromise was set in motion with the selection as his running mate of George Bush, the ultimate "pragmatist" who clearly aspired to political power without a clearly defined purpose. Reagan's Compromise continued through a failure, despite flamboyant promises, to redress the military equilibrium vis-a-vis the Soviet Union. Despite trillion-dollar spending on defense by the Reagan Administration, precious little was actually accomplished in the modernization of America's strategic nuclear forces. Indeed, his administration lacked a coherent strategy for defense. Notwithstanding all the billions invested in Reagan's pet project, the Strategic Defense Initiative (SDI), the blatant failure to realize the program's implementation underlined the Reagan Administration's bankruptcy in the defense arena, glaringly illuminating the gulf between what had been promised and what was actually delivered. In any event, the Reagan version of the Washington Compromise ended with the warm embrace of the regime of Mikhail Gorbachev and the latter's flawed *Glasnost* and *Perestroika* policies.

This book chronicles my twenty-five years of battles with the Washington Compromise in its various manifestations. Those battles more often than not relegated me to the role of outsider to the Washington Establishment, rejected by those who would disdain the vital strategic interests of the nation in favor of short-term political and/or personal advantage, shunned by others who believed that even a bad deal with an adversary was better than no deal at all, and looked at askance even by those who, while sharing basic principles and values of freedom, took refuge in illusions and wishful thinking. Most of the struggle unfortunately was waged with few allies by my side.

Still, this book is more than a tale of an immigrant's son who, possessing neither wealth nor the easy political access enjoyed by scions of the Establishment, challenges the powers-that-be. In many respects, what follows is intended as testimony to the significant role that an individual, by dint of ideas and force of conviction, can play in the foreign policy formulation process of a free and democratic society.

Born in New York City to Syrian Jewish immigrants, I had a multifaceted career as a Professor at the United States Air Force's Air University, Senior Middle East Intelligence Estimator for the U. S. Air Force, defense and foreign policy advisor to Presidential candidate Ronald Reagan, Senior Policy Advisor for the Arms Control and Disarmament Agency, and finally as President of the International Security

Council (ISC), an independent public policy institution based in Washington, D.C.

The following pages detail my past 25 years in government and political life. The cast-of-characters in the story includes such names as Ronald Reagan, George Bush, Colin Powell, Richard Allen, Henry Kissinger, Yitzhak Rabin, Meir Kahane, Muamar Qaddafi, Ferdinand Marcos and Stephan Solarz, among many others. The institutional roster embraces the KGB, the CIA, the Soviet General Staff, the Israeli General Staff, the American Jewish Establishment, and a host of other official and unofficial actors in the international arena.

From the start, I could have easily opted for the relatively untroubled and secure life of a government bureaucrat or college professor. Instead, I chose a challenging career that propelled me into crossfires of competing forces, including U. S. Government officials, intelligence operatives, communists, Arab governments, the PLO, and assorted anti-Semites. Sadly, neither the American government nor the leadership of the American Jewish community ever offered any real support. Indeed, it is ironic that at critical points they actually sought to undermine my efforts.

My battle with the Washington Compromise basically describes my life's work. After five books, hundreds of articles, and countless interviews and seminars on foreign policy, it remains my *raison d'etre*.

Perhaps it is an irony of timing, as well as another symptom of the passing of an era in international affairs, that—as this book is undergoing final preparation for publication—the International Security Council is ceasing its operations for lack of sufficient funding. The irony is underscored by what now turns out to be the final act in the life of that once vibrant organization, which I founded in 1984 and which figures prominently in the pages that follow.

On March 6 and 7, 1995, an event took place in Washington that, although scarcely noted by the press, could be considered on the order of a breakthrough in the complex and delicate evolution of a new relationship between the United States and the struggling democratic order in Russia—or at least, might have constituted such a breakthrough. The International Security Council capped some five years of close contacts and intense dialogue with the new actors on the Russian political stage—a dialogue that is detailed in this book—by sponsoring a meeting in Washington between prominent members of the Defense Committee of the Russian Duma, headed by Deputy Chairman Alexandr Piskunov, and their American counterparts in the National Defense Committee of the U.S. House of Representatives.

The meeting featured an unprecedented face-to-face exchange between legislators of the two nations on some of the issues pivotally bearing on the future of the American-Russian relationship and thereby the broader global scenario: matters relating to the ratification of the START II Treaty on strategic force reductions; the ominous problem of nuclear proliferation (with a focus on North Korea) and possible parameters of American-Russian cooperation in the defense against ballistic missiles; a potential eastward expansion of NATO; the embroglio in former Yugoslavia; and, finally, the likely course and ramifications of the bitter conflict in the Russian province of Chechnya.

The Russian and American legislators articulated disagreement on some of the issues, while converging toward agreement—or at least common grounds of understanding—on others. What both sides warmly agreed upon was the "eye-opener" function and more general utility of such a direct exchange between otherwise remote and preoccupied lawmakers, especially in an increasingly turbulent era marked by a general trend of shifting power from weakened and beleaguered national executives to legislatures. The hope was expressed that the dialogue thus begun may be sustained on a regular basis, but under continued private auspices (e.g. the International Security Council) that could avoid the clogged arteries and/or distortions of official channels. The Russians also saw in the exchange the broader promise of absorbing more directly the benefits of American legislative tradition and experience into their own fledgling legislative processes, especially on defense and national security issues. Unfortunately, with the closing of the ISC's doors, that promise augurs to be still-born.

On a much broader plane, unfortunately, the fundamental views and philosophy that the ISC reflected and purveyed continue to be validated by current events. I continue to be dismayed by the distorted prisms of our national interests, especially the chronic inability of the United States to create a coherent strategy for its defense. The problem is exacerbated by a failure of American leadership that has degenerated from mediocrity to ineptitude. In a post-Cold War international landscape that is increasingly complex and dangerous, the United States has yet to define and articulate its place and purpose in the world.

1

A Crime of Principle

I cannot separate my career from my origins in a God-fearing family and the Jewish community in Brooklyn, New York, where I grew up. My fundamental values and approach to political and social issues were strongly influenced by my father, especially the manner in which he coped with adversity. He was a deeply religious man whose character and conduct were shaped by devotion to Biblical scholarship. Part of his greatness lay in teaching his children to fight injustice without bitterness or vengeance, should that struggle fail, as it had failed for him. For the most part his children heeded that teaching, but memories of lost causes remain, as deep scars attest. Only as I grew older did I understand the gravity of the suffering inflicted upon my father by our "religious community."

Born in 1900 and raised in Aleppo, in today's Syria, my father came to the United States in his late twenties. His name was Raymond Churba; Rahamim was his Hebrew name. His passing in 1987 marked the end of a long line of unique scholars known as the Rabbis of Aleppo. They were revered for their high scholarship, piety and modesty. It is fitting that on the occasion of every anniversary of my father's death, Ovadia Yosef, Israel's former Chief Rabbi of the Sephardic Community and renowned Talmudic scholar, addresses select rabbis and students in Jerusalem.

In the United States, a scholar is considered to be one who does advanced studies and has a degree. There were no Rabbinical degrees in Aleppo, Syria. One became a rabbi not only by formal education, but also by approval of the community elders. Because Judaic knowledge was widespread, a rabbi in Aleppo had to distinguish himself among scholars on a daily basis in order to justify his rank. In many ways those tests were far more stringent than any formal education; this was a system far better in distinguishing the genuine from the charlatan. By this time-honored standard, my father was acknowledged even by his foremost detractors as the community's outstanding scholar on the Talmud (the textbook of Jewish law and commentary). Yet, this acknowledgement was a source of both admiration and envy, since the insecure lay leaders of the community feared superior standards as much as they were apprehensive of integrity of character.

The community of Aleppo, tracing its origins to the times of King David who conquered the area,[1] was for centuries a great center of Jewish learning and tradition. In all the great exchanges among rabbis—from Maimonides writing from Cairo, to an interpretation among the rabbis of Baghdad and Sephardic Spain—Aleppo played an important role. The earliest known record of the Bible—the Aleppo Codex—resided with the community until 1948, when it was partially destroyed in the course of mob violence against the Jews.

The great shift in world commerce through the Suez Canal in the mid-19th century, along with other events in the secular world, took its toll on the once prosperous Syrian community. The economic depression of the 1920s, which followed disruptions of World War I in the Levant, spurred a great Syrian Jewish migration to the United States. The pattern was a familiar one, which had applied also to other

Hacham (Rabbi) Rahamim Churba, 1900-1987.

waves of immigrants to the New World. However, while the Jewish immigrants from Europe—known in Hebrew as Ashkenazim—sought to sustain their religion and community ethos by building institutions to retain their values and traditions, the Syrian Jews tried to avoid assimilation through insularity. Regrettably, in both communities the inroads of assimilation, although different, have been deep.

---

[1] For those interested in the question of the oral tradition in history—which has proved, in the case of the Jews, to have been far more accurate than secular scholars would have believed—the legend of King David's conquest is upheld in the ancient acknowledgement of religious law (*halacha*) applying to Aleppo as it does in Jerusalem. Recent archaeological excavations at the traditional site of Dan have, for the first time, given evidence of "the House of David" outside Biblical references.

Mrs. Adele Churba with sons David (left), Sam, and daughter Rachel.

The Syrian Jews settled mostly in New York City. While clinging to religious customs, the community was—and remains—essentially clannish, anti-intellectual and material-istic in its outlook. To be sure, the merchant prince had been renowned as well in the eastern Mediterranean region (more so among Jews in Damascus than in Aleppo). In America, however, he became the role model for the community. How he acquired his wealth mattered little; only the fact of the wealth counted. Arts and the sciences were disparaged as professions, since they connoted values at variance with the commercial register. To succeed in the arts and sciences one had to assert an extra measure of individuality.

The Syrian Jews enjoyed the freedom afforded by their new country, but took little, if any, interest in the larger world around them. This attitude was a throwback to the clannish mentality they had brought with them from Syria. In particular, they had no real understanding of representative democracy. By contrast, the more numerous *Ashkenazim* contributed substantially to the arts, sciences and philanthropy of their haven country. Unlike the Jews from Arab lands, moreover, they maintained a higher sense of civic responsibility even as the bonds of religion were progressively discarded.

Enlightened members of the Aleppo community understood that tradition required the study of *Torah*, which was also the fault-line between rabbi and lay leader. Whereas my father put a premium on education and religious institutions, the unlettered but wealthy elite maintained control by minimizing religious education. This dominant elite—through collusion with a self-serving clergy—destroyed whatever promise there might have been for Talmudic scholarship among its American descendants of the once ancient and flourishing Aleppo community.

Remembering that the structure of the post-Temple synagogue is very loose, the *Ashkenazim* were right to call the synagogue in the Yiddish derivation of the German word for "school," a place of study. Mercifully, there is no religious hierarchy in Judaism. In the American Syrian Jewish community, power originates in a committee usually made up of the wealthy. They lead the congregation, usually in league with the "Chief Rabbi" who, in exchange for security in his position, makes the necessary accommodations with the lay leaders. The nominal Chief Rabbi, in my story, was particularly adept at role-playing. His much vaunted pretensions to

mystical teachings camouflaged the boastful claims to offici-
ating at thousands of marriages—for a fee.

In New York's Syrian community, the financial aspects
of family affairs and religious ceremonies, centered in the
synagogue, made the latter a source of great income. In time,
a clerical hierarchy evolved, and would-be rivals were systematically excluded. Moreover, competition was effectively
eliminated at the source; the leadership blocked potential
rivals by discouraging the establishment of educational institutions (Yeshivot) to train rabbis and teachers. Consequently,
American-born rabbis from the community still are few and
far between.

From time to time, courageous figures challenged this
state of affairs—only to beat a retreat. Any sustained challenge carried the real risk of informal excommunication. In
such a tight-knit community, in which family and commercial interests intertwined, religious values came last. For
practical merchants, dissent is easily overcome with compromise. But what of the dissenting Talmudic scholar? The serious call to reform threatens established authority. It was my
father's destiny to advocate change and the defense of religious principle, and mine to bear witness to his tragic struggle.

It was not long after settling into the Syrian neighborhood in Brooklyn in 1948 that I realized how different my
family was. The neighborhood was peopled by the affluent
who broke away to establish their exclusivity. My father took
his job as rabbi seriously, and endeavored to bring out the
best in the community. In this, his purpose was neither to
gain leverage nor to posture. He tried to hold the lay leadership true to religious and moral tradition remaining unim-
pressed with their acquired wealth. That was not what they
bargained for.

Money did not motivate this high-minded man. Still, he
was no fool when it came to practical matters. When he,

anticipating problems, was persuaded to take on his post as rabbi, a house was made available to him, purchased on his behalf by well-meaning donors. That same house was then, in a stealthy maneuver, "sold" to him, and at a much higher cost—with interest but without transfer of title to him. Mortgage payments were automatically subtracted from his salary without record or signature of consent.

My father quickly challenged this state of affairs, insisting upon his rights and delivery of the deed. The ugly matter escalated into confrontation with the community leaders, who threatened foreclosure of the mortgage. Finally, the district attorney resolved the issue (in an unofficial capacity) and, to avoid further scandal, mercifully swept it under the rug.

In the end, Rabbi Rahamim was ostracized for the "crime" of daring to invoke the civil law in the defense of his rights. My father demonstrated that acting on principle

Father and sons: Standing left to right Sam, Aaron, David, Isaac; Sitting Jack, Joe, Father, Moe and Albert.

leaves one vulnerable to being crushed. He could behave in no other way because he was a religious man.

The barbaric treatment meted out to my father taught me the high price that principled persons must be prepared to pay, in stark contrast with the "pragmatists" who make their accommodation with the powers-that-be for the sake of their own security. My father taught his children not to be afraid of the consequences of principled behavior. Above all, he taught by his example that becoming an "outsider" is an acceptable consequence of such behavior. Paradoxically, I always had a choice because I entered a professional field where I could opt for advancement at the expense of principle. For him, a man of religion, there was no such choice.

A recurring lesson was left to me: Principles meant little without the courage to uphold them. Still, the costs of upholding may be heavy. They must be calculated even when there is no choice.

My father resigned his pulpit, but matters did not end there. His refusal to be humbled "into line," along with the intervention of the district attorney, did not sit well with the pettily vindictive merchants of "Little Syria." Particularly objectionable was the intrusion of American civil law, since it nullified their self-arrogated authority. Consequently, the rabbi had to be ostracized, also as a warning to other would-be "revolutionaries." Shortly thereafter, my mother died of cancer.

Our community had the shell of outward identification with neither Jewish values nor the spirit of participation in American life. Ritual observance in the synagogue substituted for genuine religious commitment, while serving as a convenient escape from the need to confront one's sense of self-worth. Without the institutions to cultivate traditions and values, the community could not spiritually sustain itself, much less inspire the young to realize their full potential. The few Syrian Jews who pursued the professions, as I did, quickly found themselves outside the mainstream of community social life—isolated, ostracized and ridiculed.

Occasionally in later years I would meet a lawyer, doctor or scientist who hailed from the community. There was no question about the wide gulf that separated us from the business-dominated community. Indeed, it is a sad reflection that in more than a century the community managed to contribute precious few professionals in the arts and sciences to itself, let alone to the world-at-large. Even the few rabbis, teachers and cantors needed to sustain the synagogue had to be brought in from outside.

In seeking needed change and adaptation, my father emphasized the requirement for balance. He favored maintaining the community's ancient cultural roots and identity while participating in the wider world. He believed in both secular and religious education. In addition to studying the Torah, he wanted the young to attend graduate school. He loved America and its openness, believing that Judaism and freedom could coexist without friction. In the New World he fought communal rigidity, but in the end he became its victim.

I believe that what happened to my father was more than his personal tragedy, or a tragedy for myself and our family. With the events that followed the creation of Israel in the 1940s and the Israeli-Arab Wars of the 1960s, the 2500-year-old Aleppo Jewish community which had survived so many dramatic clashes in the Middle East was under siege, driven underground, and eventually dispersed. My father, the son of generations of rabbis, came out of its unique rabbinical tradition. He hoped that in the New World of freedom and culture he would keep that flame of Jewish learning alive. He hoped to found a yeshiva that would, in its own way, carry on the tradition of enlightened discourse with other centers of Jewish learning—just as Maimonides in the Middle Ages had consulted by correspondence from Toledo and Alexandria with the rabbis of Aleppo. And I believe that he had the knowledge and breadth of vision to begin to lay the foundations for that kind of institutional continuum. So when my father's role was destroyed in Brooklyn, it was also, alas, a loss for the Community and for all of Israel.

And so it was that my father, my eleven brothers and sisters and I were thrown back on whatever meager, uncertain resources we could muster for survival. The family pulled together to redeem the (inflated) mortgage on the house. Life went on, but outside the community framework. My father could not be barred from his seat in the synagogue, but to avoid encountering his detractors he attended only early morning services. The family was instructed not to be bitter or vengeful; we were not to confuse religion with the community's behavior. To me this was a request for angelic tolerance.

As an obedient son, I continued my studies at Brooklyn College and Beth Joseph Theological Seminary. Still, the bitter memories of my father's fate had the effect of strangling any residual notions I had of my own entry into the clergy.

The community experience of my youth—filled as it was with cruelty and duplicity—taught me more about Levantine psychology and cruelty than all of the books I was to read on the Middle East. Some stark memories remain in particular. In the last months of his life, my father was on a hospital life-support system. During those twenty weeks, not one member of the community, clergy included, visited him—or, for that matter, even inquired about his condition. His quiet interment in Jerusalem marked my final break with the community. I can condemn the community and its leaders on personal grounds; for the sin of their failure to respect the dying—especially a man of his stature, accomplishments and contributions—they will have to await Divine Judgment.

CHAPTER

2

The University Years, Vietnam, and Meir Kahane

In the 1950s, if you were of Jewish descent and attending an American college, you tended to mingle with those of your own religion, if only because of the pervasive anti-Semitism in those days. Matriculation at Brooklyn College brought a sharp change from my seminary experience. I was exposed more directly to liberal, often left-leaning Jews of European descent known as *Ashkenazim*. There was a rich assortment of political groups on campus, including assimilationists, Zionists, right wingers, Marxists, Communists and what-have-you—each group professing to have the solution to suffering humanity and bidding for my allegiance.

Brooklyn College had high academic standards. It was also a hive of Marxist activity. No day passed without political combat in the lecture halls or student cafeteria. Little did I suspect that such controversy would follow me for the next four decades. I had rejected the medieval cast of the Syrian Jewish community. Now I was pressed by new friends and colleagues to join the community founded by Karl Marx. I chose to stand alone.

VIETNAM FRUSTRATIONS

I graduated from Brooklyn College in 1957 with a degree in philosophy, while also attending Beth Joseph Theological Seminary. I continued my studies at Columbia

University and earned an M.A. in 1960. In 1965 I received a doctorate in international politics, law, and organization from Columbia University. My dissertation dealt with the rivalry between the United Arab Republic (Egypt) and Israel in sub-Saharan Africa.

Between 1965 and the summer of 1967, I worked as a consultant, researcher and lecturer at Adelphi University in Long Island, New York. I became involved in the great issue of the day: Vietnam. My main concern was that a Communist victory in Vietnam would make the Middle East the next flashpoint for a showdown between the two super-powers.

There were many different views of the conflict then. America faced what seemed to be a wave of Communist expansionism in Asia, which was widely seen in the context of a Sino-Soviet threat. We now know that U.S. intelligence grossly underestimated the Sino-Soviet rift. In effect, we were fighting China's war for dominance in the region over their erstwhile Russian Communist brothers. Spared this miscalculation, perhaps we might never have involved ourselves so deeply. As it turned out, the War—that is, America's defeat—in Southeast Asia did have the subsequent effect of maximizing Communist expansionist pressures on the Middle East, Africa and Afghanistan.

By the fall of 1967 I found myself teaching political science at the University of Winnipeg. What shunted me so far afield was utter disillusionment prompted by my lack of success in New York in increasing the public's understanding of the Vietnam War.

The first effort in that regard had been in May 1965, following my graduation from Columbia University. I helped launch a student organization called the "July 4th Movement." My collaborator was Meir Kahane, who was destined to become a controversial figure in Jewish life and about whom more will be said below.

Kahane and I co-authored a book entitled *The Jewish Stake in Vietnam*. Aside from the expansion of Communist influence in Asia, we were concerned that the "hawks" on the Middle East were "doves" on Vietnam.

In the broader setting, the "July 4th Movement" was to be a nonpartisan organization on college campuses favoring the American engagement in Vietnam. We planned to challenge the well-prepared, disciplined and organized leftist groups on the issues of freedom and Communist aggression. Jay Lovestone and Irving Brown, high officials of the International Department of the American Federation of Labor and Congress of Industrial Organizations, both veterans of many battles with Communists, supported our effort on behalf of the labor movement. Critics would later allege that I had close personal relationships with these two influential and controversial men. In fact, I barely knew either of them. I had encountered Irving Brown's son when he was a student. I was introduced to Lovestone, one of Stalin's few enemies who survived the early days of the Comintern, by a woman friend at Columbia University. We met occasionally, but our relationship was casual.

The "July 4th Movement" enjoyed initial success. We established a presence on the campuses of Columbia University, New York University, the City College and four or five Midwestern universities. There was much interest and support, but no funds were forthcoming. The organization collapsed after several months. The experience taught me an enduring lesson for later fund-raising efforts: Those who speak the loudest tend to contribute the least!

Meanwhile, I contracted with a publisher, Information Inc., to write a book that would profile the Viet Cong and show that the war in South Vietnam was not a civil war but one promoted and directed by Hanoi. I intended to document how the Viet Cong employed terrorism systematically to achieve the ends of their political strategy. Additionally, I planned to produce a television documentary on Vietnam based on captured footage.

Those two projects took me to Vietnam in April 1966, where I searched through government archives and met with various Vietnamese and American military officials. They included the Vietnamese Minister of Information, who agreed to release captured footage to me. He also arranged for my production costs to be reimbursed in Washington by the Vietnamese Embassy to the United States.

Upon my return to the United States, I suffered two disappointments. First, the publisher reneged on our book deal, citing the shifts in the fortunes of the war and the mood of the American public. Next, when I sought the promised production money from the Vietnamese Embassy, I was put off. I concluded that Saigon had also had a change of heart, but I would discover the truth several years later.

Meanwhile, with both of my projects frustrated, I gave up on the cause of promoting understanding of the Vietnam engagement and asked Columbia University's Placement Office for an academic posting. An opening was available at Winnipeg University in Canada. How appropriate I thought: The deep freeze of the Canadian prairies was just the place to cool off. And it was the coldest winter of my life!

After several months in Winnipeg, I was contacted by Dr. Woodford Heflin, who three years earlier had talked to me about joining the U.S. Air Force's Air University at Maxwell Air Force Base in Montgomery, Alabama, as Professor of Middle East Studies. "Woody," a Rhodes Scholar, was the Air Force lexicographer who compiled the Air Force dictionary. He again asked if I would be interested.

By then, my previous disgust and frustrations had waned under the Winnipeg frost. "The Vietnam syndrome"—as so many things connected with that unfortunate part of our contemporary history have been labeled—led me on the first step of my pilgrimage through the corridors of policy and power.

I flew to Montgomery in May 1968, and began my career in government. Recognition and promotions came quickly. For the next four-and-a-half years, I lectured at the Air War College, Command and Staff College, Squadron Officers School, and the Counter-Insurgency School at Eglin Air Force Base in Florida. This also proved to be a very fertile period in academic research and writing—perhaps the most productive I ever enjoyed.

During my time in Montgomery, my previous Vietnam puzzle gradually came into focus. I learned that money for the proposed documentary film had, in fact, been given to the Vietnamese Embassy in Washington, D.C. That it was not passed on to me conformed to a larger pattern of corruption that led, at least in part, to the fall of Saigon. Some years later, William Mazzocco, a friend and colleague who had been an AID (Agency for International Development) official, told me that the Vietnamese ambassador who withheld the money from me had been appointed to Washington, notwithstanding his known previous mishandling of U.S. aid funds. With friends like those, who needed enemies?

MEIR KAHANE—
BOYHOOD FRIENDS BUT DIFFERENT PATHS

Mention was made earlier of my association with Meir Kahane. Actually our relationship went back to our boyhood on the streets of Brooklyn, a boyhood filled with adventures among the rough-and-tough of an immigrant neighborhood. Kahane and I, almost alone among our friends, organized fellow Jewish students during our neighborhood's constant turf battles among the various ethnic groups. In a sense, we epitomized part of the duality of the Brooklyn Jewish community: he, a scion of a traditional *Ashkenazi* family, and I, the descendant of a long line of *Sephardic* rabbis.

But Kahane and I, prior to his organization of the Jewish Defense League and his more flamboyant departures into Israeli and American politics, had yet another bond: a common view of the American Jewish establishment and its relationship to the State of Israel. We believed that the American Jewish establishment was far more concerned with the threat of domestic anti-Semitism than with the security of the Jewish state.

Through charisma and oratory Kahane excited the fear of survival among a minority of American Jewish youth and thus was perceived as a threat to the American Jewish establishment leadership. No other Jewish leader aroused this wellspring of Jewish survival as effectively as he did. This gift stood in stark contrast to Kahane's flawed contention that democracy was incompatible with a Jewish state. That position stemmed from his belief that Arabs eventually would outpopulate Jews in Israel, dominate the Knesset (Parliament), and control the Jewish state. In the early days of our acquaintanceship, this subject never arose, perhaps because his whole lifeview was still forming and such dilemmas were beyond his concern at that moment. I did not share Kahane's estimates regarding the threat to Israel or the Jewish people at large. I did agree with some of his analyses, but definitely not with his overall conclusions.

My interpretation of Jewish religious teaching makes the question of some form of democratic government absolutely essential in Israel. While the precise forms of a democratic state can always be argued about in terms of their relationship to the cultural norms of the given society, every moral precept in the Prophets is a call to a democratic society as we define those terms today. Essentially, the Kahane thesis is vulgar Malthusianism. Skilled historians know the danger of projecting on the basis of existing evidence or current conditions; and nowhere have the amateur prophets been more wrong than in their extrapolations on fertility, obviously one of the most mysterious of all human conditions.[1] In any event, the West Bank population has not kept pace with the growth of the Jewish population and there has been a constant voluntary emigration of the West Bank Arab population for greater opportunities in the Gulf and the West.

I had no contact with Kahane or any of his activities after 1967. This was before the Jewish Defense League (JDL) was founded. My break with Kahane centered on his character and dogmatic outlook: neither was an appealing basis for a professional relationship. Even though we had been good friends during our youth, there were sound reasons for striking a distance. His true character emerged as he became increasingly political. I wanted no part of such a friendship. Most certainly, I could not risk identification with him while serving as a civil servant and later an intelligence estimator. As it was, he became baggage that followed me over the years as many of those who disagreed with me often referred to my earlier association with Kahane in an effort to discredit me.

Thus, PLO, Libyan, Communist, and anti-Semitic tracts have persisted in identifying me with Kahane's work. I have

---

[1] I am old enough to remember *revanche de la creche* (revenge of the cradle), a slogan of the French Canadian nationalists only a half century ago. Today Quebec has the lowest birthrate in North America with, seemingly, little hope that the French Canadian population will continue to exist in the 21st century, much less overwhelm the English-speakers in a Canadian confederation—if, indeed, that state continues to exist in its present union of French and English-speakers.

been struck by how many observers of the Jewish scene, wittingly or not, have joined that disinformation campaign. I have also been portrayed—at different times and sometimes simultaneously—as a confidence man, coward, FBI informant, CIA operative, co-founder of the Jewish Defense League, and Mossad agent. These long-standing assaults on my character, waged from both outside and inside the U.S. government, have been designed to discredit my good family name while stripping me of credibility as a specialist in Middle East affairs. I have regarded the assaults as another price one pays for principle and integrity; as such, I have ignored them.

But back to Kahane: as he became more assertive and militant, I saw less reason to reconcile or even exchange views with him. He was polarizing Israeli public opinion at a time when unity was required. Moreover, I thought his confrontational tactics were perilously wrong, for they risked tearing the fabric of relations between the United States and Israel.

Only once since 1968 did I come close to contact again with Kahane. I was on a shuttle flight from New York City to Washington, D.C. Kahane boarded and dropped his carry-on bag practically at my feet. While bending to pick it up, he searched for a seat ahead of him and did not look my way.

The Kahane story is all the more tragic because I deemed him able, even brilliant. With more restraint—and tolerance—he might have achieved great things for himself and for Israel. In November 1989 he became the first victim of Islamic fundamentalist terrorism on American soil. He will not be the last.

CHAPTER
3

The Air Force Years: The Shock of "Intelligence"

From May 1968 until December 1972, I served as Air University's resident Middle East scholar. As I have already suggested, those were very productive years: I did research and analysis, conducted seminars and lectured widely. More generally, I gained experience which proved invaluable for the next phases of my career.

In late 1971, I attended a conference in Tel Aviv on the Soviet Union and the Middle East sponsored by Tel Aviv University. Noted academic luminaries on these subjects who participated in the five-day confab included P.J. Vatikiotis, Hans Morgenthau, Richard Pipes, Bernard Lewis, Elie Kedouri, J. C. Hurewitz, among others. While the meeting consisted mostly of academicians, some Israeli officials and military officers attended, including then-Defense Minister Moshe Dayan.

It was an illuminating experience because I learned how divided the academic community was on Russian intentions and behavior. A diversity of opinion was expressed, most of it speculative. I held strong views of Russian intentions and expressed the firm judgment that Soviet strategy was to neutralize the U.S. Sixth Fleet and more generally outflank U.S. and NATO forces in the Mediterranean; after thus blunting Western military power, the Soviets would be freer to give their attention to the challenge of China. What really surprised and puzzled me was that I seemed to have a broader and more confident grasp of the situation than most of the bright academic luminaries assembled—men I had much admired from afar. Even more disturbing in that respect was Dayan. He sat there in patent confusion admitting that he had no real understanding of Russia's intentions and objectives.

It turned out that I was the only American government official among the conference participants. My comments about Moscow's strategic imperatives—to outflank NATO and the Sixth Fleet, to enhance their overall options in the Third World, and to buy time before the Chinese nuclear threat matured—made their way into *The Jerusalem Post*. The report traveled to Washington and caught the eye of Air Force Maj. Gen. George J. Keegan, head of U. S. Air Force Intelligence.

In December 1972 General Keegan brought me to the Pentagon as his Middle East intelligence estimator. I became the working representative for the Air Force in deliberations of the national intelligence estimates (NIEs). Those estimates are designed to serve high-level officials in the formulation of general policy.

Going into government, I was under no strong illusion about the internal workings of the system. Still, I was unprepared for the shocking reality of the policy-formulation process. The very first NIE to which I was assigned the day after my arrival on the job was on "The Energy Crisis." I was given the draft to read and told to participate in the deliberations at CIA Headquarters. The following day, I took my place at the table with representatives of the other intelligence agencies—the Army, Navy, Defense Intelligence Agency (DIA), National Security Agency (NSA), and CIA. My curiosity was aroused by many people in the room wearing visitor badges on their lapels. Upon inquiring, I was told that they were representatives from the oil companies. They were more numerous than the official participants at the table! The "visitors" made no comments, but at one point in the proceedings the CIA distributed production and consumption figures on oil. I asked the Agency representative about the source of the statistics. They came from the Petroleum Institute, he replied.

I asked, "Do you not have your own database on consumption and production?"

"No, we don't," he admitted.

Here was blatant evidence of an incestuous relationship between the CIA and the oil companies! The oil firms were allowed to provide crucial data, and to oversee the members of the intelligence community in the performance of their estimating task. Invariably the estimates that emerged were in concord with the prevalent interests and views of the oil industry. That was my introduction to independent U.S. government policy formulation!

For four years afterward I participated in the formulation of national intelligence estimates. In those years many dissenting footnotes were tabled by Air Force Intelligence in contraposition to the other participants, particularly the State Department, DIA, and the CIA. If ever an analysis is undertaken of the estimates during that period, General Keegan's courageous dissents from much of what was then accepted as conventional wisdom will stand out.

Unhappily, the NIEs serve Presidents and the Congress poorly. Their basic weakness has stemmed from CIA dominance of the process at the expense of the other intelligence bodies. The bureaucratic motivation is simple: With no competition, the estimates are unchallengeable. This "protectionism" has rendered the majority of the estimates useless. Judgments are hedged in such a way that responsibility cannot be fixed. Since no penalties are imposed for being proven wrong, the estimators are free to ignore evidence that challenges the conventional wisdom, particularly if the latter reflects the "policy mindset" at higher levels.

In this way, evidence in the early 1970s that Moscow had mobilized vast resources to build, fight and win a nuclear war was dismissed. After all, the conventional wisdom manufactured in the CIA held that the USSR was running out of oil for its rapidly expanding economy, and Moscow's concentration on nuclear development was thus explained away as an effort to enhance energy sources.

Only once was the CIA challenged and forced into substantial debate. In 1976, President Ford—at the urging of Leo Cherne, an "amateur" but member of the President's Foreign Intelligence Review Board (PFIRB)—convened a team of outside experts which became known as the "B Team." They were given full access to classified data in order to draw their own conclusions. The CIA team had to concede finally that the B Team was correct in its much more daunting estimate of Soviet strategic-nuclear capabilities. Since then, no competing outside analysts have been admitted into the splendid building in Langley, Va.

But if official estimates of Soviet strategic capabilities and intentions were consistently mistaken, the record was even worse with respect to the Middle East. There was a consistent failure to assess the magnitude of Soviet involvement in Middle East politics, diplomacy and conflict. The record is one of chronic understatement and miscalculation of the extent of both Soviet capabilities and interest in attempting to control Middle East oil flows, in strategic inroads in the form of military base rights, in direct involvement in hostilities and in obstruction of the diplomatic process.

American estimates fell far short of a rational understanding of the Soviet role in political processes underway in the region. In a variety of subtle and self-deceiving ways, analysts went to great pains to paint a magnified picture of problems confronting Soviet policymakers and allegedly dictating caution, restraint and responsible behavior in Moscow. Never was the Arab-Israel conflict understood correctly as a growing fissure in the foundation of world politics, and thereby as the prime arena for Moscow's challenge to the global balance of power. At critical junctures Soviet objectives, policies and intentions were perceived either as opportunistic or speculative, rather than as parts of an aggressive, unrelenting campaign entailing the investment of major resources and prestige, along with the deliberate assumption of high risks. Nor, of course, was there any grasp of how the regional conflict fitted into the strategic map of the globe and the U.S.-Soviet confrontation.

My participation in the process was that of a mouse in the cheese pantry to the generally pro-Arab officials in the Pentagon and the State Department, who from almost Day One of my arrival sought my ouster. My very presence was an affront: Here was a senior intelligence analyst on the Middle East for the Air Force who was a Jew—worse still, a believer in his faith. More aggravating to them was that my views of events were buttressed by data and logical concepts. Progressively, General Keegan was besieged by requests, and then demands, that I be removed from the process, not because of incompetence or lack of scholarship but precisely because of the reverse.

Keegan later told me: "At the outset, the State Department shared my positive impressions of you." After a few meetings, however, in which I represented the Air Force in general and Keegan in particular, they changed their tune. Keegan said they now considered me "belligerent." The real problem, Keegan agreed, was their intolerance of my "schol-

Major General George J. Keegan (USAF) Chief, Air Force Intelligence, 1972-1977.

arship and competence." Without intending to do so, I came to dominate many of the discussions, but Keegan did not admonish me to be silent.

My involvement often seemed to prove embarrassing to my counterparts in the other services' intelligence agencies that held working level sessions at CIA headquarters under the chairmanship of the National Intelligence Officer. There were several such working level discussions every month, depending on the issue. Whenever the Secretary of State or the President ordered an estimate, someone would prepare a draft. We would then huddle over it, not disbanding until we had achieved a consensus. The NIE would then be passed to the Board of National Estimates (BNE), which was a body comprising the heads of the United States intelligence services, including the Army, Navy, Air Force, CIA, FBI, and NSA. They would oversee and rule on the estimates before passing them on to the President. As Director of Central Intelligence, (DCI), George Bush was the Chairman of the BNE in 1972.

I often participated in the estimates of Soviet military capabilities as well. I became increasingly frustrated in my dealings with these bureaucrats, none of whom had my educational background and training. Through it all, I stuck to logic, data and conviction, refusing to "run with the pack." More often than not, I succeeded in forcing some changes in a given draft, but I also was forced frequently to register dissenting footnotes when unable to alter mistakes and poor assumptions. Keegan was pleased, averring that my willingness to stick to my guns was precisely why he had chosen me. Sometimes we attended BNE meetings together.

Air Force Intelligence clashed with George Bush regarding provisions of the SALT agreement on technical matters where we had special competence. An example was the issue of whether the Soviet Backfire Bomber was a strategic or a theater weapon, and whether it was long-range or intermediate-range. In order to gain a SALT agreement, Kissinger had purposely downgraded this strategic weapon (which could carry nuclear arms) to a lesser role as a tactical weapon, despite our having identified the Backfire as a crucial issue in the negotiations. For defending my (and the Air Force's) ground on this issue—and as a skeptic of U.S.-Soviet detente more generally—I was marked by my bureaucrat colleagues as a barrier to progress.

It was an immensely demanding job. I spent thousands of hours reading reports and cable traffic. My greatest frustration concerned the "politicization" of the estimates process. The CIA was lord of the roost; in what was supposed to be a give-and-take process, they preferred neither to give nor to take. The CIA officials barely tolerated expressions of dissent or correction from other intelligence agencies, whom they sought to reduce to rubber stamps.

At stake was more than just wordsmithing. The intelligence estimate loses its value if judgments are not clear, depriving the policymaker of direction. By obfuscating the judgment, the purpose of the exercise is negated. The "judgments" that emerge then are merely the globs of Washington Compromise—a muddled expression of the party-lines and proprietary notions of the agencies involved rather than of the ideas and issues under discussion.

During Henry Kissinger's successive tenures as National Security Adviser to the President and Secretary of State, the estimates process became all the more politicized as a consequence of his effort to get rid of the "hardliners." One of his victims was James Angleton, the old curmudgeon who headed CIA's counterintelligence and who through personal experience shared my concept of Israel's strategic value. From Kissinger's point of view Angleton had three liabilities: He was a hardliner on the Soviets, opposed to detente and critical of the arms control process; he was the strongest advocate of a tight U.S.-Israeli relationship in the intelligence community; and he was convinced that a mole—a secret double-agent reporting to the Soviets—was burrowing somewhere in the U. S. intelligence community. Kissinger and the bureaucracy determined that Angleton had to go, and with him those who shared his viewpoints. With his departure, the process of homogenizing the NIEs in support of Kissinger's detente policies was eased.

Like Angleton, Keegan was a man of extraordinary courage and integrity, who challenged Kissinger's policy toward the Soviet Union. Although he managed to survive for five years as head of Air Force intelligence, his "sins" would cost him his third star.

My dealings with Kissinger were indirect and related to NIEs formulation. No Secretary of State manipulated the NIEs process more than he. Keegan told me that after Kissinger's arrival, "We had a lot of arguments with the State Department people. Kissinger took exception to some of the Air Force contributions. As time went on it became impossible to negotiate with him, so we terminated our weekly meetings with State."

Keegan said that Kissinger usually got his way with the intelligence community by tightly controlling the agenda at meetings. CIA Director William Colby, according to Keegan, usually was reluctant to act because he disliked dealing with Kissinger. Kissinger went to the extent of whitewashing the Soviet nuclear threat of October 1973 as it related to the Middle East crisis. That was a monumental obfuscation because the Soviets threatened to introduce nuclear weapons in a conflict not involving the defense of their homeland for the first time since the Cuban missiles crisis of 1962. The Soviets introduced that threat at the height of the fighting to prevent the collapse of Egypt and Syria, and it remained a consideration throughout the war. So serious was the threat that the U. S. forces were put on Defcon 4 alert—the first step toward war with the Soviets.

4

The Yom Kippur War: Warning, Disaster, and the Kissinger Doctrine

It was from my privileged vantage point in Air Force Intelligence that I also observed the 1973 Arab-Israeli conflict—some details of which I am still not at liberty to discuss.

I was very much involved with the incoming reports on the crisis and in their assessment.

Perhaps "privileged" is not the right word because mine was also a vantage point of utter frustration. The low point came after the crisis was resolved and the Soviets had been turned back in their attempt to introduce nuclear weapons into Egypt. Henry Kissinger subsequently schemed to discredit all references to the latter episode, claiming that the reports of Soviet nuclear moves were "exaggerated." In fact, we received a directive from him which was, in effect, an order to misrepresent the entire affair to the American public and world media!

This demonstrated just how far Kissinger was willing to go in sacrificing historical truth—along with the vital interests of America's friends and allies—in order to justify his own policies-in particular, the cornerstone of "detente" with the Soviet Union. On the eve of the 1973 War, Kissinger demanded Israel not preempt the Egyptians, even in the face of certain knowledge of impending Egyptian attack. It was he who was responsible during the war for the withholding of American arms replenishments to Israel; his obvious intent was thus to force Jerusalem into peace negotiations. And it was Kissinger who later followed this up with the famous 1975 reassessment of U.S.-Israel relations which pointed the finger at Israel as intransigent in the so-called peace process. These are historical facts and not my conjecture.

Kissinger epitomizes the modern version of "the court Jew" of medieval times—the Jew whose presence in the royal court was tolerated so long as he behaved and paid his dues. In Kissinger's case, the dues he paid were largely in Israeli coinage.

A CASE OF TRAGICALLY UNHEEDED WARNING

My own futile attempt at warning of the threat of the Yom Kippur War in 1973 is a sad but probably typical example of the pitfalls of intelligence and the warning process. On the day war broke out, Israeli Prime Minister Golda Meir telephoned Kissinger, waking him, and told him that war was imminent. Kissinger all but ordered her not to preempt Egypt's attack. Dreading being labeled the aggressor, she complied. Three times she refused Israeli Air Force Chief Benny Peled's request to launch a preemptive strike. So confident were the Israelis of a "second-strike capability," they agreed to absorb the first blow. This acquiescence cost them dearly in human life—and very nearly their political extinction.

Earlier, in September 1973, fearing that war was imminent, I had sought General Keegan's permission to go to Israel and examine the situation on the ground. He denied my request, saying I was in too much trouble as it was. Still, there had been a war scare in May and I was deeply anxious about developments. The Egyptians, to be sure, were talking about "economic development" and not displaying warlike behavior. We would later learn this was part of a deliberate plan of deception leading up to strategic surprise. The tactic fooled many people at the time. But I noted that, at the same

Henry Kissinger, Secretary of State, Washington, D.C., 5/15/75. Henry Kissinger listens as President Ford explains options in the Mayaquez incident during National Security Council Meeting. (Consolidated News Pictures)

time, the Russians were stepping up arms deliveries to both Egypt and Syria. In March and April, the Egyptians were receiving medium-range surface-to-surface SCUD B launchers, whose missiles could reach Israeli populations centers. By using this substitute for a medium-range bomber force, the Egyptians calculated that they could deter deep penetration raids by the Israelis. Egypt was poised for a major war.

At the same time Syria began receiving Soviet FROG surface-to-surface missiles, similarly capable of hitting targets in Israel. Moreover, in July and August, Moscow rushed delivery of a surface-to-air missile system which they deemed capable of eliminating Israeli air superiority. The Soviets intended to use SCUDs and FROGs to deter Israeli deep penetration raids while neutralizing Israel's Air Force.

The war setting was furthered by the development, since 1972, of a network among Egypt, Syria and Saudi Arabia that amounted to a military alliance. Sadat later revealed that the war had been planned for May, but delayed due to the projected second Brezhnev-Nixon Summit. The "Basic Principles" agreement adopted at the first summit led U.S. intelligence estimators and policymakers to believe that the Soviet embrace of detente precluded the possibility that the various moves of 1973 pointed to war.

In September 1973, I took leave without pay and flew to London, where I polled the Middle East experts I respected: Bernard Lewis, Elie Kedouri and P.J. Vatikiotis, all at the University of London. None of them shared my fears. From there I proceeded to Israel and met with General Aharon Yariv, who had retired as Director of Military Intelligence in July of that year and now headed the Jaffee Strategic Studies Center in Tel Aviv. He was skeptical of my analysis and inclined to reject it, but offered to introduce me to his successor at Israeli Military Intelligence. I declined, because meeting an official of the Israeli intelligence organization would have exceeded my authority and given my "private investigation" an official cast.

In any case, it was apparent to me that the Israelis were convinced, notwithstanding evidence to the contrary, that war was not a credible option for the Arabs. I cut my trip short and returned home, believing even more strongly in the imminence of conflict. No one had persuaded me otherwise and the cock-sure manner of the Israelis disgusted me. Egypt attacked on October 4, 1973. Absent American policies and Israeli accommodation in September 1970, the aggression might never have been launched.

Before the war, Israel was certain that the Egyptians could not cross the canal because of their inferior air power. For this very reason, Israel had fought an air war over the Suez Canal in 1969-1970—to deny the Egyptian-Soviet attempt to move their SAM missile belt to the waterway, which would have enabled a crossing by ground forces. Clearly, at that time, Egypt considered such a forward-deployed missile belt a substitute for the air superiority necessary to effect a cross-Canal invasion. In August 1970, the United States sponsored an Israeli-Egyptian truce, according to which Egypt agreed not to advance its Soviet missiles to the Canal. On the night of the signing of the truce, Egypt, in brazen defiance of the agreement, moved the missiles forward to the Canal. Through one deceptive stroke of a pen, the Egyptians achieved what they had been unable to attain in nine months of air combat. Israel protested to the United States but made no move against the missiles in their now threatening locations. By the time Washington verified the Israeli charge, the tactical balance had tilted in Egypt's favor. As compensation, Kissinger provided Israel with a $100 million Electronic Countermeasures (ECM) package. The illegal missiles remained deployed.

Three years later, that missile defense belt on the Canal allowed the Egyptians to neutralize the Israeli Air Force and facilitated a Canal crossing by ground troops. Israel had seemingly forgotten that Egypt had the missiles in place. In two days, Egypt shot down 80 Israeli Phantoms. Kissinger's acquiescence and deal for an ECM system cost Israel their first line of pilots in the first days of the war. Once across the Canal, the Egyptians dug in, precisely as the Soviets had trained them to do.

THE WASHINGTON COMPROMISE AND ISRAEL

Unfortunately for the Israelis, they did not really take to heart their own bitter lesson of how the Washington Compromise works. Throughout the next twenty years, they would continue to trade long-term security interests for short term compensation, mostly from the United States. Notable in that category was the promise held out by President Carter to the Israelis in order to secure their withdrawal from Sinai in 1978.

Amidst the considerable speculation and controversy surrounding the Camp David Accords in 1978, the Foreign Relations and Security Committee of the Israeli Knesset, then under the chairmanship of Moshe Arens, invited retired General Keegan to testify on Israel's Sinai withdrawal as part of the ratification process. Keegan agreed, provided that I accompany him and that we both would depart Israel before President Carter arrived to close the ratification process. It was a measure of Keegan's sense of correctness and integrity not to be seen undercutting his Commander-in-Chief's efforts on foreign soil. The cost of our voyage was covered by William J. Levitt, the well-known American housing and construction magnate who had a major financial investment in the Sinai oil fields.

Rather than perform an unprecedented act of Americans "testifying" in a foreign parliament, we agreed to an informal exchange with the full committee. Although our views were generally known, we did present a formal paper setting forth our negative views on Israel's projected Sinai withdrawal. For the most part, we argued that it was not the proposed treaty that would neutralize Egypt or take it out of the existing Arab war coalition, but rather the memory of Israel's breaking of the Egyptian offensive on the fifth day of the 1973 Yom Kippur War. We were not at all sanguine that a positive peace would follow along the lines expected by Israel. It was ironic that General Keegan and I were in the position of advising the Israeli Parliament not to accept the proposed U.S. Government-led peace accord, in the form in which it was being presented.

The episode before Israel's Parliament did have a humorous aspect. Israel's Minister of Religion, Mr. Warhaftig, suddenly awoke from a state of semi-slumber to deliver a tirade against U.S. policy, demanding an explanation for our pressuring Israel to accept the peace accord. It was clear that he did not understand the nature of our presence, which was exactly the opposite. After delivering his broadside, he promptly resumed his dozing. I was told subsequently that Warhaftig voted for the Camp David Accords.

In the case of the Camp David Accords, Jimmy Carter sweetened the pill of the Washington Compromise with handsome financial incentives to the Israelis. The more general pattern of Compromise set during the Yom Kippur War—American "assistance" in return for Israel's "restraint" in the exercise of its legitimate security interests—continued through the 1980s. The Compromise was blatantly demonstrated during the Persian Gulf War, when Israel accepted essentially impotent and useless American Patriot missile batteries in lieu of directly retaliating against Iraq for the latter's SCUD attacks against Israeli population centers.

Meanwhile, my rage at the needless disaster of the Yom Kippur War was overshadowed only by a sense of tragedy and frustration. It did teach me a hard lesson about trusting my own analytical conclusions based on personal examination of the information available. In the future I would rely on them even if it meant taking an independent position against great odds. It also entailed a basic professional decision: torn between advancing my career by becoming a political "team-player" or remaining true to my integrity as an analyst, I chose the latter. Let the chips fall where they may.

THE LONGER REACH OF THE "KISSINGER DOCTRINE"

As it happened, I experienced another somewhat accidental bridge between the Yom Kippur and Gulf Wars. It occurred in 1976 at the National War College (NWC), that prestigious military institution in Washington which every year offers a nine-months course of graduate-level studies for distinguished U.S. military officers considered "comers" in their respective services. Every year also one civilian official is selected for the course from each of the military services. I was among the privileged in 1976.

Many of my fellow students in the "Bicentennial Class of '76" went on to notable careers. In retrospect, two stand out. One was P.X. Kelly, destined to rise to Commandant of the Marine Corps. The other was an Army officer named Colin Powell, who was to achieve enduring fame as Chairman of the Joint Chiefs of Staff during the Gulf War. Again in hindsight, what makes Powell's stint at the War College remarkable in my memory is its lack of remarkability. Powell made himself inconspicuous during the course, rarely commenting or even raising questions of lecturers. Perhaps, as an ambitious career officer, it was his way of "playing it safe."

Did he also "play it safe" as a commander in the Persian Gulf War? What is not commonly known is that General Powell came perilously close to failing in that conflict. The Joint Chiefs had advocated an air, land, and sea attack strategy which, if implemented, might have resulted in enormous casualties. It was Sir Peter de la Billiere, commander of British forces in the Gulf with extensive experience in desert warfare, who objected initially to a frontal assault, as did other commanders.

Fortunately, General H. Norman Schwarzkopf's bold flanking strategy was pursued and Desert Storm became a quick military success. However, Powell's inexplicable advice to President Bush to prematurely halt the successful offensive allowed Saddam Hussein to recoup his falling fortunes and to sustain himself in power.

Powell is not entirely to blame. Already at the War College, war-winning strategies were not high on the agenda. Instead, the emphasis was on crisis management, budget analysis and administration. In fact, if a military theme were propagated, it was, in effect, how to avoid a decisive victory. This defeatist theory was the prominent legacy of Henry Kissinger.

Kissinger couched his theory in a larger "world view". The cornerstone of the Kissinger conception was a "system of power balances" modeled after Count Metternich's "Concert of Europe," which had sustained a relative peace on the continent through much of the 19th Century (and which had been the subject of Kissinger's doctoral dissertation at Harvard University). Kissinger theorized that, for the sake of a new balance, the USSR should be allowed to achieve strategic parity with the U.S.—assuming, of course, that the Soviet Union wanted peace as Kissinger defined it. Parity was to be the key to detente. The Russians gratefully accepted the principle of strategic-nuclear parity, but carefully turned it into Soviet superiority for many years. Much later, Kissinger admitted in his memoirs that he had miscalculated. By then the damage was done.

It is a short logical step from parity—denial of military superiority—to the denial of victory as unacceptable to the notion of "balance." Thanks largely to Kissinger, "seek neither victory nor defeat" became the *modus operandi* of U.S. policy and its military.

Moreover, that abstract, debilitating notion was brutally imposed on our friends and allies. When Israel was on the verge of a decisive victory in the 1973 Yom Kippur War, its hand was stayed by the United States. I remember how deadly serious the United States was in its stern, little-publicized message: Unless Israel stopped its advance, Washington warned, the Americans would paradrop food, water and medical supplies to the beleaguered Egyptian 3rd Army. After all, resounding victory by Israel would have compromised Kissinger's ability to engage in diplomacy.

One must ask whether Kissinger was psychologically qualified to shape the policy of the United States at a critical juncture of its history. He had fled to the United States as a 15-year-old refugee from Nazi Germany. The roots of his personal insecurity—described by some as verging on paranoia—were thus understandable. But should this insecure man have become Secretary of State, charged with safeguarding the security of democracy and the Free World?

Those were not questions one would properly ask at the War College, but there were no shortage of themes to write about. In my required paper for graduation, I made a case for the dissolution of NATO, to be replaced by a U.S.-German security agreement. I had seen at close hand the serious problems besetting NATO: the factional rivalries, the indifference to the Third World, the reluctance of member nations to seriously arm (we had been urging them to put more of their GNP into defense), the penchant to let Uncle Sam carry most of the burden, and the backdoor German flirtation with the Soviets under Chancellor Willy Brandt's *Ostpolitik*. I understood then the implications of NATO's weaknesses, the unfairness to the U.S., and the failures of collective security.

Although it was unclassified, the Pentagon refused to allow publication of my paper. Only General Keegan's advice persuaded me to withdraw it in order to avoid further controversy. When I returned to the Air Force from the War College, I learned that I was being considered for a higher-level post—as the Defense Intelligence Officer (DIO) for the Middle East in the Defense Intelligence Agency. The final choice came down to me and an elderly man named Waldo Duberstein, who had CIA experience. Duberstein was chosen. Subsequently, he committed suicide while facing charges of having sold classified information to the Qaddaffi Government in Libya. How strange to have been passed over for a man supected of being a spy and traitor to his country! The irony was to be compounded by my own legitimate encounters with the Libyans in subsequent years. More about that later.

Meanwhile, if the handling of my War College paper or being passed over for a promotion soured me on the Pentagon, the "General Brown Affair" proved to be the last straw . . . .

The General Brown Affair

In November 1974 General George S. Brown, (USAF), Chairman of the Joint Chiefs of Staff, was reprimanded by President Ford for making public statements disparaging to American Jews. He had suggested to an audience at Duke University that Jews exercised undue influence in Congress and that they controlled the banks and newspapers in the United States.

His failure to heed that reprimand marked the beginning of the end of my government service. Early in October 1976, I was briefly hospitalized with lower back problems. I was in the hospital bed, legs hoisted in traction, when the phone rang. It was Bernard Gwertzman, the diplomatic correspondent of *The New York Times*. "What do you think about General Brown's latest comment?" he asked me. According to *Newsweek International* magazine, Brown had told an Israeli cartoonist that Israel was a "burden" to the United States.

My anger hit the boiling point. I decided it was time to speak out. Knowing that I was being quoted in a major story in the "newspaper of record," I described General Brown's remarks as "dangerously irresponsible because it is precisely what the Soviets and Arabs are telling the United States." I added that the Joint Chiefs of Staff's Chairman's comment was further evidence of an increasing "tilt against Israel in the Defense Department." The story appeared in the *New York Times* the next day, October 20, under the headline: "Pentagon Is Accused Of Anti-Israel Stand; Air Force's Mideast Intelligence Expert Criticizes Gen. Brown."

The reverberations came swiftly. I was informed by the Pentagon that my special security clearances were suspended on the grounds that I had "technically violated" Defense Department regulations. The nature of that "violation" was never explained to me. Be that as it may, the suspension of clearances made it impossible to discharge my official duties, and my hand was thus forced. In any case, I had already decided to resign, but wanted to wait until I could leave the hospital and discuss the whole matter and my motives with General Keegan. I felt that I owed that to my "patron," all the more so because Keegan was a close personal friend of George Brown.

The *New York Times* ran the obituary of my government career on November 11th, 1976: "Air Aide Who Complained Is Out," proclaimed the headline. The first few paragraphs of the article clearly described the cause of death:

> A civilian intelligence officer of the Air Force who publicly criticized the views of General George S. Brown, Chairman of the Joint Chiefs of Staff, resigned today after being stripped of his special security clearances because he talked to a *New York Times* reporter.
> Joseph Churba, The Air Force's senior intelligence officer for the Middle East, said in a telephone conversation that his superior, Maj. Gen. George Keegan, told him on Monday (Nov. 8) that because of his newspaper interview his special clearances for signal and satellite intelligence had been suspended and that he was no longer of any value to the Air Force as an intelligence estimator. As a result, he said, he resigned.
> The Air Force confirmed the facts, but a spokesman said that Mr. Churba knew when he took the job in December

1972 that as an intelligence officer he would be unable to speak publicly.

What had fueled my response to Gwertzman's question was that over the preceding year-and-a-half, the Pentagon's position on the Middle East had steadily shifted toward the Arab side. The key force behind the shift clearly was Brown, who had demonstrated his personal views in his ridiculous 1974 statement about Jews controlling America.

There is another facet to the Washington Compromise which has to do with the caprices of the bureaucracy. Ambitious careerists are quick to discern the weather-vanes of policy-thinking above them, and to adapt their own thinking—and "analyses"—to the prevailing winds. During that period I had my hands full trying to cope with the pro-Arab assessments of the Middle East emanating from within the Air Staff of which I was coordinator. It was open season on Israel.

I traced the growing anti-Israel sentiment in the Pentagon, beyond the personal bias of General Brown, to the aftermath of the 1973 War. Had Israel been allowed to establish a clearly victorious position, its standing as a strategic asset of the U.S. would have been similar to what it had been in 1967. I was a witness to the process both before and after the war, and the pro-Arab orientation of papers flowing within the Pentagon after the conflict sharply contrasted with the general objectivity of assessments before 1973. But more was at stake than "mere" bureaucratic bias. I later explained in a book the main motives behind my decision to speak out:

> General Brown had in fact said precisely what the Soviets and the Arabs have been telling the world in order to advance their own global strategic designs. In lending his high office to the Soviet-Arab stratagem of isolating

the United States from Israel, General Brown sent the wrong signals to Moscow and the Arab capitals. He thereby increased uncertainty as to whether the United States would respond in the event of renewed hostilities in the Middle East.[1]

In any event, the decision cost me my job. The career I began in May 1968 ended in October 1976.

My last task before leaving the Pentagon was to conduct a post-mortem on the intelligence estimates concerning the Middle East since 1955—a practice normally performed by the CIA. For several weeks, I documented with chapter and verse just how wrong the estimates had been, focussing principally on the Soviet factor in the region, and I delivered the findings to Keegan. I can imagine the consternation in the CIA when it was learned that I had undertaken this project.

So, after nearly nine years of government service, I found myself not only unemployed but virtually without friends. Still, I had no regrets then; nor have I entertained any since. To be sure, the practical course for me would have been the established bureaucratic road—to "go with the crowd." I could have kept silence on General Brown, and be collecting my government pension today. I did not have to disagree with flawed national intelligence estimates. I could have kept my counsel and—who knows—risen in time to a lofty level within the Defense Intelligence Agency.

The reality is that I truly could not have done otherwise. Quite simply, my upbringing did not prepare me to place career or job security above integrity and principle. Indeed, I considered it my obligation to challenge the established but dangerously mistaken U.S. policy "mindsets."

---

[1] Joseph Churba, *The Politics of Defeat*. New York: Cyrco Press, 1977, p.20.

More specifically, the Brown affair reaffirmed to me that American Jews, irrespective of their scholarship and other qualifications, have no future in high U. S. policy positions dealing with Middle Eastern affairs—unless, that is, they hold the basic views that Israel should be reduced to its pre-1967 status. If they are willing to go along with the latter notion, they can become useful tools for any administration, Republican or Democratic. Noteworthy in that context was President Clinton's retention of James Baker's three top Middle East aides—Dennis Ross, Daniel Kurtzer, and Aaron Miller—who have become known as the State Department's "Jewish Arabists." Responsible for shaping the Bush-Baker policies on Israel, they remained key figures in charting President Clinton's Middle East policies. However much they might resent the sobriquet "Israel-bashers," they know that because of their past history of support for the Arab view their integrity will always be suspect.

I often wondered after October 1976 why my blast against General Brown drew a cool reaction from the American Jewish establishment, especially since there had been earlier condemnations of him as an anti-Semite. I found the answer only some thirteen years later, when I learned that immediately after my denunciation of Brown, the Israeli Prime Minister Yitzhak Rabin himself had ordered the Israeli Embassy in Washington to keep a distance from me, lest Israel's relations with the Pentagon be compromised. That leads to larger questions about the U.S.-Israeli relationship and the role of the American Jewish establishment in that relationship.

6

Israel And
The American Jewish Establishment

The American Jewish establishment essentially consists of the thirty-eight organizations that make up a large umbrella organization called the Conference of Presidents of Major American Jewish Organizations. All are self-anointed in their claim to "leadership" of the American Jewish community. The average American Jew does not have much awareness of their existence, let alone their role on the larger policy stage where they generally claim to speak for the entire American Jewish community.

Despite the fact that these organizations' memberships combined represent less than half of the U.S. Jewish Community, plus the fact that many in the individual organizations do not necessarily share their leaders' views on particular issues, these organizations are recognized by the White House as representing the views of most Jewish people in the United States. Given the American system of lobbying, this kind of claim can be made because there are no organized opposing or competing voices. Consequently, whether the organizations are assets for the United States, for American Jews, or for Israel is a matter for debate.

THE TRUE MEANING OF U.S.-ISRAELI PARTNERSHIP

A strong case can be made that the American Jewish establishment has played a role detrimental to a healthy U.S.-Israeli strategic relationship. Strength in such a relationship is a measure of the self-reliance of the partners: indeed, that is the definition of sound partnership. A corollary is that the less dependent Israel is on external power, and the more confidently it can act on its own, the greater the regional respect it receives and the more effectively it can function in furthering common U.S. and Israeli interests.

Measured by those criteria, the high point in the U.S.-Israeli strategic partnership coincided with the independent power Israel displayed in the 1967 War. After the trauma of the 1973 Yom Kippur conflict, however, successive Israeli governments became addicted to U.S. financial aid. This "recuperative" relationship was started by a Labor government. Begin's Likud party not only continued the addiction but deepened it substantially after the 1978 Camp David accords. The real profiteers at Camp David were the Egyptians, who gained the Sinai, oil, airfields, plus generous American assistance, and paid nothing in return. The Israelis surrendered the Sinai and became more addicted to U.S. aid.

The American Jewish establishment has been a major player in this addiction process, by dint of its presumptuous dealings with the U.S. and Israeli governments. The more financial assistance Israel gleans from the U.S. government, the greater the standing of the establishment—notably the American-Israel Public Affairs Committee (AIPAC)—in Jerusalem and in Washington, D.C. But there has also been a reverse flow of the current: whenever the U.S. Government has sought some policy modification from the Israelis, it has leaned on the American Jewish leadership to "use its influence" in Jerusalem—in other words, it has "lobbied the lobbyists". Over time, the self-anointed American Jewish leaders have been elevated into an essential two-way link between the two countries.

In the larger process described, however, Israel is declining as a strategic asset to the United States, despite its military capabilities. As Israel strips itself of needed space for territorial defense, and becomes increasingly reliant on the flow of American military technology, its freedom and capacity to make decisions are commensurately impaired. Both the United States and Israel would be far better served if the latter acted independently in its own defense without indispensable support from the former. Especially in a contingency of American embroilment in conflict elsewhere on the globe, the Israeli capability as an independent power would be the true measure of its value to the United States.

It is this view of the broader strategic context for the U.S.-Israeli relationship that brought me into sharp conflict with the American Jewish leadership. I have spelled out those differences over the past 15 years. Thus, in *The Politics of Defeat*, I wrote:

> for America, Israel is not an end in itself as some pro-Israel and anti-Israel forces would see it, but rather a means for fostering stability, peace and progress. Israel should not be viewed in the context of the problem of Palestine, but rather in relation to the American strategic need for a strong asset in the region.

Israel as an end in itself: Herein lie the sins of the self-appointed leaders of the American Jewish establishment. They have "parochialized" Israel, making the problem of Palestine the key to their uneasy self-image as Jews in America. Their narrow view has helped convince Americans that Israel is the problem rather than the solution in the Middle East. In this way, the American Jewish establishment inadvertently feeds the anti-Israel forces in America.

The devaluation of Israel reached new depths in 1990, when American Jewish authorities, witnessing the collapse of the Soviet Empire, believed the time ripe to "bring Israel home"—to sustain it as their personal "precious little flower," unsullied by the realities of international power politics. That approach nurtured the image of American support for Israel as a function purely of American domestic politics, rather than of vital U.S. national security interests in the Middle East.

AMERICAN JEWISH PAROCHIALISM AND THE GULF CRISIS

During the Persian Gulf crisis, the liberal American Jewish establishment went to the very brink of, in effect, declaring Israel to be a burden to America. They did so not because they believed in the Arabist line that our relationship with Israel threatened to undermine the anti-Iraq coalition, but in the misguided notion that Israel would do best by staying out of the fracas. Yet any American, Jew or Gentile, who was not fooled by the Arabist line, and who understood the long-term threat posed by Iraq to global security, would have welcomed a quick and massive military response by America with Israel's assistance. Some even remembered that had it not been for the heavily criticized Israeli raid on Iraq's nuclear facilities in June 1981, the crisis a decade later would have taken on a much more ominous cast.

What would have happened had the United States and Israel moved in military concert against Iraq during Operation Desert Storm in 1990? Some American and Israeli soldiers and airmen would have died together, but would have prevented many more American and Israeli casualties in the future. There would have been no need for a build-up of troops in the first place. True, in some Arab countries the "souk"—the mobs so easily ignited in impoverished and embittered Arab cities—might have mobilized for a few days of rioting. But the Arab elites, after initial protests, soon would have adjusted to the reality of a dismembered Iraq. In the end, those Arab elites—particularly in the virtually defenseless Gulf states—would have been comforted by the security provided by America and Israel. A telling lesson would have been imparted to Syria's leadership lest it try its own hand at pan-Arab imperialism in the wake of Iraq's failure.

Let us stretch the scenario of a combined U.S.-Israeli military action against Iraq further. From the ashes of Arab imperial dreams would have arisen a Palestinian Arab state—but in Jordan rather than in Western Palestine, where the Arabs, the U.S. government, and liberal American Jewish leaders have artificially projected such a state. King Hussein's alignment with Saddam Hussein should have cost him the monarchy, and the Palestinian majority might have declared their republic in Amman. By thus adapting a realistic policy to the problems of Palestine, America and Israel would have finally solved that conflict: two states, one Jewish and one Arab. This could have marked a long stride in addressing the fundamental issue in the area: how to create, for the first time since the demise of the Ottoman Empire, free and democratic national states in the Middle East, able and willing to live in peace and stability with one another. Additionally, it would have buried once and for all the last two dreams—Arab and Russian—of empire in the world.

These have always been the fundamental issues deserving attention, not such peripheral ones as the problem of an Arab minority in Israel. How absurd-from the perspective of American national interest as well as humanitarian concern-is the abiding obsession with the lot of the Arab minority in Israel, when the much more terrible fate of many nationalities elsewhere—in Tibet, in former Yugoslavia, in Lebanon, let alone in Africa—is ignored or rationalized!

But the road to a stable peace in the Middle East is foreclosed so long as Israel remains a parochial concern, and the American Jewish establishment works overtime to insulate its "precious little flower" from the harsh realities of the region and from the need for Israeli-American cooperation in making the Middle East safe for democracies. Nor should we forget that the call of liberal Jews to protect their "precious little flower" is the inverse side of Yassir Arafat's call for America to punish "its naughty little baby."

Under the influence of its liberal "leaders," Prime Minister Shamir in 1990 bit into the bait offered by the anti-Israel forces. America was encouraged to "protect Israel" from Saddam Hussein, while Israeli generals argued for self-defense. The legacy is a bitter one. Even before he left office, President Bush had already accused Israelis of "ingratitude" for failing to offer sufficient thanks to him for "saving" them. Remembered well is the reality of those early days in the crisis when Undersecretary of State Lawrence Eagleburger was in Israel, alternately begging and threatening the Shamir government not to intervene, not to go after the Iraqi Scud missiles targeted at Israel, because that might disrupt "The Arab Coalition."

FUNDAMENTAL ISSUES AND PRIORITIES

A stable Middle East is not possible as long as the virus of parochialism continues both to distort and to debilitate Israel's true potential. In fact, Israel could be the principal provider of peace and security to the region. In the aftermath of the Gulf War, one cannot emphasize enough the flawed presumptions of American Jewish leaders and their detrimental impact on the strategic interests of both America and Israel. I stress the words "liberal" and "establishment" because, at the American grassroots level, Jews and Gentiles alike support a valiant, democratic, freedom-loving country battling against military dictatorships and absolute monarchies. Let Israel be freed from the stifling embrace of the liberal American Jewish establishment, and watch it fully serve its true vocation as America's strategic ally in the region!

Both America and Israel must be wary of schemes that entail sacrifices of real security in the whimsical pursuit of "peace" in that volatile region. It may be that true peace simply is beyond reach. How often has it been said that Israel wants and needs peace? Whereupon the question follows: What price is it prepared to pay for a peace that also benefits the Arab states? This is a poor opening position for negotiations.

There is another issue: Does not Israel have to be saved from an Arab demographic time bomb? Here, the aforementioned radical Rabbi Kahane, was the choice strawman of the liberal establishment. He was exploited to vindicate the position that Israel would be neither Jewish nor democratic if it retained territories heavily inhabited by Arabs.

Thirty years ago, then in Israel's loyal opposition, Menachem Begin explained to his audiences that the Zionist enterprise envisioned millions of new Jewish immigrants, especially from the Soviet Union, who would make the Arab population of Western Palestine an ever *smaller minority*. A majority of Israelis came to believe him. But liberal circles remained, and remain, impervious to the concerns of the majority of the people of Israel. "How can Israel remain truly Jewish when it oppresses another people?" they asked. Swept away are the immediate imperatives of a country in a state of war, struggling with insurrection within its borders. Forgotten are the visions of pragmatic early Zionists in the West who wanted Israeli society to mirror other nation-states in the world balance of power. Dismissed is the unique opportunity for Israel to show it can defend and even nurture the civil and religious rights of minorities—that it can be an example to nations in the region that have not assimilated the basic meaning of human rights or democracy.

Even more to the point is the inability of liberals to distinguish between civil and political rights when discussing minorities. The Arab-Jewish crisis will end only when Israel's Arab minority makes its own peace with the sovereignty of Israel on the West Bank of the Jordan River.

In the eyes of someone who has observed the demoralization of some of America's Jewish youth—their ventures into drugs and aberrant behavior, vaunted secularism, and abandonment of traditional Jewish values and ethics—such liberals would make a greater contribution to the community if they were concerned more about the Jewish souls of their own children than the soul of Israel. Indeed, with the notable exception of the Orthodox community, their problems of intermarriage, secularism and assimilation combine to render them a shrinking people. While the overall population increased 22 percent between 1970 and 1990, Jewish demographic growth was an insignificant 1.8 percent. As the only group in America to diminish in numbers, perhaps it is time that the secular Jewish leaders review their chronically liberal positions on traditional Jewish values. But to do this they might have to surrender their deep and passionate commitment to another religion—liberalism.

DISTORTED LEGACY OF THE COLD WAR

For the American Jewish leadership, accepting the thesis that Israel is a strategic asset of the United States would have meant accepting also a fundamental proposition of the Cold War: that the West faced an imperialist enemy in a systemic struggle of global dimensions. The Jewish leadership did not accept the reality or implications of this proposition. They were, on the whole, "detentists" and accommodationists and critical of U.S. defense spending. They did not want to see Israel as an extension of American power in the global contest with the Soviet Union.

There was never a possibility of convergence between Communist and capitalist systems. The great volume of literature and rhetoric that for years encouraged Americans and the West to accept Soviet tyranny as a reality and to "live with it" as it "matured" was nonsense. The Soviet Union had no "legitimate security concerns," only imperialist objectives. It was indeed the "evil empire" that Ronald Reagan described. There was no "shared responsibility" for the Cold War. Communism was never more than a totalitarian rationale for dominion over man and his soul, and for the pursuit of world power. However, none of this is acceptable to the fashionable liberal, who for more than half a century regarded anti-Communism as aberrant behavior.

My life and career have been devoted to fighting this revisionist mindset among American liberals, particularly fellow Jews. But given the liberals' chronic inability to accept the brutal reality of power politics in the nation state system, they generally deny that there ever was a contest of life and death in the Cold War, or that America won. They are even less inclined to accept that America won with the help of its valiant ally, Israel. The commissars in Moscow, however, cognizant of the century-old Zionist revolution, understood quite well the threat that the Jewish national liberation movement posed to their new socialist order and empire. Nationalism, indeed, has vanquished communism.

It is no coincidence that the very same liberals who believed that Israel had to be "spared" from involvement in the Cold War are also those who today bemoan a relative decline of interest in Israel in U.S. policy circles. They refuse to acknowledge the debt owed to Israel, and to the Russian Jews who bravely attempted to emigrate, for their role in our victory in the Cold War. Instead, the liberal media abound with references to America's "moral obligation" to Soviet Jews on the grounds that it actively championed their emigration for many years. If it is only "a moral obligation," then the average American can be excused when he argues:

"Haven't we done enough for Soviet Jewry? We got them their freedom, and now the Jews want us to pay their room and board. What ingratitude! It's time we worried about our own!" Only through enhancing public recognition that the Cold War was won in no small part because of American-Israeli collaboration, along with Jewish forces of dissent within the Soviet Union, is it possible to establish solid and durable understanding and support based on mutual respect and shared historical experience. A dramatic example of such collaboration was the Israel destruction of the Syrian Air Force in a matter of minutes in the skies over Syria in the 1982 War. In Consequence, the more knowledgeable Soviet elite—led by Andropov, and later, his protege, Gorbachev—concluded that only radical "reform" of the Soviet system would save it from implosion.[1]

I warned President Reagan's advisors of the dangers in viewing Israel through a parochial prism. In a memorandum to National Security Advisor Richard Allen, dated December 1, 1980—that is, after the election but before the Administration took office—I stressed the importance of a wise choice for the new ambassador to Israel. I pointed to the pivotal importance of that post if Israel were to be enlisted effectively in the global U.S. strategy *vis-a-vis* the Soviet Union. I wrote:

> the future American ambassador to Israel must not be one whose claim to such a position rests on political favors rendered or a special place in the hearts of American Jews . . . We simply can no longer afford a moralistic, parochial, more-of-the-same approach in our relationship with Israel . . . The new U.S. ambassador must insure the Israelis against probable Soviet inducements to neutrality (e.g.,

---

[1] See "The Russia-Israeli Rapprochement," a report on a conference between Russian military and Israeli officers, Jerusalem, in the International Security Council quarterly, *Global Affairs*, Fall 1992.

offers of increased emigration of Soviet Jews as a *quid pro quo*) . . . Together with their counterparts in the liberal American Jewish establishment, a Labor government might be tempted to revive the discredited (Israeli) social- ist dream of pursuing a mediating role between East and West. Their cry may go up to remove Israel from the dis- tasteful Cold War, especially if the Soviet price appears right. In such circumstances, the U.S. ambassador will be required to steady Israel's hand on the Western side of the table.

Part of the motive behind the memo was to remind those in power to ensure that the ambassadorship to Jerusalem under the Reagan Administration not be co-opted by the liberal Jewish establishment.

In 1976, when I confronted General George Brown over his statement about Israel as a strategic liability, I received absolutely no support from the American Jewish establish- ment. It was brought home to me then that the establishment could not or would not understand. How could the Chairman of the Joint Chiefs of Staff be blamed for playing into Soviet hands by belittling Israel, when the American Jewish leadership itself was devaluating Israel's geopolitical importance in the Cold War?

7

The Reagan Campaign: Revolution to Betrayal, Act I

For all the reasons enumerated in the preceding chapter, I was hurt, but not surprised, by the total silence from the Jewish establishment concerning the Brown affair and my abrupt departure from the U.S. Government in late 1976. I knew that I would have to rebuild my career all over again. But first I had to get off my chest my view of the larger issues that had been involved in my duel with General Brown. Subsisting on the modest amount that had accumulated in my pension plan, I focused on writing *The Politics of Defeat*, which was published in the fall of 1977.

I began lecturing and writing op-ed pieces, notably for the *Baltimore Sun* and *Christian Science Monitor*. Then came the glimmer of an opportunity. With support from Sidney Maduff, a prominent Democratic fund-raiser and commodities trader whom I had befriended, I established the Center for International Security in the spring of 1978. The Center's avowed mission was to convey to the U.S. public greater awareness of a generally rising Soviet threat and of the importance of Israel to America in the global struggle. From personal experience I knew that, notwithstanding General Brown and his ilk, there was strong support for this viewpoint among America's professional military men. It was to them that I initially turned.

The enterprise got off to a running start with the willingness by courageous military men—my former patron and now deceased Chief of U. S. Air Force Intelligence, Major General George J. Keegan, former Chief of Naval Operations Admiral E. R. Zumwalt, Jr., and Major General D. A. Thompson USA (Ret.)—to take a public stand against the defeatist policies of President Jimmy Carter, which threatened to undercut Israel as America's ally in the Middle East. It was the first time in recent history that senior military officers joined together in open protest against a serving president's policies. Israel is "a matchless strategic asset for the West . . . at no cost to U. S. manpower and at a military supply expenditure amounting to less than one percent of the U.S. defense budget," the officers asserted in a *New York Times* advertisement in April 1978. The statement, which also carried the signatures of distinguished civilians, was designed to counter Carter's policy of massive arms deliveries to the Arab states.

By the end of 1978, the effort had snowballed into an "Open Letter to President Carter" signed by more than 170 retired generals and admirals. We warned that the Soviets were "heading for superiority, not parity, in the military area," and that the President therefore should desist from "any new arms control agreement that would threaten to perpetuate the current strategic imbalance." The letter published in *The New York Times*, like its predecessor, went on to state that the "Soviet focus on the Middle East . . . represents a real and growing threat to Western security."

ENTER THE REAGAN CAMPAIGN

In early 1979 I was still writing articles for the *Baltimore Sun* and other newspapers critical of the Carter defense policies. One of my writings, on SALT and the Middle East in The *Christian Science Monitor*, caught the attention of Richard V. (Dick) Allen, who had been Richard Nixon's principal foreign policy aide in the 1968 campaign (before being shunted aside after the election in favor of Henry A. Kissinger) and who was now filling that role for presidential candidate Ronald Reagan. Allen wrote to me, inviting me to lunch. And so it came about that several days later, in the elegantly subdued atmosphere of Washington's Sheraton Carlton Hotel, Allen and I discussed what we agreed was the unmitigated disaster of Jimmy Carter's foreign policies. I questioned him about Reagan's political philosophy. Allen averred that Reagan would agree with me on the paramount need to restore the credibility of the United States' nuclear arsenal.

Allen then told me that he was assembling a small team of specialists on defense and foreign policy to advise the coming Reagan campaign. At the time the group included William Van Cleave, Richard Pipes, William Casey and retired Lieutenant General Daniel Graham—all known for their previous antagonism to Kissinger's detente policies. Allen asked me to join the team.

The proposal took me by complete surprise. I had never met Reagan. I was not terribly impressed by what I had observed of him at long range, e.g. by his intellectual stature. Still, he seemed level-headed, with an instinctive sense for the proper stance on major issues. More important, he understood the priority need to redress a military balance that was tilting in favor of the Soviet Union. Given the utter disarray of Carter's domestic and foreign policies, I had no doubt that Reagan could win the election decisively. I realized that a Reagan victory could mark an historic turning point with respect to the fundamental issues relevant to national defense and the Middle East which I championed. Although I had always prided myself on nonpartisan independence as an analyst, I had no reservations about aligning myself with a political party or candidate who shared my concerns. Indeed, I felt honored to be able to help in fashioning what promised to be a new, rational departure in American foreign and defense policies.

As Allen and I agreed, I moved my office immediately adjacent to his in a building on Sixteenth Street, just one block from the White House. Bill Van Cleave, Reagan's principal defense advisor, and I immediately struck up a strong kinship. Columnist Morton Kondracke was to describe our group as follows:

> In foreign policy, . . . Reagan's innermost group of advisers tends to be rigidly hardline—though certainly not of the kooky-right fringe. Their most common single characteristic (beside suspicion of the Soviet Union) is a record of opposition to the policies of Henry Kissinger. Reagan's chief issues coordinator on foreign policy is Richard V. Allen, who performed the same function for Richard Nixon in the 1968 campaign, then joined Nixon's administration as Kissinger's deputy at the National Security Council. Apparently fearful of Allen's independent access to Nixon, Kissinger froze Allen out of policy action at the White House, and Allen quit, though he later came back as a Nixon adviser on international economic policy.
>
> Some of Reagan's other key foreign policy briefers: Fred Ikle, who argued against Kissinger's SALT II proposals from his post as President Ford's Arms Control Director; retired Lt. Gen. Daniel O. Graham who fought against Kissinger's detente policies as head of the Defense Intelligence Agency; William Van Cleave, who was special assistant to Defense Secretary Melvin Laird, Kissinger's bureaucratic arch-rival in the Nixon days; and Joseph Churba, a former Air Force intelligence analyst and critic of Kissinger.[1]

No one in our advisory group had contact with Reagan's campaign staff. Allen served as the only contact point while protecting our ability to concentrate on the main

---

[1] Boston Globe, April 4, 1980.

task: formulating Reagan's foreign and defense policy positions. We were essentially the architects of his declaratory policies.

As the campaign gathered momentum, and the chances of an electoral victory swung upward, more and more people sought to hop aboard the bandwagon. There came a steady stream of bids to join our team. At this stage very few were admitted. Allen fielded all inquiries, consulting me frequently.

THE "MIDDLE EAST BIBLE" OF THE CAMPAIGN

I handled most of the work on the Middle East for the campaign. A month or so after I joined, Richard Allen approached me one morning: "I want you to do an article that would be the bible on the Middle East. It will be published under Reagan's byline, and serve as the campaign's position paper." I sat down and essentially condensed my recent book, *The Politics of Defeat*, into an article. "Recognizing The Israeli Asset," appeared in *The Washington Post* under Reagan's name on August 15, 1979. It gave me immense satisfaction to feel that my views were being propagated by the likely next President of the United States.

The article quickly became one of the most talked-about statements of the campaign. Copies were reproduced by the tens of thousands. There was nothing really startling about the contents of the article. What it did, however, was to lodge a challenge to the prevailing misguided view of Israel which had long characterized U.S. policy. As a candidate he said: "The paramount American interest in the Middle East is to prevent the region from falling under the domination of the Soviet Union" and even argued that the endangering of Persian Gulf oil supplies might invite the neutralization of Western Europe and Japan. He also noted that Soviet inroads were quite independent of Israel, and said firmly: "Our own position would be weaker without the political and military assets Israel provides." American policymakers, he said, "downgrade just those three attributes of Israel that are potentially beneficial to the West: its "geopolitical importance as a stabilizing force," its ability to serve as "a deterrent to radical hegemony," and its capacity to be a "military ofset to the Soviet Union." Further, "the fall of Iran has increased Israel's value as perhaps the only remaining strategic asset on which the U.S. can truly rely; other pro-Western states in the region, especially Saudi Arabia and the smaller Gulf kingdoms, are weak and vulnerable."

The article argued that Israel's democratic system guaranteed that it would not be ruled at some future time by a radical anti-American government. Moreover, Israel's intelligence services provide critical guidance and information for ongoing regional developments; the technical know-how of Israeli specialists could be used to assist American forces in a crisis; and Israeli facilities and airfields could provide a secure point of regional access for U.S. forces in an emergency. Further, Soviet planners constantly had to take into account the effective dominance of the Israeli forces, and especially its air force, over critical zones of access and transit in the region.

Subsequently, many people in and out of the Reagan camp claimed credit for the celebrated article. They included Richard Allen. I remember Richard Pipes telling me in a restaurant in New York: "That Israel article was a superb piece of writing by Dick Allen."

"By whom?" I asked.

"By Dick Allen," Pipes repeated. "He told me he wrote that article. He did write it, didn't he?"

Contending claims of authorship aside, the article did serve as the basis for my first encounter with Ronald Reagan. Arranged by Allen, the meeting took place at the Atlanta Airport Hilton Hotel in February 1980. Others in attendance, in addition to Reagan and Allen, included Congressman Jack Kemp, Edwin Meese, William Casey, Professor Robert Pfalzgraff of the Fletcher School of Law and Diplomacy, and Mrs. Reagan. Meese took copious notes but did not participate in the discussion.

In Van Cleave's absence, I offered an assessment of the U.S.-Soviet nuclear balance, warning of America's growing vulnerability to a Soviet nuclear first strike. I'm not sure that in this respect I told Reagan anything that he had not heard before. Still, what I said seemed to confirm his fears, because he remarked wryly: "When those people out there [the waiting reporters] ask me how this meeting went, I think I'll tell them I decided I'd better go find a cave to hide in!"

Reagan demonstrated a lively interest in my discussion of Israel as a strategic asset, posing a number of probing questions. Our dialogue was interrupted by the arrival of a telegram from Governor John Connally, in which he conceded his loss in the primary race. The timing, I thought, could not have been more fortuitous.

I left the meeting feeling good about my exchange with the candidate. Governor Reagan came across as gracious and confident. He more than met my expectations of a worthy Presidential candidate. I took heart from my exchange with him. Regrettably, I could not place the same confidence in the campaign staff, or in the nominee for Vice President.

BEGINNINGS OF THE BUSH POLLUTION

In May 1980, I received an invitation from the South African ambassador in Washington to visit his country. I accepted, primarily because of what I saw as South Africa's importance to the West in the global rivalry with the Soviets. While I was in South Africa, the Republican National Convention was held in Detroit on July 14-17, 1980. With

Reagan's candidacy assured, the only remaining question befell the choice of running mate. Henry Kissinger, hoping for another tenure as Secretary of State, pushed hard to put former President Gerald Ford on the ticket. Reagan refused. The decision was made in favor of George Bush, whom we had battled hard in the primaries.

That was Reagan's first big mistake. Reagan could have won the 1980 election just as decisively without Bush. The nagging fear among Reagan advisors, however, was about a repetition of the debacle of 1964, when large-scale defections by self-avowed Republican "liberals" insured the defeat of Barry Goldwater. Incredibly, in the negotiations over the vice-presidential nomination, Bush was secretly given the right to fill at least 18 of the key positions in the White House, including Chief of Staff. It was a misbegotten deal with the Republican "liberals" which, in time, would spell the ruin of Reagan's policies and achievements. The Washington Compromise was alive and well!

Detroit, 7/17/80. GOP standard bearer Ronald Reagan (C) bids farewell to the final session of the National Republican Convention with vice-presidential running mate George Bush (R) and former President Gerald Ford (L). (UPI)

My appraisal of George Bush as a man of doubtful honesty, weak character, and narrow vision had been shaped well before the primary battles of 1980: they went back to his tenure as Director of the Central Intelligence Agency. As I mentioned earlier, I had often accompanied General George Keegan to meetings of the Board of National Estimates. There I witnessed first-hand the debate over the exclusion from the SALT treaty of the Soviet Air Force's Backfire Bomber—an aircraft capable of delivering nuclear weapons over long distances. Incredibly, Bush argued the totally phony Soviet line that the Backfire was a tactical, not a strategic weapon. He thereby lied brazenly for political purpose to push the agreement through. A strategic weapon would fall under the SALT agreement, while a tactical weapon would not. Bush's motive in defining the Backfire as tactical was to skew the SALT numbers making them look more favorable for the U.S. so as to minimize resistance to the SALT agreement in the Senate—even to the detriment of U.S. security. This was Kissinger's game at the time, and George Bush was his compliant lackey.

I was in South Africa when the Reagan-Bush ticket was announced. Upon my return, a distraught General Keegan telephoned: "Joe, it's all over! The Reagan revolution is dead! He picked Bush! It's finished! It's over and done with!"

Later in October 1980, I was invited to speak at a political rally in Baltimore as a stand-in for Campaign Manager William Casey. I gave my speech, then braced for questions from the audience. A young man stepped up to a microphone: "If George Bush were to come into office, would he continue the Reagan program?"

Searching my conscience, I mustered the qualified answer: "One would hope that he would." That caused an uproar in campaign headquarters the next day. That was the last rally I was asked to address.

Unfortunately for the United States and many other parts of the world, I was fully vindicated in my early judgment of Bush by his performance as President after 1988.

Bush had no yardstick of values and principles to guide him; therefore he did not know how to exploit the unprecedented opportunities history presented to him. It was a tragedy that he was at the helm of the ship of state at the time of the most fateful event of the 20th Century: the collapse of the Soviet Empire. Bush's inability to take advantage of the historic watershed toward the creation of a global order based on freedom and democratic ideals attested to his myopia, as did—on a smaller scale—his failure to bring down Saddam Hussein's regime in Iraq following America's resounding military victory.

Bush had generally been tabbed a "foreign policy expert" by the media because of his experience as ambassador to China and the UN, and as director of the CIA. This was utter nonsense! Bush was living proof that a curriculum vitae does not an expert make. His true vocation was that of a manager of power—and a mediocre one at that.

THE JOHANNESBURG INCIDENT

Already while I was in South Africa I had my first skirmish with the Reagan campaign. The best way to set the stage is to cite at length from an article that appeared in the *New York Times* on June 13, 1980, under the byline of John F. Burns in Johannesburg, and headlined, "Aide to Reagan in South Africa Says Embargo Should End":

> One of Ronald Reagan's defense advisers said at a news conference here today that he would urge Mr. Reagan, if elected president, to end the United States arms embargo against South Africa, set up a Navy presence at the Simonstown base and help the South African armed forces to strengthen themselves in aspects relating to the

security of the Cape sea route, particularly in the field of helicopters.

The adviser, Joseph Churba, is president of the Center for International Security, a conservative research body in Washington. He said he was expressing his own views, not speaking for Mr. Reagan. But he said that Mr. Reagan, if elected, would, be certain to order a "fundamental re-evaluation" of the Carter Administration's policies toward South Africa, which have combined harsh strictures against apartheid with restraints on some aspects of trade.

Mr. Churba, a ranking Middle East specialist in Air Force intelligence during the Ford Administration, is visiting South Africa as a guest of the Foreign Ministry and was introduced at the news conference by the South African news media, which emphasized his connection to the probable Republican candidate in the November election.

Mr. Churba charged the Carter Administration with "criminal neglect" in failing to take account of South Africa's importance to the United States as a supplier of strategic minerals and as the guardian of the sea route around the Cape.

Reaction from the Reagan(Bush) campaign staff was swift. The same edition of the *New York Times* carried the following story datelined Atlanta, June 12:

Mr. Reagan's press spokesman said by telephone in Los Angeles today that Mr. Churba's trip to South Africa was not related to his role in the presidential candidate's foreign policy advisory group.

"We had nothing to do with it," said the spokesman, Joe Holmes, "and we don't subscribe to his thinking on lifting the embargo on supplying arms."

He added that Mr. Reagan did not subscribe to Mr. Churba's views about establishing a United States naval presence in South Africa or providing aid to South African armed forces in the Cape area. As for Mr. Churba's prediction that Mr. Reagan would order a "fundamental re-evaluation" of American policy toward South Africa, Mr.

Holmes said, "I think we would prefer to let Mr. Reagan make that decision because that is one of the things that has not been discussed."

The incident should have served as warning of my likely future—or lack thereof—in the Reagan-Bush constellation. As Burns faithfully reported, I stated the clear qualifier at the news conference in Johannesburg that I was speaking strictly for myself, and not for the Reagan campaign. Nevertheless I later learned that Allen reacted angrily to my statements. I received a cable from him advising me "to cool it." I was stunned to realize that the Reagan camp was flailing me in order to propitiate its liberal critics. Interestingly, the word *apartheid* had never once been uttered in the Johannesburg press conference.

As it was, the campaign quickly dispatched none other than a Bush supporter, Chester Crocker, to undo the "damage" I had perpetrated in South Africa. Crocker, Director of African Studies at the Georgetown University Center for Strategic and International Studies, arrived in Johannesburg while I was still on the scene. He gave an interview in which he denied any and all implications that could be drawn from my statements. Crocker was to be rewarded with the post of Assistant Secretary of State for Africa throughout the Reagan years and one year into the Bush Administration.

In retrospect and from a career vantage point, my trip to South Africa might have been badly timed. But I had no regrets over my assertions, and I made that clear to Allen upon my return. While no overt action was taken against me, the incident did indicate the sudden influence projected by Bush advisors into the campaign. That infusion was also reflected in the dramatic expansion of our small and cohesive policy team into a horde of almost 70 "advisors."

Ironically, at the time I was more concerned about Dick Allen's career. In September-October 1980, *Mother Jones* magazine ran an article revealing that Allen had once served as a consultant to a lawyer for the fugitive financier, Robert Vesco. In the post-Watergate era, Vesco was someone the Republicans wanted to forget: he had contributed illegal donations to Richard Nixon's 1972 campaign. The article, leaked to *The Washington Post* before it was published, alleged that Allen was paid $10,000 per month, for six months, by Vesco's attorney, Howard Cerny, to analyze prospects for establishing an offshore operation in one of the Azores Islands. Allen admitted to *The Washington Post* that he had arranged a meeting between Cerny and the-then Securities and Exchange Commission (SEC) Chairman, William Casey, but that he was "terribly embarrassed" when during the meeting Cerny brought up the subject of the SEC investigation of Vesco. He claimed not to have known of the investigation.[2]

The barrage against Allen widened. Jody Powell, President Carter's press secretary, told *The Washington Post* that the real issue was that Allen was "a top national security adviser working for the Japanese."[3] Newspaper accounts had noted that upon leaving the Nixon Administration in 1972 and establishing a consulting firm, Potomac International, Allen had represented Nissan, USA, Tokyo Electric Power, and the Industrial Research Institute of Japan.

On October 30, 1980, Allen offered to remove himself from the campaign. I mobilized the entire advisory team and drafted a telegram to Reagan, urging him to retain Allen. Reagan responded positively to the appeal.

Only after the election did I realize that my efforts on Allen's behalf had been overly generous. Allen would show neither comradeship nor gratitude when I needed his help in

---

[2] Washington Post, July 15, 1980, p. 12A.
[3] Washington Post, Oct. 31, 1980, p. 1A.

fending off the attacks against me from anti-Semitic groups, the PLO, and above all the "Bush crowd." There would be no room on the NSC staff for the author of Reagan's "Bible" on the Middle East. And, as it turned out, the rhetoric would be Reagan's, but the actual policy was in the hands of Caspar Weinberger, the designated Secretary of Defense. The Washington Compromise was to be triumphant once again.

8

The Reagan Campaign: Revolution to Betrayal, Act II

The disappointments during the campaign notwithstanding, Reagan's landslide victory in November 1980 offered the hope for the real turnaround in national security policies that candidate Reagan had espoused on the campaign trail. Unfortunately, the prospects of such a turnaround had been devalued even before the voters went to the polls. Many deals had been struck without the public's knowledge, including the aforementioned gift to the Bush forces of 18 key slots in the White House, headed by Bush ally James Baker as Chief of Staff.

EARLY PERSONAL BETRAYAL

This was the backdrop for a remarkable meeting with Dick Allen. As a very active member of the transition team, and one who played a not inconsiderable role in framing policy during the campaign (including the "Bible" for the foreign policy on the Middle East which, reproduced and distributed in the hundreds of thousands, had surely garnered a large number of votes for Reagan), I was given every reason to expect a commensurate role in the administration, with the authority to help implement that policy. I called on Dick Allen, already ensconced as National Security Adviser in the West Wing of the White House, and asked him:

"Will there be a position for me in the new administration?"

Allen hesitated, then offered: "Well, you pick what you want and I'll help you campaign for it."

I was taken aback. "I thought the campaign was over," I rejoined.

I felt betrayed. I was getting the obvious cold shoulder from the man under whom I had labored, without any remuneration whatsoever, for a year and a half. I had, of course, no intent to engage in such a "campaign."

The message was clear that I had served my purpose. There was to be no place for me at the table of the political victory that I had worked so hard to achieve. I later realized only too clearly that the episode was but a small, if personally painful, example of the Washington Compromise.

I couldn't resist the temptation to nettle the newly installed National Security Advisor by calling his bluff. I sent him a memo in which I indicated my interest in becoming Assistant Secretary of State for the Middle East or Ambassador to Israel. I knew that, for any number of reasons, there was not the remotest chance of Allen "campaigning" on my behalf for either job. Despite our two-year working relationship, Allen never even gave me the courtesy of a reply. I had no further interest in continuing to be used by him, and I began preparing for my next career move.

The irony, in retrospect, is that Richard Allen was in poor shape to campaign on anyone else's behalf; he had enough trouble securing his own job. He had survived the "Mother Jones expose" and post-election infighting, but in a badly weakened position. Partly in deference to that weakness, he proposed that the National Security Advisor, after the ego-driven Kissinger and Brzezinski years, assume a "lower profile." That may have made some sense in the larger scheme of policy-making. But Allen not only reduced

Washington, DC, 1/28/81. Richard Allen, National Security Adviser, (L), talks with President Reagan (2L) and Chief of Staff James Baker, along with Asst. Chief of Staff Michael Deaver (R), as they head back into the White House after saying goodbye to Jamaican Prime Minister Edward Seaga. (UP)

his profile; he also reduced the quality of the National Security Council staff—to the point where its effectiveness was crippled for years to come. He filled the staff with mediocrities, including even some holdovers from the Carter Administration; the noted Russia specialist, Richard Pipes, was an exception that proved the rule.

But if Allen thought that by thus weakening his office he would make himself personally more acceptable to his rivals, he was sadly mistaken. By November 30, 1981, Allen was forced to take a leave of absence while the Justice Department investigated charges involving Japanese gifts and $1,000 in cash found in an NSC file cabinet. By Christmas 1981, when Attorney General William French Smith cleared him of wrongdoing, James Baker and Michael Deaver had spread the word that Allen was a political liability. He resigned on January 11, 1982, having lasted barely a year. Ironically, he was victimized by essentially the same forces that had blocked my entry into the Administration.

In any event, my own state in January 1981 was not a commendable one. I had worked for the Reagan campaign for a year-and-a-half, with no compensation whatsoever to show for it. My only income came from lectures and publishing, and support from Chicago commodities trader Sidney Maduff.

In retrospect, I have to note again the strange absence during that period of any kind of support, moral or otherwise, from the American Jewish community. I had no exaggerated notion of my importance; still, from the vantage point of Jewish community leaders, here was someone who had been highly placed on the Reagan advisory team with the potential of influencing top-level policy. Yet, not one word of encouragement came from the Jewish establishment. The silence was even more glaring than the lack of support when I left Air Force Intelligence following my criticism of General Brown's anti-Israel remarks. After all, then I was simply a civil servant who had lost his job. In 1981, however, I was ostensibly positioned to play a major role in the policy process. I raise this because I am certain that the politicians in the Reagan camp were well aware of the lack of support on my behalf, and therefore could more easily leave me in the cold when the time came for appointments. The way the game was played during the Reagan Revolution required you to either "get along" by agreeing with the team, or "get lost," unless you had a powerful constituency that wanted you in the Administration and would push for your inclusion so that you could represent their interests.

Meanwhile, the State Department adjusted with its own customary ease to the incoming Reagan Administration. The careerists in Foggy Bottom assumed that, campaign rhetoric notwithstanding, nothing much would change in U.S. foreign policy, especially in the Middle East. And they were right. Only later, under Secretary of State George Shultz, did the Reagan Administration make some move toward closer relations with Israel. It was, after all, Shultz who brokered the peace pact between Israel and Lebanon that was then scuttled by Syria's President Hafez Assad.

THE BETRAYAL OF WILLIAM VAN CLEAVE

I was not the only early victim of the Reagan Administration's version of the Washington Compromise. During the 1970's, Professor William Van Cleave of the University of Southern California had established himself as a foremost nuclear strategist in the United States. It was he who coined the term "window of vulnerability" to describe the emerging period of risk for the United States in the strategic-nuclear equation with the Soviet Union. In 1980, Van Cleave proposed to candidate Reagan that he develop an

Washington, DC 11/23/83. Secretary of Defense Caspar Weinberger as he prepares to make a statement before his press conference. (Consolidated News Pictures.)

(Left to Right) Professor William Van Cleave with Dr. Vitaly Shlykov, former Russian Deputy Defense Minister, co-chairmaen of 12 ISC Conferences.

eight-year defense plan to be ready by Inauguration Day. Reagan told Van Cleave to proceed.

Headed by Van Cleave, the defense-oriented members of the foreign policy advisory team now became the nucleus of a "Defense Transition Team." We were busily drafting the promised defense program. Among the first items put to the attention of the team was a proposed multi-billion dollar sale of military equipment, including a super-sophisticated AWACS (Advanced Warning and Control System), to Saudi Arabia. This was the first we heard of the proposal, which was being pushed by oil, banking, construction, and arms interests. Van Cleave dismissed the proposed deal. In the aftermath of that decision came the announcement that the next Secretary of Defense would be Caspar Weinberger.

No one was more shocked by the announcement than the members of the defense transition team. No one had anticipated it. Few of us knew Weinberger, whose role in the campaign had been minor. Weinberger had been part of

Reagan's "Kitchen Cabinet" when he was Governor of California. He had earned the reputation as a cost-cutter ("Caspar the Knife"), but had no credentials whatsoever in defense matters.

In the waning days of the campaign, Van Cleave and Weinberger had become embroiled in a debate over defense spending.[1] That debate must have convinced a basically insecure Weinberger that Van Cleave constituted a personal threat to be disposed of. He clearly was intimidated in particular by Van Cleave's credentials in the highly complex world of nuclear strategy, a world in which Weinberger was a complete novice.

Interestingly, Weinberger soon revealed himself as basically antagonistic to Israel, notwithstanding the strong pro-Israel stance of the President and other members of the administration. The inevitable inference is that discomfort stirred by his own Jewish ancestry played a role in this view.[2]

It is testimony to Van Cleave's patriotism and integrity that he did not withdraw from the Reagan cause even after Weinberger had been named incoming Secretary of Defense, and selected the former State Department bureaucrat, Frank Carlucci, as his deputy. The two veteran Washington columnists, Rowland Evans and Robert Novak, depicted the scene when Van Cleave visited Weinberger on December 20, 1980, to brief him on the work of his transition team:

> At Weinberger's plush office in the Bechtel Corporation, the atmosphere was cold. Van Cleave explained

---

[1] *The Atlantic Monthly*, Oct. 1984, pp. 74-75.

[2] A high official in the Reagan Administration told an amusing anecdote about the visit of a high Korean official to the Pentagon brass. In small talk during the meeting, the Korean remarked on what he considered the large number of Jews in the Administration. He then listed several names, and in Weinberger's presence, his name as well. There was considerable embarrassment on all sides when it was explained that Weinberger is not a Jew, despite his name.

that he was not trying to "usurp" the secretary of defense-designate, but recalled Reagan's instructions to Van Cleave that he wanted "to hit the ground running on January 20 with his new defense plan." Weinberger, smarting from the reports that Van Cleave was trying to force him to accept a new defense budget written by Van Cleave was glacial. "As of December 22," he told Van Cleave, "you and your team are finished."[3]

Weinberger then dismissed the entire Defense Transition Team, myself included. This was already early warning that I would not be a part in any way of the new administration. Despite his dismissal, Van Cleave continued to promote the basic defense posture proposal that his team had put together. Within a month, according to *The Atlantic Monthly*, Weinberger "became an ardent proponent of the views about the Soviet military that Van Cleave, the Committee on the Present Danger, and other conservatives had put forth for so long."[4]

No one had labored harder and longer in the campaign than Bill Van Cleave. He was treated shabbily, and had only the partial satisfaction that some of his ideas formed the basis for the new Administration's overall policies toward the Soviet Union. Moreover, Van Cleave had to run the gauntlet of another disappointment. He later revealed to me: "Dick Allen and I had an explicit handshake agreement in 1980 that if I did not receive an acceptable offer by the Department of Defense, then I would become his Deputy National Security Advisor. After Weinberger's appointment, and when it was clear that I was not welcome in any significant position at the Pentagon, I told Allen that I was available. But Allen

---

[3] Rowland Evans and Robert Novak, *The Reagan Revolution*, Dutton, 1981, p. 192.
[4] *The Atlantic Monthly*, op. cit., p. 76.

reneged." According to Van Cleave, Allen offered him an ordinary staff position on the National Security Council, and Van Cleave told him to "forget it."

THE SECRET AGENDA OF CASPAR WEINBERGER

Looking back, I believe that there were several reasons for my being jettisoned by the Reagan Administration before it really got started. First, Dick Allen knew that he could not keep me under tight control, especially on Middle East matters, and he was apprehensive of anyone with strong views. Next, the State Department and the CIA would have been very upset had I come into a strategically placed policy spot vis-a-vis the Middle East; they no doubt remembered the rigorous dissents that I registered when I represented the Air Force on the National Intelligence Estimates. Yet another factor was my association with Meir Kahane, even though that association had ended in 1967, long before Kahane himself became a center of controversy. In the Republican Party, circles sympathetic to the PLO opposed me and my positions. There was also the episode in South Africa. Incidentally, I later learned that the FBI had performed on me probably the most thorough background investigation of any candidate member of the Reagan Administration, without turning up any obstacle to my appointment.

All these factors, may have played a role. I am absolutely convinced, however, that the main reason I did not receive an appointment in the Reagan Administration had to do with the proposed sale of AWACS to Saudi Arabia. The sale was among the first items on the agenda of the new administration. It was also only the opening gambit in a huge financial deal involving a variety of aircraft and other weapons and services. The interests of munitions, shipping, oil, banks, and construction industries were lined up behind it. And at the center of the deal was the Bechtel Corporation which supplied a number of Reagan appointees, notably Caspar Weinberger.

When the proposed AWACS deal made the news in 1980, the big guns of these interests swung into action. Even I received a phone call from an official in Saudi Arabia lobbying for my support. I could never endorse the proposed sale of a weapons system that would give the Saudis the ability to track and target Israeli military aircraft. There is no question in my mind that I was marked as an obstacle to the deal, and therefore had to be kept out.

I had calculated before the election that even if I did not join the Reagan Administration, at least I could hope to exert an influence on its policies in ways that had been barred during the disastrous tenure of Jimmy Carter. Yet, looking back at the Reagan legacy of two terms in office, I see a squandered opportunity for fundamental change. Appeasers, capitulationists, and defeatists wormed their way into the administration—with George Bush holding the door open—and eventually took control of the policy-making process. The "Reaganauts" were progressively pushed out, to nurse memories of the "revolution" that foundered on the Washington Compromise.

The reins of power grasped by the Bush forces essentially were used to turn the Reagan Administration around on all key issues, specifically the Middle East, the Soviet Union, and arms control. In the end, the Administration opposed Israel in Lebanon, recognized the PLO, and returned the United States to the path of unilateral disarmament—in the name of arms control! By the time that happened there were no advisors still present who would honestly inform the "hands-off President" how his original policies had been subverted and his "revolution" betrayed.

Especially reckless were Secretary Weinberger's maneuverings to strip Israel of its qualitative military superiority over the Arabs as a precondition for a regional peace agreement. A strong Israel was viewed in the Pentagon not as a deterrent to Arab aggression, but a threat to the Arab states. And, following the Kissingerian abstraction, in the interest of "balance," the weaker players' strength had to be upgraded, just as Kissinger tolerated—indeed seemed to welcome—the Soviet Union's rise to military parity with the United States in the interest of detente. In the language of the Pentagon, Weinberger sought to "level the playing field." In plain terms, Weinberger did his best to accord Syria what the Soviet Union denied it: strategic parity with Israel.

While the Reagan declaratory policy on the Middle East embraced Israel as the primary strategic asset in the region, the actual policy, in the hands of Secretary Weinberger, aimed at cultivating a strategic alignment between the United States and the Arab states, both moderate and radical. The depressing list of Weinberger's misdeeds is long and tragic. First, Weinberger consistently dishonored the U.S.-Israel Exchange of Information Agreement of 1983, which was signed by President Reagan as an effort to pacify the Israelis *after* the $8.5 billion AWACS sale. Next, he *inter alia* withheld critical intelligence information from Israel and the U.S. Congress; provided the Saudis with direct access to U.S. satellite intelligence on Israel; failed to inform the U.S. Congress and Israel of Syrian access to F-15 technology in violation of guarantees from the Saudis to safeguard this technology; suppressed information on Iraqi efforts to develop atomic, biological, and chemical weapons with the assistance of American companies, specifically U.S.-Iraq trade in nuclear and biological weapons technology; and provided to Saudi Arabia detailed U.S. intelligence assessments of Israeli Defense Forces, which they then relayed to Syria and Iraq.

Yet, these were hardly the limits of Secretary Weinberger's secret agenda. When Congress opposed his proposed sale of long-range strike aircraft and Pershing missiles to Saudi Arabia, the Saudis purchased CSS-I "Eastwind" IRBMs from China. Neither Israel nor the Congress knew of their arrival, but the CIA was certainly aware of it. Similarly, the CIA was aware that Egypt, together with Iran and Argentina, was developing the IRBM known as the BADR 2000 (later known as CONDOR II) in violation of the Camp David Accords. By making Israel's non-NATO ally status conditional on Egypt's being accorded an equal footing, Weinberger cleared the way for Cairo to obtain co-production of the American M-1 Abrams tank. This independent tank production would allow Egyptian armor formations to be massed on the Israeli border within 24 hours after a decision to repeal the Camp David Accords.

It should be remembered that during Weinberger's watch, 247 marines were slaughtered in Lebanon, the American Embassy in Beirut was bombed, and both went unavenged. We aligned with Iraq in its war with Iran—to our own detriment. We did not know how to play the balance of power in the Gulf. This laid the foundations for the future confrontation between the United States and Iraq.

It is supremely ironic that President Reagan came to embrace the rhetorical objective of Soviet arms control, which was the elimination of all nuclear arms. Yet, the Strategic Defense Initiative, which Reagan had launched in 1983 as the centerpiece of true nuclear disarmament, never got off the ground. Even more ironic is that Reagan declared his overwhelming success in defeating the "evil empire," believing that it was all his doing, when none of his major programs against the Soviet Union succeeded, and all his major positions were reversed. Reagan was a fortunate President because America's economic growth was sustained throughout his tenure. But that growth was stimulated less by "supply-side" measures—"voodoo economics," as George Bush called it—and more by the collapse of OPEC. Oil became cheap and this spurred an economic boom. Even then, under Reagan, the governmental debt grew tremendously. Fortunately for him, in the boom times the rising debt was hardly noticed.

Unfortunately for Bush, the economic engine ground to a halt, and we confronted the national deficit in its numbing magnitude. Bush's fortune was that, despite his foreign policy disasters and his support for Gorbachev, the Soviet Union imploded under the weight of its systemic failures. But for Bush to take credit for this development is the height of demagogy. Still, we know that on the Washington exchange the only currency is success—whether real or counterfeit.

9

Arms Control and Ferdinand Marcos

There was a "consolation prize" for me in the Reagan Administration, which I achieved strictly on my own. Eugene Rostow, whom I admire immensely, appointed me Senior Policy Advisor to the Arms Control and Disarmament Agency. Rostow, a former dean at the Yale Law School, had served as Under Secretary of State for Political Affairs in the 1960s and more recently as President of the Atlantic Treaty Association. He was an experienced diplomat and historian, and we shared a common view of the Soviet threat. But I quickly recognized that most of the key bureaucrats retained at ACDA would be working against implementing Rostow's views.

Rostow invited William Van Cleave to serve as Chairman of the President's Advisory Committee on Arms Control. Bill immediately began service as acting chairman. Because of his continuing criticism of Weinberger's Strategic Force Modernization plan, the nomination never reached the confirmation stage.

More generally, internecine politics and policy differences led to ACDA's being downgraded within the Administration. Rostow appointed as his deputy a Foreign Service Officer named Robert Gray, who had been his assistant when Rostow was Undersecretary of State. Gray represented in the eyes of Reaganites the old view of arms control.

They wanted to block him, but Rostow, as a matter of principle, insisted on his right to appoint his deputy. In the end,
ACDA was simply shunted by the White House off the main
tracks of policy.

In January 1983, President Reagan dismissed Eugene
Rostow as head of ACDA because of his disagreements with
Secretary of State Shultz on Middle East policy, as well as on
arms negotiations with Soviet Union. Dissent, however consistent, reasoned and compelling, was of dubious value to an
administration pandering to Arab and Soviet susceptibilities.

While at the ACDA in December 1981, I received
through a mutual friend an invitation from President
Ferdinand Marcos to visit him in the Philippines. It was a
rare opportunity to meet a major player on the world stage
in general and in Southeast Asia in particular. I took a short
leave without pay and traveled to Manila. Marcos and I met
privately several times at his presidential palace; most of the
meetings included his wife, Imelda. In the discussions
Marcos did not seem fixed on any specific subject; apparently he just wanted a general exchange. Indeed, we covered
a wide range of topics, from Gen. Douglas MacArthur to
mutual strategic interests between Israel and the
Philippines—after all, the only two nations in Asia that based
their national identities on Judeo-Christian values.

Whatever may have been the ultimate failings of the
Marcos regime, I was strongly impressed by his strategic
vision. He came across as a first-rate analyst who well understood the importance of the American presence in Southeast
Asia, which is acknowledged even today by virtually all
powers in the region, even though the Cold War is over. He
firmly believed that the Philippines could play a significant
role in U.S. strategy. We even discussed the possibility of a
rapid deployment force raised and based in the Philippines
to handle emergencies in the Far East. Such a project

promised dual benefits: It would make the Philippines an active American strategic asset by exploiting its location to protect the sea lanes of Asia—a critical factor especially for Japan—and it would bring badly needed capital into the country.

I emphasized repeatedly to Marcos his need for better public relations in the United States. Whereas his emphasis was on Congressional lobbyists, I suggested he direct a public relations campaign addressed to editorial boards and U.S. media. I warned him, too, that he might be abandoned, just as the Shah of Iran had been, and that U.S. diplomacy often fails to distinguish between friend and foe. In retrospect, I think his failure to heed this advice contributed to the downfall of his regime and the subsequent U.S. loss of its important navy and air bases in the Philippines.

Marcos and I hit it off well. I was flattered by the attention he bestowed on me. For example, at a large reception for a U.S. official, Marcos pointedly bypassed everyone and came directly to me to ask how my day had gone. Later, he threw a party for me and invited many people of note in Manila, greatly irritating the American Embassy.

Although I had the advantage of several meetings with Marcos on U.S. security posture in the Far East, no one at the U.S. Embassy took the initiative to debrief me on our discussions. Indeed, there was more hostility than curiosity from that quarter. The State Department also ignored my meetings with Marcos and the opportunities they offered because they were held without their own involvement. It was another example of how the Washington Compromise is not limited geographically to "inside the (Washington, DC) beltway," but is part of the mindset of the American bureaucracy more generally, encompassing even our "diplomats" abroad.

The encounter in the Philippines engendered a personal understanding of the bankruptcy of America's Far East policies. On his part, Marcos revealed a keen understanding of how U.S. policy was developed, formulated, and implemented. I can only wonder how that contributed to his growing cynicism and pessimism about his own place in American policy vistas. The episode expanded my vision: I recognized that the State Department's bumbling was not limited to the Middle East. From then on, I took a more active interest in East Asian affairs.

Upon returning to Washington, I learned just how irritated the U. S. Embassy in Manila had been. The State Department asked me whether I had compromised any secrets or classified materials—an accusation that I could only laugh at. My ACDA "colleagues" told me pointedly: "Well, you're going to have to be investigated." It was clear that the investigation was designed to keep me "secure" in my office, surrounded by the bureaucracy. The move was orchestrated by Rostow's chief aide in concert with his counterparts in the State Department.

I had already decided to resign. I told Rostow of my plans, but he advised me not to resign "under a cloud of uncertainty." The affair had started in December 1981; it dragged on until May 1982. I was isolated from the staff during the "investigation." My only contact was with Rostow.

I used this period of "quarantine" to begin drafting the book, *The American Retreat*—a critique of the Reagan foreign policy. My brief tenure at ACDA thus was not a total loss. In the end, since I had decided to resign anyway, the "investigation" was dropped.

The following dispatch by the Reuters News Agency on May 26, 1982, made it official:

> A conservative analyst has resigned as adviser on strategic issues to the Reagan Administration, accusing President Reagan of not giving leadership on defense and national security.

Joseph Churba, a senior policy adviser specializing in Middle East and nuclear arms policies, told Reuters he resigned from the Arms Control and Disarmament Agency (ACDA) because he was disillusioned with the administration.

He said the President, whom he also served as a campaign adviser in 1980, had shunted aside true representatives of "Reaganism" and staffed his administration with unqualified people, holdovers from Democrat Jimmy Carter and the "worst elements of the Nixon-Ford period."

Singling out Secretary of State Alexander Haig and his two top deputies, Walter Stoessel and Lawrence Eagleburger, Mr. Churba said that "these people were all identified with the politics of defeat" and the unratified SALT II arms limitation treaty.

"What we have here is a failure of presidential leadership. It stops at Reagan's door," he said.

Mr. Churba said the real problem arose "not so much because we are weak in arms but because we are weak in our strategic thinking. We have no strategy to arrest the Soviet threat."

He said President Reagan had put conservative strategists like himself in strictly advisory posts and given the real policy roles to members of the "Liberal Republican Establishment" . . . .

ACDA Spokesman Joseph Lehman told Reuters today Mr. Churba had quit earlier this month "as a result of disagreement with current policy."

My subsequently published book, *The American Retreat*, had been preceded by my work on the Carter Administration, entitled *Retreat From Freedom*. That had followed *The Politics of Defeat*, an indictment of U.S. foreign policy during the Nixon-Ford period. Therefore, this completed a trilogy of foreign policy studies. Their common denominator was that U.S. policymakers in succeeding administrations—Republican and Democratic—had forfeited the will and wherewithal for the positive achievement of U.S. objectives on a global scale.

Indeed, I was happy to be out of government service
again once I realized that the vaunted "Reagan Revolution"
was a sham. *The Washington Post's* depiction of my motives
on July 4, 1982, was accurate:

> They were outsiders who finally became insiders, but
> many of the conservative crusaders who came into office
> with President Reagan have grown frustrated and are
> resigning in increasing numbers . . .
>
> [Some lament that] "there are a lot of Republicans in
> Washington, but not a lot of Reaganites." Joe Churba puts
> it another way: "Reagan without Reaganism." Churba
> wrote background material on the Middle East for Reagan
> the presidential candidate in 1980, and later went to the
> Arms Control and Disarmament Agency. Churba takes a
> hard-line view of the Soviets and said he went into the
> administration with the conviction that "arms control in
> itself" should not be the centerpiece of Soviet-American
> relations.
>
> But he became "gradually disillusioned," he said,
> because, for one thing, "Arms control became the admin-
> istration's panic reaction to the nuclear freeze movement."
>
> Churba resigned May 7 to return to the Center for
> International Security, a hawkish think tank here. He has
> no regrets about leaving the government: "Outside is the
> only place to be."

10

The Lebanon Quagmire

Thus, in 1982, the time had come once again to try to influence international affairs and foreign policy from outside the U.S. government. There was a difference from the period after my first resignation from government in 1976. Then I could count on no allies and few friends, and everything seemed bleak. In May 1982, the opportunity to apply effective leverage on developments from the outside was far more promising. I reorganized the Center for International Security (CIS) with a focus on the Middle East.

THE "ARABIST" ROMANCE IN WASHINGTON

From the time the Reagan Administration took office, U.S. policy in the Middle East reverted steadily from candidate Reagan's avowed appreciation of Israel's strategic value into the old backwaters of "Arabism." The term "Arabist" has come to describe those in the U.S. government who see the Middle East essentially as an Arab region. Arabists gloss over the reality that the region is an ethnic mosaic of Iranians, Turks, Israelis, Maronites, Copts, Kurds, and other minorities in addition to Arabs. They argue that U.S. policy must align itself with the interests of the Arabs who command the greater population, territory and oil resources.

Ever since World War I, the ranks of Middle East specialists in the U. S. Department of State—and, indeed, in the

American academic community more generally—have been dominated by people steeped in Arab and Muslim history. Many are cultured men with considerable knowledge of the Middle East. But almost from the beginning of America's involvement in the region, a strange romanticism about the nature of Arab society has colored views. Some have called it the "Lawrence of Arabia syndrome," based on an idealist elevation of Bedouin culture. This is a tributary of the broader and enduring Western philosophical preoccupation with the "noble savage." Eighteenth-century French philosophers wrote that man in his most primitive state was "noble," and that he fell from grace when society became more sophisticated. Applied to the Middle East, that "nobility" is equated with the Bedouin on his camel in the desert, whereas the citified Arab has been corrupted by influx of Western-style civilization. This romantic view holds among Arabists to this day. It suggests, for example, that the Saudis, whose origins are so close to nomadic tribes, represent relative virtue in regional politics. A policy geared to protect their interests, therefore, also pursues a noble purpose.

No doubt many of the virtues ascribed to the desert nomad are, in fact, real: He is often hospitable, brave, and his loyalties are steadfast. But like all romantic ideas when put to the test, these are no more the reality in the desert than in the souk (the bazaar) of Cairo.

Now, Arabists in and out of the State Department have always believed, as have Arab governments themselves, that Israel is a purely domestic American concern—that is, U. S. policy toward Israel is simply a function of domestic electoral politics in which politically active American Jews hold a disproportionate influence.

Armed with this belief, the Arabists, while pushing the line that American interests lie with the Arabs because of their resources, also pretend to accept that the United States government cannot embrace an openly Arab position because of the powerful domestic lobby of American Jews. The terrain of argument over proper U.S. policy in the Middle East is, to be sure, a complex one. Basically, however, to reiterate my own view: I have consistently argued that Israel is a U.S. national security asset, *independent* of any relationship to the Jewish factor in the U.S. political arena. Unfortunately, to the extent to which Jewish lobbyists in Washington flex their muscles in Congressional battles (more recently, in "exposures" in the media), the Arabist contention—that Israel is essentially a domestic issue—is reinforced.

LEBANON 1982 AND CONVULSIONS IN WASHINGTON

All this is background to the train of developments that began with the Israeli push into Lebanon in June 1982. It is worth noting that five months earlier, on January 6, 1982, while still at ACDA, I had forecast an eventual Israeli move into Lebanon, which I projected would be a sweeping operation to change the political map of the Levant. Eugene Rostow had passed my memorandum to Caspar Weinberger, who responded with a sarcastic, "We know Dr. Churba," deeming it "doubtful" that a military operation would take place. Weinberger may have deliberately adopted this position to discourage Israel from any military operation it was planning.

On Monday, June 7, 1982, one day after the Israeli thrust into Lebanon, I proposed on the popular television news program, the "MacNeil-Lehrer Report," that the Israeli presence in Lebanon "be used as military and political leverage for the withdrawal of Syrian forces from this state, thereby permitting the reconstitution of Lebanon's integrity." In the subsequent weeks, I issued a barrage of statements to the media on the U.S. strategic stakes in both Israel and Lebanon. What I said then remains true today: Syrian hegemony over Lebanon must be eliminated if there is ever to be peace in the Levant and peace between Israel and its neighbors to the north.

On June 25, 1982, I declared that the resignation that same afternoon of Secretary of State Alexander Haig was, in part, precipitated by the growing power of Arabist and petrodollar interests in the Reagan Administration. Speaking again on the "MacNeil-Lehrer Report," I warned that the pro-Arab forces in the Reagan Administration, headed by Weinberger, were misjudging the confrontation in Lebanon. Over the previous several weeks, Haig had overruled pro-posals of the Near East Bureau at the State Department, which urged punitive action against Israel. I speculated that this must have infuriated the entrenched Arabists, and that this certainly had impaired Haig's capacity to deal with the bureaucracy.

I contended that certain elements in the Reagan Administration were in conflict with Haig over the future of the armed PLO then occupying West Beirut. The Arabists and petrodollar interests linked to Saudi Arabia were still trying to salvage the PLO politically, if not militarily. "The issue in Beirut is the terms under which PLO withdrawal will take place, and this was a very lively issue between Mr. Philip Habib, Deputy Secretary of State, and Mr. Haig," I argued. "If the Reagan intention is to preserve the PLO as a (prospective) negotiating partner in the West Bank Autonomy talks, then this would set the stage for a wider confrontation with Israel." The anti-Haig forces in the Administration were seeking "political gains for the PLO despite their military defeat."

When George Shultz was nominated to replace Haig as Secretary of State, I interpreted that to mean "the triumph of petrodollar diplomacy and the demise of the school of thought that Reagan had promoted, mainly that Israel is the primary strategic asset in the Middle East. It means that the Department of Defense and the State Department will have one voice on the Middle East"—a pro-Arab voice.

Earlier that week, on June 22, Jack Anderson's column in *The Washington Post* carried a full report on my reaction to the bankruptcy of strategic planning in the Reagan Administration, and the reason for my resignation:

> Some five months ago, before the Israeli move against the PLO occupation of Lebanon, Dr. Churba had correctly forecast the scope and political character of the Israeli operation. However, Secretary Weinberger dismissed both the probability and the implications of such action.

My worst fears about the men Reagan chose to manage foreign policy proved well-founded. The following excerpts from an Associated Press story of June 26, 1982, told the story:

> George P. Shultz, if confirmed by the Senate, will take over as Secretary of State with a reputation as being more sympathetic to Arab interests than Alexander M. Haig Jr. . . .
>
> White House officials maintained Friday that no foreign policy changes are contemplated despite Haig's resignation. But Joseph Churba, a former Arms Control and Disarmament Agency official who resigned last month, predicted an administration tilt toward Arab countries under Shultz's leadership.
>
> Appearing on PBS's "MacNeil-Lehrer Report," Churba said Shultz and Defense Secretary Caspar Weinberger hold similar views on the Middle East.
>
> Both disagree with Reagan's view that Israel is a strategic asset for the United States in the area, said Churba, who is known for his pro-Israeli views.
>
> Churba is said to have participated in the drafting of a staunchly pro-Israeli speech delivered by Reagan in September 1980 during the election campaign.
>
> Shortly after the election, Shultz said, "If I have any differences with Reagan, it's about Middle East policy based on (that) speech." He gave no details of his differences.

As I expected, Shultz entered office with a pronounced pro-Arab bias. He modified that bias after Syria nullified the agreement between Israel and Lebanon that he had brokered on May 17, 1983, and the tragic bombing of the Marine barracks in Beirut. Only then did Shultz look more objectively upon Israel.

Incidentally, on November 3, 1983, I wrote a letter to Stephen D. Bechtel, Jr., President of the Bechtel Group Inc., the largest U.S. industrial firm in the Middle East, offering to brief him on the Lebanon crisis and suggesting that he should "hear another view." On November 15 I received a reply not from Bechtel, but from Samuel M. Hoskinson, the firm's Executive Representative. I had known Hoskinson when he was the National Intelligence Officer (NIO) for the CIA when I was working in the Pentagon. Given the incestuous relationship between the CIA and the giant oil, construction and banking industries, I was not surprised to see Hoskinson reemerge as the Middle East authority for Bechtel. With characteristic arrogance, Hoskinson wrote back: "Through myself and others, we already have access to the *full* range of information, views and analysis on developments in the Middle East. I am sure that you do have a 'rather different perspective' than the so-called Arabists, but it is one that we are very familiar with."

The record is clear that there is a powerful pro-Arab lobby in Washington representing vast U.S. oil, banking, construction, and arms interests. It is worth recalling that George Shultz was a former President and Caspar Weinberger a former Vice President of the Bechtel Corporation, which was deeply involved in Arab construction interests, particularly in Saudi Arabia.

Time magazine, on June 28, 1982, carried my assessment that the Israeli move could reap political dividends for the U.S. interest in permanent Middle East peace. On the same day, the media continued to feature reports on the George Shultz-Bechtel-Saudi connection. In a segment on NBC Nightly News that evening, I declared: "There will be one point of view between State and Defense and that point of view will be anti-Israel."

On July 2, I warned in a press release that whether or not President Reagan himself was implicated, there was little question that the American people were being misled about Administration policy in Lebanon. In his press conference on June 30, Reagan pretended an understanding of the Israeli position in Lebanon. Behind this facade, the dominant Arabist interests in the State and Defense Departments were formulating policy in ways inimical to Lebanese, Israeli, and, indeed, U.S. security interests.

All this represented a sustained effort to make political gains for the PLO, notwithstanding its military defeat. The intent was to secure a PLO role as a potential negotiating partner in the autonomy negotiations for the West Bank. American and Saudi support for Lebanese Christian leader Bashir Gemayel's presidential aspiration was conditioned on his acceptance of a PLO presence and political role in Lebanon. An Israeli pullback in Lebanon—prior to a political settlement—was pressed in the guise of "separation of forces." The resulting politico-military vacuum was filled, in part, by PLO-Saudi surrogates thereby maintaining pressure on the Christian community in Lebanon.

These steps assured continued chaos and division within Lebanon. Its land remained the battleground for the Arab-Israel conflict, deflecting attention away from the more fundamental conservative-radical dichotomy characterizing Arab politics. The less attention was focused on the feudal character and exorbitant wealth of the Saudi regime, the more secure it deemed its position. Petrodollar interests in the Reagan Administration were mobilized accordingly.

On July 7, 1982, I warned that the Reagan Administration was courting military and political reversals by proposing the use of U. S. Marines to evacuate the PLO from Beirut, where they were holding the civilian population hostage. Speaking on ABC's Nightline, I warned that even if the PLO gave every assurance of cooperation:

> Arafat does not have complete authority over the rival factions within the PLO who are competing for position and influence. And these maverick groups can easily open fire on American troops, at which point we will be confronted with two prohibitive choices: a) we can return the fire with the certainty of civilian casualties, and then be in precisely the same position the Israelis are today; or b) not to return this fire and accept our casualties, thus demonstrating the impotence of American military power. There are many bitter enemies of the United States who want to entangle the United States in the Lebanese quagmire, and what better way than to shoot at American troops? If we had any intention of contributing militarily to this situation, the United States should confine its activities to training the Lebanese National Army, down to the NCO level. I would suggest very strongly that the Lebanese army take full responsibility for the policing of its own area under its own sovereignty.

In the same interview, on the question of the political danger inherent in the Administration's proposal, again I warned:

> There is no alternative to the surrender of the PLO units and their withdrawal from Lebanon. The American escort would be a terrible and damaging blow to our diplomatic process in the area. If we proceed according to this arrangement, we will have given the PLO political victory after its military defeat, because we would have recognized, in a formal relationship with them, something we had denied them in the past. And we would have done this in violation of our commitments to the Israelis and

even in violation of our commitments set down by the Camp David process.

The discussion also turned on the capacity of the Lebanese to govern and police their own country. On this point I said:

> With the Israelis in the background and with American political influence coming to the fore, there is more flexibility for the Lebanese national government to develop its own credentials. After all, we are trying to reconstitute the Lebanese national state, and there is no substitute for the Lebanese National Army. No one else should do this job for them but the Lebanese, including the withdrawal of Syrian troops, Israeli troops, the PLO, and even U.S. forces.

In sum, during the critical early weeks of the war in Lebanon, I tried to explain, at every opportunity, what I saw as the geostrategic content of the conflict. My counsel was not requested in government, and my arguments in the media went unheeded. It is fair to suggest that the failures of U.S. policy in 1982 would come to haunt us more directly eight years later.

The Israeli incursion had provided an historic opportunity to change the political map and spell the end of PLO and Syrian aggression. But the U.S. would not allow Israel to finish the job (just as the U.S. itself would not finish the job in Iraq a decade later). It would seem that since the Korean conflict, we Americans are psychologically incapable of living with victory. In Lebanon the Reagan Administration could have quietly used Israel as a surrogate; instead, we intervened in an "even-handed" manner in order to prevent an Israeli victory.

Ironically, it was then Vice President George Bush who, while in Saudi Arabia at King Fahd's birthday celebration, conveyed to the Syrians and the PLO the message that the

United States would not allow a decisive Israeli victory. As a consequence, the PLO left Lebanon with their weapons, while the Israelis watched.

THE BITTER HARVEST OF REAGAN MIDDLE EAST POLICIES

What I wrote in *Politics of Defeat* in 1977 held true during the Reagan years, and in many respects continues to be valid:

> The same diplomacy of defeat which would obfuscate the true source of the Arab-Israeli conflict is also sealing the fate of Christian Lebanon. Through American toleration of open military moves in Lebanon, Damascus has achieved a new dominance in the Arab East despite the fact that the Lebanese battlefield is within short reach of Israel. We have lost our ability to distinguish between friend and foe, between truly appendant pro-Western powers and between radical totalitarian elements that one day smile at us and graciously allow the evacuation of our citizens from war zones and the next day connive with the Soviets in their separate designs for dominance. Under the debilitating influence of the United States politics of defeat, we have lost opportunities to bolster American security through a number of countries, each with a mature and circumspect sense of its national place in the region and a vested interest in stability stretching from Israel, through a Christian Lebanon, to Turkey and Iran. We dare not place our security in the hands of Arab powers such as Syria and Iraq, who suffer from a crisis of national identity, endemic sectarian instability and social fragmentation. Such states . . . are frustrated revisionist powers which thrive on the instability in the territory they covet—Lebanon, Jordan and Arabia.[1]

---

[1] Churba, Op. Cit., P.198.

What did the Reagan Administration gain with its policy in 1982? We reaped the bombing of the Marine barracks in Lebanon, the destruction of Pan Am 103, an 8-year epidemic of hostage-taking, and a continuation of the politics of defeat in the hopes of "reaching out" to radical forces in order to do business with them. Instead, they gave us the business.

In the latter context, on March 21, 1983, I delivered a warning via United Press International that proved tragically prescient:

> A former adviser in the Reagan Administration said Monday the United States soon may face a dilemma in Lebanon.
>
> Joseph Churba, founder of the nonprofit Center for International Security in Washington, told a news conference at the Jewish Community Center that at some point, U. S. troops in Lebanon either will have to be increased, or withdrawn.
>
> "The United States has frozen itself into a position of paralysis," Churba said, saying the United States is in an awkward position because it has only 1,800 troops as a peacekeeping force in Lebanon. He added the U.S. has not established any superiority for respect in the area, partly because of U.S. policy forbidding fraternization with Israelis who he said are treated "as the enemy".

On April 18, 1983, the U. S. Embassy in Beirut was bombed. Sixty-three people were killed, including 17 Americans. On October 23, 1983, a truck bomb destroyed the Marine barracks near the Beirut airport. Several days later, the death toll had reached 241. Soon thereafter, the U.S. peacekeeping force quit the troubled land. Just as we were later bombed onto Iraq's side in the Iran-Iraq War, we were bombed out of Lebanon as a result of our inability to read the play of forces on the ground. The supreme irony here is that the guns of the U.S. Sixth Fleet were trained more on Israel than on Syria during this period. No one who lived through it could forget the widely publicized photograph of an American marine facing off an Israeli tank. Talk about Israeli "intransigence" showed an inability to differentiate between enemy and friend.

In March, 1983, the CIS published an open letter in *The New York Times*, signed by 280 retired admirals and generals. The advertisement stated that the Israeli technology displayed during the 1982 Lebanon war was forcing the Soviet Union to reconsider basic strategic concepts for the defense of its own major population centers. The letter called upon NATO to apply these insights to its strategy for deterrence and defense against the Soviet Union.

"The profound military significance of the decisive defeat of Soviet arms in Lebanon is being obscured by the political turmoil surrounding Israel's armed intervention," the advertisement said. "The Israelis have made major breakthroughs in conventional and electronic weaponry" with their startling downing of more than 80 Syrian warplanes above eastern Lebanon. Israeli tactics and technology employed in the Lebanon war offer "exciting prospects for arms control and disarmament negotiations as well as the intriguing possibility of reducing the reliance on escalation to tactical nuclear weapons," the statement concluded.

Earlier, on September 10, 1982, I had been quoted by Reuters on that issue as follows:

> Israel displayed startling new war technology during the recent fighting in Lebanon, some of which is superior to anything that the United States has in its arsenals, the head of a private research group said today. Joseph Churba, Director of the Center for International Study, said U.S. officials undoubtedly recognized that these advances had reduced Washington's leverage for controlling Israeli actions in the Middle East.

> If the Israeli advances were made available to NATO,
> Dr. Churba said, "We would probably be able to deny
> Soviet superiority on the central front in Europe by con-
> ventional means alone, reducing the need for tactical
> nuclear weapons."
>
> In an interview with Reuters, he said the Israeli tech-
> nology demonstrated prowess over Soviet-made planes,
> armor, surface-to-air missiles and command and control
> communications used by the Syrians in Lebanon.
>
> In particular, he said Israel had developed a 105-mm
> armor-piercing shell which destroyed a dozen of Mos-
> cow's premier T-72 tanks. "Nothing in our inventory can
> penetrate the T-72," he said.

Only later did I learn that similar conclusions had been
drawn by Marshal Nikolai Ogarkov, the Chief of the General
Staff, credited with triggering a "revolution in Soviet military
thinking" in the 1980s. Ogarkov concluded that the Soviets
would have to make a concerted move toward high-tech pro-
ficiency in conventional weapons. He argued that Israel's
destruction of electronic countermeasures in Lebanon, had it
been applied in a war on the Central Front in Europe, would
have effectively nullified Soviet defenses and strategically
opened the way to Moscow and Leningrad.

A BRIEF RUN AT CONGRESS

But if the State Department exhibits a chronic inability
to distinguish friend from foe, the orthodox Jewish establishment of Brooklyn behaves little better. My statements and
high profile on Middle East issues drew the attention of some
well-placed and well-to-do citizens in my home district in
Brooklyn who had become thoroughly disillusioned with
both the politics and personal duplicity of their representative in Congress, Stephen Solarz. I was encouraged to make
a run for his Congressional seat, which represented the
largest Jewish constituency in the United States.

Solarz and I had met before. Shortly after the Brown incident in 1976, I accepted his invitation to lunch. He told me then that he felt my remarks on General Brown were an attack on the U.S. military establishment (the farthest thing from my mind). Subsequently, in the early 1980s, Solarz took the position that Israel should withdraw from the West Bank; indeed, he was among the first in the Congress to take that stance (although he later disavowed it). Luckily for Israel, Solarz soon stopped ministering his nostrums for the Middle East and turned his attention to Africa and East Asia, with equally dismal results. He made a name for himself with frequent junkets to the Far East. He later made a bigger name for himself as one of the top ten "check-bouncers" in the Congressional banking scandal.

I was encouraged to enter the race for his seat on the strength of my position that Israel should be regarded as a strategic asset rather than a ward of the United States. I had never before considered elective office. Still, it seemed logical that I should propagate my view in the U.S. Congress, and do so while representing the largest Jewish constituency, thereby gaining the chance not only to have an impact on policy, but also in shaping a better message for the American Jewish establishment.

The setting in 1983 seemed favorable. Solarz was vulnerable. I received endorsements from right and left (literally so). Roy Cohn, leader of the powerful East Side Conservative Club, hosted a reception for me and pledged the "unreserved support of conservatives." There was support as well in the mainstream Democratic Party, largely because of distrust of Solarz, who had developed his own little machine. Meade Esposito, a colorful figure in Brooklyn politics, invited me for dinner in Little Italy. He was most gracious, and unexpectedly endorsed my candidacy. Support suddenly flowed from all sides—Jews, Catholics, Italians, Democrats, Republicans, and Conservatives.

Word began to spread in the community that my candidacy was serious, and Solarz quickly moved to block me. He met with community leaders and cut his deals, using his favorite currency of social services to be provided. One fateful day came the denouement: a well-known writer was sent as an emissary by the community leaders. We met in the courtyard of a Manhattan hotel. The message was that they wanted to support my candidacy—in an adjoining district. They wanted me to run, not against Solarz but against his rival, Charles Schumer. I patiently explained that my motivation was as much to dislodge Solarz as it was to become a Congressman. But Solarz, notwithstanding his questionable record on defense issues and Israel, had the Orthodox Jewish leadership back in his corner. I lost all interest and abandoned my candidacy.

The Washington Compromise thus took a side-trip to Brooklyn. In the end, the only satisfaction I drew from my dip into electoral politics, brief as it was, was the knowledge that it had cost Solarz. He was forced to pay a higher price in the many deals he made with his manipulative constituents who used me as leverage.

My education also benefited. I relearned that there was no correlation between what Brooklyn Orthodox Jewish community "leaders," touted as religious and moral principle and the reality of their behavior.

11

The International Security Council

The high profile struck by the Center for International Security during the Lebanon conflict attracted the attention of Israel's Ambassador to the UN, Moshe Arens. Our emphasis on Israel as a strong ally of the U.S. was obviously appealing to Israeli leaders. For American Jewry, the publication by the CIS of open letters signed by hundreds of retired U.S. generals and flag officers was significant: it removed some of the fear of being castigated for expressing support for Israel as Americans.

Ambassador Arens sponsored a luncheon on my behalf to help the CIS raise funds for a stable operating budget. The affair took place in New York in July 1982. Some 30 wealthy Jews, mostly of the liberal persuasion, attended. They pledged a substantial amount. It was not long, however, before I determined that the money was drying up. When I investigated, I learned that the would-be contributors lost interest when I began talking about the Soviet threat. They worried that the activities of the CIS would adversely affect U.S.-Soviet detente, preferring that our work be an appendage of the American-Jewish Lobby for Israel. For reasons that I have amply described, however, this would have defeated the whole effort by playing once again into the hands of the Arabists. When I informed Arens that the pledged support for the CIS was not coming through, he merely shrugged. I was advised by many wellwishers: "Focus on Israel and forget the Soviet Union." Mindful of my father's example, I turned my back on the merchant princes.

THE UNIFICATION CHURCH TO THE RESCUE

Fate intervened in the person of the Reverend Sun Myung Moon, leader of the Unification Church, who agreed to support a newly established International Security Council (ISC). As successor to the CIS, it would address foreign and defense policy issues. It would do so in complete independence, without any editorial or political direction whatsoever from the Unification Church.

Why did I get involved with an organization with a controversial religious message and roots in far-away Korea? At stake were considerations that went beyond the comprehension of bureaucrats and businessmen; they also transcended U.S.-Israeli relations. There was, first of all, logic in an "Asian connection" the economies of East Asia were booming and its political leaders were more keenly aware of geopolitical realities than many of the "sophisticates" in Western foreign policy circles. As for being associated with a controversial religion, that was part of my heritage. Simply put, there was a correlation of long-term security concerns, and the Unification Church was willing to do what my own co-religionists were not: give financial support—without strings attached—to an organization that would bring to bear the best minds available in the study and analysis of global strategic realities, and to make these findings available, without compromise, to a broad policy audience in the U.S. and abroad.

A few words are in order about the principal benefactor of the International Security Council. Sun Myung Moon was born on January 6, 1920, in what is now North Korea. He received his revelations, so to speak, at the age of 16 and became a practicing missionary for his own "Unification" church. This made him a rival to the other sects of Christian Koreans.

During the Korean war, Moon was imprisoned by the North Koreans for his missionary work and sentenced to death. He was saved by American troops on the day before his scheduled execution. After the war, Moon continued his activities as a fervent anti-Communist. He mobilized resources based in Japan and worldwide, and sponsored seminars and meetings around the globe against the doctrines of Communism and Socialism.

Reverend Moon knew of me because of interviews I had given to *Newsworld,* a New York newspaper owned by the Unification Church, well before the Reagan campaign. I was one of the few people who would talk to their reporters. Concerned with the Soviet threat, I did not discriminate among those interested in my views.

Dr. Bo Hi Pak was Reverend Moon's right-hand man. At one time he had served as an assistant defense attache in the South Korean Embassy in Washington. I had been introduced to him during the Reagan campaign by a *Newsworld* reporter, Ted Agres, who had interviewed me several times.

I reached an understanding with Bo Hi Pak whereby the Unification Church would provide funding, and I would run the International Security Council program free of editorial or political interference from the Church. To this day, I am happy to say that the agreement was always scrupulously upheld. The church never interfered in ISC deliberations or positions taken.

To underline the scope of ISC concerns, an Advisory Council was created. The list of advisors has included, at one time or another, some of the most distinguished names in the political, military, and academic professions world-wide. Serving at this time of writing are the former U. S. military

THE WASHINGTON COMPROMISE

service chiefs Admiral Elmo Zumwalt Jr., USN(Ret.), General Alfred M. Gray, USMC(Ret.), General Michael J. Dugan, USAF(Ret.), General Carl E. Vuono, USA(Ret.), along with such outstanding civilian analysts as Bill Van Cleave, A. James Gregor, Walter Hahn, William J. Mazzocco, Leon Goure and former Ambassadors David G. Jordan, John Norton Moore, and William R. Kintner. There has been an equally long list of distinguished personalities in Europe, East Asia and Latin America, including former NATO Secretary General Joseph Luns.

THE ISC'S SELF-ASSIGNED MISSION

From the beginning, the ISC defined its role by affirming the existence of a global threat targeted against the United States and the Free World, and calling that threat by its proper name: the drive by the Soviet Union for global hegemony. The ISC also would describe the shape of the Soviet strategic design as it appeared in various regions around the world. It was to alert the national leadership and public of the Free World to the dimensions, intensity and urgency of the common challenge.

In the wake of the collapse of the Soviet Union, there may be some fashionable, "revisionist" notions about the aims of the men in the Kremlin. However, there can be no controversy, even in retrospect, however, about Soviet military power. The Soviet leaders commanded the largest military machine in history, with five million men under arms at its peak in 1988. It had warships and submarines stalking the seven seas, manned spaceships permanently in orbit, and enough nuclear missiles to pulverize the planet several times over.

The ISC was founded not only to define the threat in all of its global dimensions, but to formulate an affirmative response by the West—a response that was also equal to the challenge of leading the international community of nations into the post-Communist era. "What the Free World requires above all else is a common political will," was the Council's motto.

It was a demanding agenda we thus undertook, but one we deemed absolutely essential. In free, open and pluralistic societies, consensus on even the most fundamental, life-threatening issues evolves slowly, if at all. And because free societies are basically non-ideological, they find it especially difficult to understand and defend themselves against regimes driven by ideological orthodoxies.

A telling example of this inability to grasp the true identity of the adversary was the continuing emphasis in the United States on disarmament as the road to peace. What most Americans failed to realize is that disarmament is at best the consequence of peace established between systemically compatible nations—e.g. the United States and Canada—but that in the absence of fundamental changes in the Soviet system, "peace" in the nuclear age resembled at best a military armistice behind which the struggle continued, pending a final showdown. Americans thus found it difficult to embrace a long-term strategy that took as its fundamental assumption the fact that true peace with the Soviet Union, as it was then constituted, was unachievable. Appreciating this, the Soviets periodically launched peace overtures with an overriding purpose: obstruct and prevent a strategic consensus within the United States on the Soviet threat.

Western resolve was further weakened by failure to understand the integrated nature and global reach of Soviet strategy. The Soviets' most valuable ally was Western disunity, beginning with disunity of fundamental understanding. Given this disunity, the Soviets were free to adjust their global strategic design as expedient, cutting losses on one front in line with priorities, while moving forward relentlessly on other fronts or opening new ones.

Basic to the West's disunity of understanding was the tendency to compartmentalize the world and its conflicts. Instead, policymakers had to look upon each manifestation of threat in a global context, and synthesize a responsive strategy accordingly.

Indeed, the need for a "global view" was paramount. U.S. policy-makers tended to look at conflicts as if their implications and costs were confined to the given region. But a U.S. defeat in Central America or Southern Africa could exert rippling effects into other geographical theaters, encouraging the Soviets to employ similar tactics.

American policy-makers brought to bear a similarly compartmentalized view of "levels of conflict." They seemed to assume that the principal stakes of U.S.-Soviet competition were those relevant to the direct dealings between the superpowers, notably issues of nuclear weapons and their control. In contrast, the Soviet view of conflict did not draw sharp distinctions in terms of magnitudes of weapons or sizes of combatants involved. Similarly, the Soviets did not differentiate between developments that directly affected the superpower relationship and those that did not. The Soviet strategic view, rather, stressed that the collective effect of small but "ideologically proper" policies would register on the larger stage, where the end-game between socialism and "capitalist imperialism" would be played out. The Soviets operated on the assumption that successes in such high-level fields as nuclear weapons paved the way for successes on the local level, and that local breakthroughs could strengthen the Soviet position versus the United States at the level of superpower confrontation.

An affirmative Western strategy was even more fundamentally obstructed by the misperception that the West and
the Soviets spoke the same language and held the same
vision of peace; that the Soviets could be "persuaded" to
change their behavior in the interest of a "stable coexistence;"
and that there were "moderates" in the Kremlin who merited
Western encouragement and support.

Such self-debilitating attitudes were especially conspicuous in periods of ostensible U.S.-Soviet detente, when the
political fortunes of U.S. national leaders were inextricably
linked with the "success" or "failure" of openings to the
Soviet Union. The phenomenon also became pronounced at
times of real or rumored leadership change in the Kremlin.
The Soviets, well aware of their audience and the latter's
predilections, used disinformation of "internal struggle"
with substantial tactical and strategic effect.

The Soviets clearly believed that by lowering the salience
of conflict in some arenas, and by establishing a moral equiv-
alence between the superpowers, they could acquire greater
leeway to maneuver internationally while stifling minority
voices of strategists within the United States. Unquestionably,
if the United States were to move in the direction of an affirmative strategy, the Soviets would make an early effort to persuade the American body politic that a U.S. counterstrategy
against the Soviet Union was both dangerous and unneces-
sary. The Soviets appreciated Chinese philosopher Sun Tzu's
dictum about the desirability of defeating the enemy's strategy. But why not strangle it in its crib?

What was to be the core of an affirmative strategy?
Given fundamental weaknesses of the Soviet Union, and its
increasingly pronounced inability to compete politically or
economically with democratic systems, the Free World had
the opportunity to effect changes in Communist regimes so

as to render them less of a threat to the international order. But that entailed a disciplined Western policy of diplomatic "linkage" addressed to real Soviet concessions in human liberties. The Soviet system itself would be made the issue in East-West dealings. The West would reject joint political and diplomatic ventures, for they implied a moral equivalency and a shared agenda. By waging war with other means, the Free World would constantly create new demands upon the Soviet system, new issues requiring satisfaction and institutional change in the Soviet Union.

Shifting the focus of international diplomacy from world peace to world order, the Free World would make a collective effort to demand Soviet compliance with the agreements to which it was a signatory, such as the UN Charter, the Yalta Agreement, the Universal Declaration of Human Rights, memoranda on consultation by Presidents Nixon and Brezhnev, and the Helsinki Final Act. These demands were to be given diplomatic primacy.

On the military level, an affirmative strategy called for seeking to limit the political utility of the Soviet military arsenal by denying the Soviet leadership confidence in its military capability. The United States would in this context have to make its nuclear weapons *useable* to deter attack but, if necessary, actually to defend U.S. interests and allies. It would have to arrest the trend toward unilateral nuclear disarmament.

This is the challenge that the ISC set for itself as we started on our journey . . . .

12

Trouble in America's Hemispheric Backyard

Soviet machinations in Central America and their implications for U.S. global strategy, especially in NATO, preoccupied Reagan Administration officials in the early 1980s. With minimal resource investments in that region, Moscow was managing both to preoccupy U. S. policy with a growing problem close to its borders and to stir dissonance in the Western Alliance. Even before the founding of the International Security Council, its predecessor, the CIS, had published a newsletter and produced TV and radio commentaries to inform the American public about the repression of civil liberties in Nicaragua and the Sandinistas' links to international terrorist networks.

While some Americans were quick to recognize Soviet strategic encroachment into the hemisphere beyond their well established base in Cuba, Europeans tended to see the evolving crisis in Central America as a combustion of social and economic problems endemic to the local countries, much like those afflicting some areas in Africa and Asia. They generally failed to recognize the Soviet Union's growing influence in the area as a part of a global strategy against its superpower rival.

CARRYING THE CARIBBEAN TO EUROPE

It was to educate Europeans about the true significance of the Central American developments that the International Security Council staged its very first conference in February 1985 in Paris. The conference addressed the strategic implications of the Soviet threat in the Caribbean basin. In attendance were more than 100 retired and active senior military officers and national security experts from 21 countries on four continents. The meeting brought home to Europeans for the first time the extent of the Free World's combined stakes in the security and stability of the Caribbean basin.

At the time, public opinion in Europe was divided in its perception of the Sandinista regime in Nicaragua. By and large, conservative parties and media were sympathetic to the U.S. Administration's view that Nicaragua had fallen under a Marxist-Leninist regime, with massive support from the Soviet Union, Cuba and other Communist countries. The strong left-of-center political parties and media in Europe, however, took up the drumbeat that a democratic revolution had taken place in Nicaragua and that U.S. support for the Contras constituted an intervention in Nicaragua's internal affairs. Indeed, Nicaragua was becoming the new rallying ground for the easily mobilized hordes of student protesters in Western Europe.

On the more responsible level of argument—which the ISC conference addressed—the demand that Central American states determine their own future without outside interference not only failed to take into account the nature of the emerging regime in Nicaragua, but also U. S. security interests and treaty obligations. It also minimized Cuba's role in Latin America as the stalking-horse for Soviet designs. The emerging problem was all the more potentially divisive for NATO because of the prospect that the United States might

ICS Advisors (left to right): General Michael J. Dugan, USAF (Ret.) former Chief of Staff, USAF, Dr. Norman Polmar, noted naval authority.

ultimately have to call upon naval forces earmarked for the North Atlantic to deal with the Soviet-Cuban challenge and secure sea lanes in its own backyard. The drain of naval power might negatively affect NATO's overall capability to deter aggression and maintain the essential nexus of sea lines communication across the Atlantic.

Statistics presented to the conference by retired U.S. Army Gen. Michael S. Davison further illuminated the implications of a deepened projection of Soviet power into the Caribbean Basin. In peacetime, 47 percent of all U.S. trade passes through U.S. ports in the Gulf of Mexico and the Caribbean, along with 57 percent of all U.S. oil imports. In an European emergency, 50 percent of the U.S. forces dispatched as reinforcements would embark through those same ports.[1] Moreover, most of the United States' largest military installations, military equipment manufacturing and storage depots are located west of the Appalachians, placed

---

[1] ISC Conference Report on The Caribbean Basin and Global Security: Strategic Implications of the Soviet Threat, Paris, March, 1985, pp. 29-36.

there in the pre-nuclear age to provide strategic depth, and for ready access to Gulf ports through the inland river system. Then-Secretary of the Navy John Lehman estimated in the early 1980s that in a wartime contingency some 85 percent of military logistics would cross the Gulf harbors.

The sea lanes for oil imports were crucial as well for bauxite coming from Surinam, Guyana, Haiti and Jamaica, iron ore from Brazil and Venezuela, copper from Peru and Chile, tin from Bolivia and other metals from western South America which transited the Panama Canal. The Caribbean states provided 75 percent of U.S. aluminum needs. And, ultimately, there was the problem of Mexico: its unique domestic difficulties, historic border troubles with Central America, and a populist left, heavily infiltrated by Communist propaganda, always ready to take up the latest line against the United States. The U.S.-Mexican border—the only land border in the world between the Third World and the industrialized West—was largely undefended and under constant "attack" by impoverished Mexicans and other Central Americans seeking illegal entry into the U.S.

Therefore, from a U.S. national security standpoint, unhampered access to the sea lanes that traverse the Caribbean and adjacent waters was essential. This geopolitical axiom continues to be valid in the post-Cold War era. Were the Panama Canal to be blocked or the Caribbean shipping lanes threatened during a crisis in Europe or the Middle East, U.S. capacity to meet its defense commitments could be seriously impaired. Similarly, in the event of a major crisis in the Far East—e.g. in Korea—upward of 40 percent of U.S. reinforcements would have to cross the Caribbean and the Panama Canal in a westward direction. Without the Canal, forces and supplies from the West Coast destined for Europe or the Far East would have to be diverted around Cape Horn, adding as much as three weeks to minimum ship transit time.

The United States also maintained a vast network of communications, navigational and tracking facilities throughout the region, including listening posts monitoring ship and submarine activity in the Atlantic Ocean and approaches to the Caribbean. There are major naval training facilities in Puerto Rico and at Guantanamo Bay in Cuba, which has the best anchorage in the Western Hemisphere. Finally, and important to the continuing development in U.S. anti-submarine capabilities, the Navy's Atlantic Underseas Test and Evaluation Center was located in the Bahamas and the Virgin Islands.

Speakers at the 1985 Paris conference identified three interrelated threats in the Caribbean to American and NATO security interests: the proliferation of low-intensity conflicts, such as in El Salvador, where left-wing guerrillas sought to topple a democratically-elected government; the militarization of Cuba and, progressively, of Nicaragua; and the growing power projection of Soviet and Cuban military capabilities.

Nicaragua aside, an insurgency victory in El Salvador threatened to accelerate the flares of conflict northward toward Mexico and southward toward Panama, with all sorts of international security implications. Adverse regional trends were weakening the global posture of the United States. As Gen. Davison summarized: "Simply stated, there is a direct relationship between events in the Caribbean and NATO. As security conditions deteriorate in the Caribbean, more U.S. attention and resources will necessarily be focused away from NATO and toward the Basin. In an era of increasing resource constraints, it becomes, in a sense, a zero-sum game in which the NATO alliance wins only if the adverse security trends are reversed in the Caribbean."[2]

---

[2] Ibid.

COUNTERING THE SOVIET TENTACLES
INTO THE HEMISPHERE

In the post-Cold War era, statements such as the one above by General Davison may sound like exaggerated echoes of alarmists proven wrong. "Revisionists" of the Cold War may argue more generally that there was never any real threat to the U.S. interests in the region. There is always comfort in hindsight. But hindsight also raises another question: Had the U.S. not responded in Central America—and elsewhere—would the Cold War be over?

It is clear in retrospect that Soviet leaders keenly understood that the Caribbean and the Gulf of Mexico constitute an inland sea that can be bottled up by hostile air and naval power deployed in or near the vital sea lines of communications. Soviet strategy in the region therefore was directed at gaining sufficient control, directly or through surrogates, over critical "choke" points and the capacity to interdict the major maritime routes crossing the region. The linchpin of Soviet strategy was, of course, Cuba.

Concern about Soviet activity in Central and Latin America, therefore, wove through much of the ISC's activity in the 1980s. In a 1987 conference held in Hawaii, the ISC warned that the Soviet-backed "Cuban-Nicaraguan axis poses a major challenge to Mexico." External ideological forces could provoke chaos in a Mexico already rife with economic and political unrest. Such a development would have the effect of tying down substantial U.S. military forces and triggering a flood of immigrants into the United States. At the same time, the Soviets were also working hard to effect the removal of U.S. forces from Panama.[3]

---

[3]ISC Conference Report on The Hawaii Declaration, *Geopolitics of Security in the Greater Pacific Basin*, Hawaii, March 1988, p. 7.

At an earlier conference in Quito, Ecuador, in 1986—addressed to collective security in the Western Hemisphere—an ISC declaration called attention to the growing Marxist-Leninist threat. Terrorism and insurrection, often aided and abetted by drug trafficking, had reached crisis levels in several American countries. A Soviet-backed propaganda drive, distorting cherished historical and cultural symbols, endeavored to subvert an entire generation. The emergence of the Soviet Union as a global maritime power posed a potential military threat to those countries bordering the South Atlantic and Pacific waters.

The ISC suggested that the inter-American system be provided with adequate mechanisms to cope with the "vertical" war of transnational subversion, guerrilla actions and terrorism that characterized the effort of Marxist-Leninists to extend their power in the Americas. As a guiding principle, the ISC declared that "security without economic and social development is not enough—just as development without security is unattainable." A revitalized Organization of American States should seek to resolve, behind the shield of collective security, measures to deal with such festering issues as poverty, injustice, inequality, human rights abuses and the huge Latin American debt burden.[4]

As the Reagan Administration wound down in 1988 and Americans prepared to go to the polls to elect a new president, the ISC published a strategic assessment of the situation in Central America that could serve as a guideline for future U.S. policy in the region. It recommended:

> Any effective U.S. strategy would have to involve the removal of the Soviet Union and Cuba from develop-

---

[4] ISC Conference Report on The Quito Declaration, Collective Security in the Western Hemisphere and the OAS, Quito, Ecuador, October 1986, p.5.

ments in Central America by raising the cost of their meddling in the hemisphere.

To do that, short of direct military action, requires both a subtle and tough policy of linkage: What the Soviet bloc most needs, it cannot get without retiring from the region. Whether it is a credit or a new arms control agreement, all would be denied without such a decision.[5]

A New and Foreboding Hemispheric Scenario

Since that time the Nicaraguans have thrown off Sandinista rule—at least partially so. A 1990 ISC advertisement in the *New York Times* credited Violetta Chamorro's electoral victory over the Sandinistas to the Nicaraguans themselves, but also to the pressure applied by the United States over time. But the ISC statement also warned the Bush Administration not to focus too hastily on a demobilization of the Contras. Instead, the U.S. government should make it absolutely clear that game-playing by Sandinista leader Daniel Ortega and his discredited junta would not be tolerated—and that the U.S. would take whatever action it deems appropriate to guarantee the success of the Nicaraguan people's revolution for freedom and democracy.

The warning was not heeded. At this writing the Sandinistas, while ostensibly out of governmental leadership in Nicaragua, still dominate the army and manipulate the politicians — the ultimate arbiters of power. More generally, despite the enormous material and human expenditure on the whole Central American problem during the years of the Reagan and Bush Administrations, the U.S. continues to face in the region a welter of deep and interlaced problems, all impacting on the U.S. Beyond a campaign of interdicting the narcotics flow from and through the area, which has been

---

[5]Central America: A Political Strategic Assessment: International Security Council, Washington, D.C., August 1988, p. 32.

woefully ineffective, no overall U. S. game-plan, let alone strategy, is in place. Personalities in the Carter Administration who were responsible for the disastrously myopic policy of easing the march to power by the Sandinistas in the late 1970s are again prominent in the Clinton Administration in shaping Central American and Caribbean policy.[6]

To be sure, in Central America as in other realms, the U.S. is in a decidedly better position than it was in the 1980s. The long arm of Soviet intervention into the area has withered. Fidel Castro's Communist dictatorship seems to be on the verge of disintegration——or implosion. Mexico, under President Salinas de Gortari, moved away from autarchical economic policies and toward some measure of political liberalization with the promise of economic integration in a North American trading bloc; still the chaotic violence of more recent Mexican politics once more becloud the future course of our neighbor to the south. Just as the demise of Communism on the Eurasian land mass has left behind a seething mass of problems for the successor regimes and for American policymakers, not only are fundamental, inflammable issues in the Caribbean-Central American region unresolved, but new ones are multiplying.

Much as it would be welcome, a collapse of Castro's dictatorship in Cuba bodes substantial problems for the United States. A mass exodus from Cuba to the southern United States would add staggeringly to an already debilitating problem of illegal immigration. American policymakers got a taste of that in the Castro-instigated and controlled Mariel Exodus in 1980, when in less than a month, a quarter of a million refugees entered South Florida; and Castro pro-

---

[6]For example, A. Lawrence Pezullo, instrumental in the 1970s in putting together the Sandinista coalition government in Nicaragua, served as President Clinton's chief negotiator in Haiti.

vided a forceful reminder in the "rafts armada" of 1994. The turmoil in the former Soviet Union and in Central-Eastern Europe presents a preview of a post-Castro Cuba. And those problems will explode not on another continent but on our very doorstep, intruding deeply into our domestic politics.

These problems were repeatedly pointed out in ISC documents over the past decade, yet there is little sign that their truly disastrous potential has been grasped by policy-makers and legislators inside the Washington beltway. In the process, enormous opportunities opened in the post-Cold War era are being neglected in pursuit of less than "the vision thing," as President Bush was wont to call it.

CHAPTER
13

Libya's Qaddafi: Confrontation and Dialogue

I described earlier how I was passed over for a post in the Defense Intelligence Agency by one Waldo Duberstein, who is memorable only for his subsequent suicide while under a thick cloud of charges that he had sold secrets and services to the Qaddafi regime in Libya. In a way, I returned the favor to the Libyan strongman. *The New York Times* on December 22, 1983, carried the following story under the headline: "Aid to Qaddafi in '71 Charged"

> A former American intelligence analyst said today that United States Embassy officials in Tripoli, Libya, betrayed military officers plotting to overthrow the Libyan leader, Col. Muammar el-Qaddafi in 1971 and that this led to the execution of the plotters.
>
> "They were betrayed by the Americans," said Joseph Churba, who had served as the senior Air Force intelligence adviser on the Middle East in the early 1970's.
>
> Mr. Churba, who heads a private conservative research group, said at a news conference, "In 1971, military officers told our Embassy that they would overthrow Qaddafi."
>
> He said the plotters were apparently seeking aid from the United States and assumed that Washington wanted the ouster of the radical leader, known for his anti-American views.
>
> But according to Mr. Churba, the American officials "handed the information over to Qaddafi and these men were eliminated."

Asked what motive the Americans might have had for thwarting the coup, he replied: "Oil is a very big interest. There are economic oil interests in Libya that did not want to see the change."

I am still not at liberty to reveal the source of my disclosure. Suffice it to say that the grave charges I made were never really repudiated by the U.S. Government. Unfortunately, they could not be repudiated, because they were true.

Unfortunately, also, the 1971 incident which I disclosed was totally consistent with my own experience in Government. I recounted earlier the easy access enjoyed by representatives of American oil interests to one of the most sensitive and highly classified activities within the Government: the compilation of National Intelligence Estimates, which in turn provided guidance to the U. S. policy formulation process in general. If the commercial oil interests could penetrate the NIE sanctuary, they certainly found even more accessible doors in the State Department, the Pentagon, and the White House itself.

Call it the economic dimension of the Washington Compromise.

FILLING A WASHINGTON VOID ON LIBYA

What I revealed in 1983 was another problem: Few in the Washington bureaucracy were aware of the extent of the Libyans' support of international terrorism, or if they knew, cared about it. I determined to try to rectify that neglect and force our policymakers to confront the problem.

Again, I turned to the media, giving interviews right and left. One interview, on C-Span, took up 45 minutes, and ran nine times. Almost overnight, I found myself the sought-after media expert on Libya. That in and of itself underscored the lack of attention—let alone expert attention—paid to Qaddafi in Washington.

In 1984, I began publication of a monthly newsletter, *Focus on Libya*. As the only authoritative source on Libyan developments, *Focus* filled a glaring void. It was published regularly for five years, from 1984 to 1989. The White House was a steadfast and interested subscriber, judging by the recurrent inquiries from that source whenever the newsletter was late in arriving.

Meanwhile, I decided to escalate matters. *The Philadelphia Daily News* on December 22, 1983, reported my calling for Qaddafi's removal:

> Joseph Churba, a former national security adviser to President Reagan, urged yesterday that the U.S. government and CIA give open and covert support to the removal of Libyan leader Col. Moammar Khadafy—not excluding assassination. Calling Libya an "outlaw state," Churba said the Khadafy regime is "a malignancy in the international body politic, which should be excised at the source."

This was a bold statement indeed—especially in light of the law that had been passed by the U.S. Congress prohibiting the CIA from carrying out assassinations (in the wake of information that Fidel Castro had thus been targeted by the Agency). Still, law or no law, I recognized that the American people would raise no objections to the elimination, by whatever means, of a man who spawned massive terrorism throughout the world. I must also admit, however, that I deliberately thus "raised the ante" in order to produce some tremors for the State Department and its policy of business-as-usual with Qaddafi.

At the same time, I also recognized that it would be foolish to engineer the removal of Qaddafi, by whatever means, without first preparing the ground for a successor regime in Tripoli more amenable to human rights at home and civilized behavior abroad. Unfortunately, in 1986, the man clearly marked for the succession was Abdessalaam Jalloud, who was also the Soviets' clear choice. It was tragic that when the U.S. launched its air strikes against Libya in 1986, we had no political answer to Qaddafi.

OPERATION MALTA

Meanwhile, the ISC waged its own battle with Qaddafi, and won. The story of that encounter is one of those little-known skirmishes of the Cold War, which, however, played a part in the larger battle. It began when Joseph Licari, a Maltese then serving as an international civil servant at the UN, anguished by what he saw as the damage being wrought by Malta's pro-Moscow socialist government, approached the ISC. Licari was particularly concerned with the close relations between the regime in Valletta and a host of radical countries, like Libya, and more generally with Malta's deteriorating image in the international community.

Joseph Licari's visit to my Washington office in mid-1986 was prompted by a detailed expose of Libya's growing involvement in Malta that had appeared in the May issue of *Focus on Libya*. Licari wanted to talk about Libyan-Maltese relations and what could be done to prevent his strategically located island from sliding into the Soviet orbit and becoming an international pariah. His visit would lead six months later to an historic ISC-sponsored conference.

Focus on Libya had quoted the French journal *Valeurs Actuelles* to the effect that Malta had "become a support base for the Soviets . . . The Soviet objective is to turn Malta into a Cuba of the Mediterranean which enables Moscow to penetrate the Western defense system."[1] The newsletter concluded that the Soviet Union was exploiting the tightening

---

[1] The Libyan-Maltese Alliance, in *Focus on Libya*, Washington, D.C., May 1986.

Libyan-Maltese relationship in order to wean Malta away from the West.

Two years earlier in 1984, Malta's Labor government had signed a Soviet-style treaty of "friendship and cooperation" with Qaddafi's Libya which stopped just short of a mutual defense pact. "Malta can no longer be regarded as an eccentric nuisance but rather as a potential base of Colonel Qaddafi's far-reaching plans . . . ," commented a long-time observer of Maltese affairs, John J. Metzler. Qaddafi had already declared that his country's newly-established military ties to Malta were designed to protect the Mediterranean island nation from "imperialist forces and their stooges."

Qaddafi's declaration was backed up by the aforementioned treaty, in which Libya had agreed to "assist Malta whenever the Government of the Republic of Malta explicitly requests so, in case of threats or acts of aggression against Malta's territorial integrity and sovereignty."[2] It also called for the two countries to harmonize their views on political, economic, security and international issues, and for the training of the Maltese military by Libya. Significantly, the treaty was signed on the same day that Egypt announced the arrest of two Maltese nationals on suspicion of attempting to assassinate an exiled Libyan opposition leader, Abdel Hamid Bakkush.

Malta's rapprochement with Libya dramatically showed how far it had moved from the time it hosted NATO's Mediterranean headquarters, and even from the nation's 1981 declaration of neutrality and non-alignment once the Western alliance was asked to leave. The consequences of the Libyan-Maltese agreement were soon evident: When U.S. and Libyan forces neared the point of confronta-

---

[2] Ibid.

Ambassaador Charles Lichenstein, Chairman of ISC Conference on Malta, Nov. 23-25, 1986, Milan, Italy (Standing) on the left, Dr. Joseph Churba on right.

tion in early 1986 during U.S. naval maneuvers off the coast of Libya, Maltese Prime Minister Carmelo Mifsud Bonnici—a Marxist known as "Dr. Zero" because of his austere personality—flew to Tripoli to express support for the Qaddafi regime. But Bonnici did not leave it at that: at Qaddafi's behest, he warned Italy that Libya would strike at NATO bases in Sicily if Rome supported the use of American military force against Libya. And "Dr. Zero" took it upon himself to invite Italian Prime Minister Bettino Craxi to meet with Col. Qaddafi in Malta.

Nor did Bonnici ingratiate himself with the Reagan Administration by offering to mediate in the dispute between Libya and the United States. The offer was dismissed out-of-hand. Several months later, Bonnici was busily trying to harness international support for Libya as tensions with the United States mounted. In late March and again in April, supported by the Soviet Union and Iraq, Malta called for an emergency session of the United Nations Security Council to discuss the situation in the Mediterranean. The Maltese leader criticized the United States for "the mustering of a formidable array of aggressive air and naval armaments in disputed waters under the pretext of military exercises." He urged the Reagan Administration to "desist from using its naval might in the Mediterranean to hold maneuvers in disputed waters under the pretext of military exercises."[3]

Earlier, Maltese newspapers had carried full-page advertisements inviting Maltese recruits to join the struggle "against imperialism, U. S. aggression, and the provocations coupled with international terrorism" and "to work in technical and installation fields in all types of weapons—the naval, land and air one as well as air defense."[4]

Concern grew in the United States and elsewhere that Bonnici had mortgaged the independence of economically dependent Malta to Libya in return for ensuring the survival of his regime. Legal experts read the wording of the Maltese-Libyan friendship treaty to mean that Qaddafi could intervene in Malta at the request of whatever government he deemed legitimate. Fears rose that Qaddafi would do just that if Bonnici, as was widely expected, lost the elections scheduled for early 1987. "Such an occurrence [a Libyan intervention] would be tragic not only for the Maltese people but for the security of the entire region," we concluded in *Focus on Libya.*

Italy seemed the logical place to gather world experts on Malta to assess mounting dangers from the association between the Island's socialist government and Libya, North Korea and the Soviet Union. The timing seemed right. Growing popular criticism of the government's foreign and

---

[3] Ibid.
[4] Ibid.

domestic courses offered the Maltese conservatives their first real hope for electoral victory in almost two decades.

The conference took place on November 23-25, 1986, in Milan, Italy. Speaking on behalf of the Maltese-American community, Paul C. Mifsud warned that Malta had deviated from its neutral and non-aligned path and called on the government to cancel the military and security aspects of its treaties not only with Libya, North Korea and the Soviet Union, but also with NATO-partner Italy. He suggested that to enhance its role as a mediator and international peacemaker, Malta should refrain from statements such as it had made with regard to U.S.-Libya relations.

The French academician Richard Sola described the infiltration of Malta by Soviet, Chinese and North Korean elements. He noted the growing Soviet influence in the island's General Workers Union, with its stronghold in the shipyards from which the Labor Party derived its power, and the government's invitation to the Maltese Communist Party to participate in the elections. Chinese recognition of the importance of the island's shipyards was reflected in the presence of 200 Chinese advisors to help Malta construct a breakwater and Beijing's order of seven 1,000-ton naval vessels. Particularly worrying, Sola said, was the arming and training of the Maltese military by North Koreans and Malta's willingness to allow the Korean Communist regime to use the island as a base of operations.

"Malta is only partly free and is becoming less free with the passage of time. The regime is not as repressive as those which rule the countries of Eastern Europe. However, the standards of freedom and democracy enjoyed on the island are far below those prevalent in West European countries, despite the facade of democratic institutions that only deceives foreign observers," concluded freelance journalist Bruno Cartier, citing a report by the International Helsinki

Federation for Human Rights and the State Department's annual human rights report. Cartier warned that a socialist victory in the upcoming election would result in nationalization of schools and property belonging to the Roman Catholic Church and suppression of a free press. "All in-depth analysis of the experience of the last 15 years shows unmistakably that the Maltese socialists have been following a long-term plan to turn Malta into a totalitarian state with little or no concern for democratic values or Western interest."[5]

The final declaration of the Milan conference made it clear to dissatisfied Maltese that the outside world shared their concerns and was willing to stand by them. The declaration cautioned that "while the Atlantic Alliance neither needs nor seeks a military base on Malta, Western interests would be severely harmed if the island were to become subservient to a hostile power." It noted that the West would respect Malta's 1980 agreement with Italy affirming the island's neutrality and its subsequent Declaration of Neutrality ratified by the Maltese parliament, but that this policy should be reflected in the government's actions.[6]

The Declaration went on to assert: "Unlike the earlier agreement with Italy . . . those with Libya and North Korea contain secret protocols of military consequence apparently in violation of Malta law. In these circumstances, there is mounting concern that Malta's actions in the international arena reflect an ominous anti-Western drift." It argued that Malta's 1981 agreement with the Soviet Union to coordinate positions in case of situations that "create a threat to peace and security or the violation of international peace" could not be reconciled with the island's official policy of nonalignment.

---

[5] ISC Conference Report on Malta and the Security of the Mediterranean Region, Milan, November 1986.

[6] "The Malta Declaration," *The Washington Times*, Jan. 23, 1987.

The declaration charged that Malta was violating the European Convention of Human Rights and the Helsinki Final Act, both of which it had endorsed! "There has been an alarming deterioration in the standards of human and civil rights which the Maltese traditionally have enjoyed." It noted "cases of unchecked mob violence against critics of the government, including trade unions, independent newspapers, the Catholic Church, the courts and opposition parties. Radio and television, a government monopoly, have been used systematically as a partisan instrument. The independence of the judiciary has been fundamentally compromised."

The Maltese government was called upon to eliminate all technical and procedural barriers to a genuinely democratic electoral process that would be both fair and perceived as fair by the international community. The declaration urged the Valletta government to provide access and facilities to journalists and international observers during the elections and to create an environment that encourages social, cultural and economic ties with the West:

> We call upon the government of Malta to reconsider the political and military provision of its agreements with the Soviet Union, Libya and North Korea which place Malta in an anti-Western alignment, notwithstanding its formal declarations of neutrality and non-alignment.

The declaration was widely distributed to members of the Maltese American community, and to media organizations, prominent journalists and politicians and institutions in the United States and Europe. In January 1987, it was published as an advertisement in prominent newspapers on both sides of the Atlantic.

The declaration clearly was a thorn in the side of Malta's ruling socialists. "This declaration was signed by reactionary persons known for their right-wing views," blared the Maltese newspaper *L'Orizzont* on January 21, 1987, charging that it was a "senseless and unbridled attack on Malta's name." The paper averred that the declaration was "full of lies and inexact allegations."

Such fulminations notwithstanding, the damage was done. The declaration was cited in hundreds of thousands of leaflets distributed throughout the island nation. Dr. Zero was defeated. Malta altered its foreign policy course, steering back in a westerly direction.

The ISC cannot take full credit for the developments in Malta; still, we were able to make a sharp impact in a critical time. Subsequent acknowledgement of our role came in an invitation given to me, personally, by Malta's appointed Ambassador to the European Community, Joseph Licari, to make a visit to the island. Unfortunately, I could not find the time to accept.

Acknowledged or not, we knew what we had accomplished. The episode demonstrated the capacity of a small but rapidly reactive think-tank, working "in Washington but not of it," to harness the enormous potential of the Free World's private sector for worthwhile ends, unrestricted by blundering bureaucracies. It was an exciting foretaste of things to come.

A 1992 DIALOGUE WITH LIBYANS

The ISC's integrity and capacity for "getting things done" obviously were noticed in Tripoli as well. Some six years after the fateful Milan conference came a surprising new twist in the ISC's continuing "Libyan Saga."

In the spring of 1992, representatives of the Qaddafi regime approached me in the International Security Council with the question: Would I be interested in arranging a meeting with important officials of the Libyan regime on an unofficial basis? I was aware that the Libyans were fishing for contacts in the West. Was this just another Libyan ploy to obscure the real issues between the regime and Washington? Or, had Qaddafi in fact taken a new look at the post-Cold War environment and realized he had no choice but try to come to some accommodation with the U.S.?

It presented me with a tricky scenario. My contacts in Italy assured me that they themselves, Libyan Jews who had been victims of Qaddafi, were being given concrete assurances and incentives to recognize a fundamental change in Qaddafi's attitudes. On the other hand, it was official U.S. policy that there could be no contact with Libya until Qaddafi met some minimum requirements posed by the U. S. government.

In the end, my ISC colleagues and I decided to put the Libyans to the test. Given our record, we could not be suspected of harboring any illusions about the nature of the Qaddafi regime, and I felt that we had little to lose in going ahead.

The meeting was held April 8-9, 1992, in the pre-World War II splendor of the Grand Hotel in Rome. It was billed as dialogue between "unofficial" Libyan representatives and a group of Americans assembled by the ISC. In reality, the Libyan team included a close advisor of Qaddafi, as well as highly placed officials involved in foreign policy. The ISC delegation numbered high-ranking retired U.S. military officers.

The basic theme pushed by the Libyans in the discussion was that the world situation had changed, that the U.S. was now the only superpower, and, the Cold War being over, Libya needed to adapt to the new situation. At least implicitly, the Libyans conceded that the U.S. was seeking peace and stability—also in the Middle East. The bottom line seemed to be that Libya wished to end the confrontation with the U.S.

The U.S.-Libyan confrontation had largely come about, the Libyan members admitted, because Libya had chosen the

Soviet side in the worldwide conflict. They implied that in retrospect this had perhaps been a mistake. But there was also a plaintive tone: the United States had now changed its own attitude toward some of Libya's former Cold War allies and friends, but Libya was kept out in the cold.

The Libyans acknowledged that, in the early post-World War II years, American attitudes toward Libya had been generally benevolent. Still, the Libyan Revolution unfolded at a time when Libya had to choose sides, and the U.S. was not supportive. To be sure, the immediate Libyan demands after the revolution, which included nationalization of oil and the expulsion of U.S. bases, were met "without great difficulty." Confrontation with the U.S. had arisen later because of lack of contacts and dialogue, they argued. Their purpose in Rome was to reestablish a dialogue with Americans in an effort to solve the frictions between the two countries.

Interestingly enough, charges by American delegates at the meeting that Libya had engaged in international terrorism were not rejected out-of-hand. Instead, Libya's actions in that regard were rationalized in the contexts of the Cold War, the pursuit of policies of national liberation, reactions to the intrigues of neighboring countries, and, again, the machinations of their Soviet mentors.

In any event, the Libyans contended, all that was now no longer valid in the light of global changes. Libyans were at peace with their neighbors; they accepted the Palestinian-U.S. peace process in the Mideast; and they could no longer afford the cost of confrontation with the U.S. As proof of their good intentions they pointed out how much worse conditions in Egypt, Sudan, or Algeria would be if Libya chose to fan the fires of Islamic fundamentalism in those countries. But Libya wanted an Islamic world that was not fundamentalist, and an Arab world that was not extremist. They argued that their new attitudes were "proven" through cordial relations with their neighbors and even a *modus vivendi* with America's allies in Europe. In the latter context, they pointed to Libya's working relations with the British in the wake of termination of their support of the IRA, and to exchanges of information on terrorism with Great Britain and Italy.

The Libyans explicitly acknowledged a barrier of distrust which they would have to overcome with initiatives toward the West. They asked for advice from the American side on what those specific initiatives might be.

On the issue of the Libyans accused of the Pan Am 103 bombing, however, they were inflexible. They stuck to the insistence that the two indicted Libyan intelligence officials implicated in the bombing could not be surrendered for trial in either the U.S. or Britain, where allegedly they could not receive fair treatment. Faithful to the official Libyan position, they proffered the "compromise" of trial in a third country, e.g. Canada or Switzerland.

As seems always to be the case in dealings with authoritarian regimes, particularly those in the Arab-Muslim world with their one-man style of rule, it was difficult for my colleagues and me to determine just what concretely had been accomplished at the meeting. Still, the American participants departed from the confab with a general consensus about the signals that we had received.

It seemed to us that the Libyans, and presumably Qaddafi himself, wanted an accommodation with the United States. They did so for a number of reasons and motives, some of which they presented honestly at the meeting, e.g., a recognition that the demise of the Soviet Union left the U.S. as the major player in world affairs; the fact that Western economic sanctions, along with the declining oil prices and the general world economic recession, had hurt them; and the new situation in the Middle East in the wake of the Gulf war, which left Libya on the sidelines.

The Libyans, we also concluded, were in a bargaining stance with respect to the price they were prepared to pay for an accommodation with the U.S. In general, they seemed willing to offer economic incentives: i.e., a better deal for the five American oil companies still operating in Libya, and inducements for other new investors. They were less willing to give in on the issue of Pan Am 103 and the two indicted defendants. Second, they indicated a readiness to make declarations forswearing chemical, biological, nuclear and terrorist programs, but they were noncommittal on the repeated insistence from the American side that arms inspection would have to be unconditional. Finally, they appeared willing—at least for the time being—to stay away from the Arab Palestinian issue, "leaving it to the Palestinians" and accepting Egypt's recognition of Israel.

The meeting also left an overall impression: we had been dealing with frightened men. As an American participant, former U.S. Ambassador to NATO Robert Strausz-Hupe, put it: "These are men who see themselves hanging from lamp-posts." The fear they reflected, personalized as it may have become in accord with Strausz-Hupe's imagery, betrayed more broadly the puzzlement and apprehensions of a once bold regime that now found itself not only swamped by global tides but—worse yet—shunted into the backwaters. The Libyans were looking for more secure ground.

Indeed, following the conference, we received entreaties from Libyans, again through our Italian-Libyan middlemen, for a resumption and intensification of the dialogue started in Rome.

There were no assurances, however, that they were willing to make the kinds of concessions on major issues which would make any new meeting a fruitful undertaking.

Incidentally, while exploring the possibility of another conference, we received a warning from the State Department to the effect that a meeting may be in violation of U.S. law barring contact with Libyans. I asked, "What law may we be in violation of?" I never got an answer—although we did receive an anonymous telephone call threatening an IRS audit of the ISC. Later that year, returning from a visit abroad, my luggage was minutely searched upon arrival at JFK airport. A coincidence?

QADDAFI TREADS THE WATER

With the benefit of hindsight and more information, we can posit that in general our appraisals of 1992 were correct: The collapse of the Libyans' Soviet ally and the post-Cold War breakup of an essentially bipolar world into unstable regional theaters left the Libyans at the mercy of a host of unpredictable developments, some of them uncomfortably close to home. Qaddafi has followed a policy of keeping his head down and letting his old competitor, Hafez al-Assad of Syria, play the role of the prodigal son vis-á-vis the West. But at this writing (mid-1995), Qaddafi faces an increasingly volatile Egypt to the east, along with growing turmoil generated by Muslim fundamentalist forces in Algeria to the west, and even in his immediate neighbor, the once "moderate" and stable Tunisia.

The Libyans must reconcile their pretentious policies with the tides of developments in the larger post-Cold War international scene as it has evolved since the fall of the Soviet Union. Our Libyan respondents appear to have underestimated the chaotic nature of the "new world disorder," and overestimated U. S. policymakers' ability to use

America's new "only superpower" status to focus on major issues, much less on relatively smaller matters like Libyan terrorism and its pariah regime. That, perhaps linked with the basic problem of separating himself from his past as a flamboyant leader of world terrorism, has forced Qaddafi to postpone his fundamental choices. Meanwhile, Libyan terrorist activities continue against dissidents to the regime operating from abroad. That combination of factors has put the Libyan question on hold while the world's attention focusses more on the Balkans, North Korea, and disintegration in the former Soviet Union.

14

Highway
(and Byroads)
to China

The idea seemed totally preposterous: a highway linking London and Tokyo that would cut straight across China. Hard-line Communist China could hardly be interested in opening up to the degree that such an international highway would require. Yet, the highway would bring in badly needed foreign investment and significantly improve the Chinese transportation system.

The father of the Great Highway Project was none other than the charismatic benefactor of the ISC, the Reverend Sun Myung Moon, who saw the concept as a key to the unlocked potential of East Asia. It was part of the Reverend's mystique that, despite his staunch anti-Communism, he enjoyed access to the highest echelons of the Chinese leadership.

His initial approaches to interest the Chinese in the idea were rebuffed by Beijing. But Moon was tenacious. One day in late May 1988, his representatives unfolded in my office a map which illustrated the project as well as Moon's earlier idea of a railway link between the British and Japanese capitals. Business interests connected with the Unification Church had already taken the project a practical step beyond the futuristic blueprint by starting construction of a tunnel across the Tsushima Strait from Japan to South Korea. They had not, however, secured Chinese agreement to extend the project. The Reverend hoped that, given my own contacts in China, I could help win over the Chinese to the scheme.

On June 18, 1988, at the New Otani Hotel in Tokyo, I met with Zhi-yuan Ding, then vice president of the Chinese Association for International Friendly Contact, with whom I had earlier constructive contacts. He was quickly convinced that the envisioned project could give a badly needed boost to the Chinese economy and improve the country's transportation and communications system. At a dinner that evening, wealthy Japanese and South Korean businessmen were taken by surprise when Ding informed them that he would persuade his government to accept the undertaking.

Within weeks, China's Ministry of Transport and Engineering embraced the project. It involved an initial investment of up to $400 million—ultimately as much as a $3-4 billion in total investments. For Moon, the project represented an opening for other investments in China.

How truly serious the Chinese were about the highway project remained to be seen. For one, Professor A. James Gregor, an Asia specialist at the University of California, political scientist and member of the ISC Advisory Board, expressed skepticism of Chinese motives: "The Chinese are perfectly willing to let Moon pave the road. All they have to do is nod and they get the money. What is Moon going to do, take the road away?"

Gregor's skepticism was justified. The highway project lingered, but nothing concrete came of it. Meanwhile, however, the Unification Church and its interests reaped some benefits. Almost immediately after the Tokyo meeting, the Church's Bo Hi Pak was invited to China, where he established an office of the *Washington Times*, the Panda Auto Works, and some cultural exchanges.

STRATEGIC UNDERTOWS IN EAST ASIA

For the International Security Council, the initial break-through in the highway project was important in strengthening our contacts in China without in any way compromising our stance on the despotic character of the Chinese regime or its threats to regional security. The continued ideological distance notwithstanding, at the level of strategic discourse, ISC members had become impressed with the acumen of Chinese analysts, whose assessments, particularly of the Soviet Union, seemed substantially more accurate than those circulating in the State Department.

There were also useful distinctions to be made between the two large Communist powers. Unlike the Soviet Union, China lacked the capability to destroy the United States or even to seek global hegemony. China, it is true, did have the potential for regional mischief-making, but the Soviet Union's threat to U. S. interests had global dimensions. Maintaining the gulf between Moscow and Beijing was important to the security of democratic societies in both Europe and Asia.

These perspectives guided a number of conferences organized by the International Security Council in East and Southeast Asia. For example, one meeting, held in Bangkok in July 1986, explored the implications of the Soviet-Vietnamese alliance for the security of Southeast Asia. The conference issued the warning that Soviet surface vessels, submarines, and long-range aircraft operating out of Vietnam's Cam Ranh Bay and Danang could interdict the sealanes vital to the security and economic viability of China, Taiwan, Japan, South Korea and the countries grouped in the Association of Southeast Asian Nations. With that threat now seemingly ended, or at least in abeyance, the Chinese effort to build a blue-water navy—and its provocative actions against Japanese shipping in the Taiwan Straits in the recent past—have enhanced question-marks about China's prospective role in the post-Soviet world. A steadfast strategic imperative was clearly the security of the sea lanes in the Pacific Basin.

A FATEFUL ISC MEETING IN BEIJING

Winning Chinese endorsement for the highway project was not the ISC's first accomplishment in the People's Republic. In March 1987 the ISC persuaded the Beijing Institute for International Strategic Studies (BIISS)—which has close links with Chinese military intelligence—to engage in an unprecedentedly free and open exchange of views on global and regional strategy with former senior American military officers and prominent scholars. The meeting was to address the balance of power in Asia, with each side presenting ten papers. At the last minute, the BIISS objected to references to Taiwan and human rights violations in China in the American papers.

The attempts by the BIISS to backtrack from the agreement to publish the presentations were rebuffed by the ISC. Trouble flared already during the opening reception on March 22. One of the top Chinese participants, the chief of the People's Liberation Army Intelligence, strode into the room and promptly convened on the spot a meeting with me and several other senior American participants. As nonplussed conference participants, Western diplomats and junior Chinese staffers of the BIISS watched guardedly over their cocktails, the Chinese official demanded that the conference be taken off the record. We refused. Negotiations continued after the welcoming banquet and into the night.

To his credit, the-then U.S. Ambassador to China, Winston Lord, joined in the talks and advised us to stick to our guns. He informed us later that in previous weeks other

Washington think tanks had held meetings in Beijing, all of which had been off-the-record. We were the first group of Americans, he said, to prove themselves tougher than the Chinese at their own game.

Talks were still going when the time came the next morning to convene the conference. When I advised our delegation in Beijing to prepare for an impromptu cancellation of the conference and departure for home, the Chinese caved in. "Friendship has to be earned," commented one of the Chinese participants at a banquet that night.

This did not keep the Chinese, however, from adopting a hard line in the conference. They constantly looked for guidance to the conference co-chairman, BIISS Secretary General Xu Yimin, and never budged from the party line. Tension rose again when the Chinese broke the agreement not to raise the issue of Taiwan: one of their delegates suddenly lambasted the island republic and U.S. policy. It was an obvious attempt to test our defense of principle. The Taiwan issue quickly vanished when the Chinese realized that the U.S. participants would not give an inch. General Yimin covered the Chinese retreat as follows:

> The U.S. government has already explicitly recognized that Taiwan is an integral part of Chinese territory and a province of China . . .   The question has thus been resolved by the two governments and is known to the peoples of both countries . . . It would be inappropriate to consider these settled issues at academic gatherings such as this.[1]

Chinese and American participants agreed on the seriousness of the Soviet military threat emanating from the massive buildup and modernization of Soviet military forces

---

[1] Report on *The Balance of Power in Asia*, International Security Council, Washington, D.C., May 1987, pp. 15-16.

ISC Symposium Beijing, China, March 1987.

in the Pacific region. There was agreement more generally that the situation in Southeast Asia was a reflection of Soviet and Vietnamese hegemonical ambitions and the overall strategic threat posed by the Soviets. The Chinese appeared to accept that the U.S. military presence in the Philippines was a stabilizing factor in counterbalancing Soviet power.

The Chinese put their own spotlight on Soviet support for Vietnamese military operations in Kampuchea, the Soviet occupation of Afghanistan, and the deployment of Soviet forces along the Sino-Soviet border. "The Chinese were pessimistic about the voluntary Soviet removal of these obstacles . . . . They saw no evidence of a fundamental change in Soviet policy," said Eugene Rostow in his remarks on behalf of the ISC at the conclusion of the conference.[2]

Unlike the Americans, however, the Chinese characterized Soviet military strength as a political and strategic lever rather than an immediate military threat. They believed that the military situation had been largely stabilized with the Reagan Administration's military buildup, which created a

---

[2] Ibid, p. 20.

military balance of power in Asia, with the two superpowers' nuclear forces offsetting each other. This allowed the Chinese to take a long-term view of military problems and the issue of modernization of the Chinese military. Nevertheless, the Chinese described U.S.-Soviet rivalry as a threat to security and castigated the arms race between the superpowers.

Furthermore, the Chinese voiced strong objections to America's Strategic Defense Initiative, describing it as an attempt to militarize space. Their arguments prompted Professor Gregor to remark: "It was evident that the Beijing Institute was hopelessly ignorant [about SDI]." In fact, the Chinese allegations were not very different from those of American critics of SDI. In any event, American participants pointed out that Soviet strategic defense programs were older and more advanced than those of the United States, positing that the West could not allow the Soviet Union a monopoly on strategic defenses to accompany its already enormous offensive nuclear threat. The Chinese had no response as to why they were more concerned about American than about Soviet strategic defenses.

Interesting in retrospect is that already in 1986 Korea was a particular bone of U.S.-Chinese contention. The Chinese at the Beijing conference appeared to differ with their American counterparts on the importance of the increased flow of sophisticated Soviet arms to North Korea that had enhanced North Korean military capabilities, Soviet overflights of North Korean territory, and the access to North Korean naval facilities outside the checkpoints at the Korean and Tsushima Straits that were provided to Soviet naval vessels by Pyongyang. Instead, the Chinese termed the U. S. military presence in South Korea "provocative." American arguments that those U.S. forces were a critical element in regional stability seemed to make little impression on the Chinese.

The Americans sought to allay Chinese fears that increased Japanese defense spending may lead to a revival of Japanese militarism. While both sides agreed that Japan was a major factor in the Pacific balance of power, the Americans argued that Japan's democratic system and its dependence on U.S. security guarantees precluded reassertion of an independent Japanese military role.

U.S.-CHINA RELATIONS AFTER TIANANMEN SQUARE

The ISC sustained its emphasis on China as a primary factor in the power balance of Asia. At an ISC conference in Tokyo in April 13-15, 1986, on "The Security of Northeast Asia," participants deplored the fact that China refused to cooperate in regional security arrangements. The conference struck a warning note about possible dangers in U.S. arms transfers to Beijing: "U. S. military sales to the People's Republic of China are intended to contribute to its military deterrent capability against the USSR. However, those sales must be evaluated cautiously in an overall Asian context, because they have the potential of destabilizing the security of other nations in the region."[3]

The issue of military sales came into sudden focus when the Bush Administration had to respond to the Chinese suppression of dissidents with massive violence in Tiananmen Square in June 1989. Outrage over the brutal repression prompted the United States to impose sanctions, including a ban on military sales.

As the call for a review of U.S.-Chinese relations grew stronger in the months after Tiananmen Square, the ISC convened a meeting, in June 1990, of Republican and Democratic

---

[3] *ISC Conference Report on National Security in Northeast Asia*, 1986, p.4.

political leaders, officials of the State Department and economic agencies, as well as academicians for a discussion of America's China policy. Most believed that the Chinese regime would not last long following the events in Tiananmen Square—that China's economy and political institutions had been irreparably damaged. Participants argued that U. S. policy should be designed to ease the suffering of the Chinese people as their nation makes its transition from a fatally flawed system to one that is more democratic, efficient, and rational. Economic sanctions would only have the opposite effect and would reduce the survivability of those elements—reformist politicians and entrepreneurs—best capable of guiding their nation to alternative economic and political approaches. Others presented exactly the opposite case: economic sanctions would hasten the advent of a new China.

If anything became clear during the deliberations, it was that conscientious and informed Americans found it very difficult to recommend specific policies toward China with any great confidence. But that is an old story: confusion about what could be expected in U.S.-Chinese relations has abounded ever since the rapprochement between Washington and Beijing in the 1970s. In security terms, some in the United States were convinced that China would serve as a military counterweight to Soviet capabilities in East Asia. For its part, China believed that a "united front" with the industrial democracies would afford it security against Soviet military initiatives. In retrospect, both expectations were on weak ground.

Soviet capabilities along the Sino-Soviet border were so superior to those of China that prudence and national interest commended to Beijing a policy of restraint and accommodation. As a result, the United States could not expect China to actively support any policy calculated to deter

Soviet initiatives in Asia or to engage in conflict with the Soviet Union should deterrence fail. China, however, provided the anti-Soviet alliance with an important, if passive, security asset by its very existence.

Amid the uncertainty, the remarks of Ted Galen Carpenter, director of the Cato Institute's Foreign Policy Studies, at our June 1990 conference on U.S.-China policy held out hope: "The current (Chinese) leadership is aged and will not hold the reins of power much longer. We cannot be certain about the views held by the successor generation of leaders, but there is at least a reasonable likelihood that the revolutionary changes that have swept through the Communist world will not leave China unaffected."

Designed to coincide with the conference, the ISC published a "Global Perspectives 1990" statement as an advertisement in *The New York Times* criticizing the Bush Administration for renewing China's most-favored-nation trading status despite its arms shipments to the Khmer Rouge in Cambodia and to Middle Eastern nations. Responding to concern about driving China into isolation, the ISC noted that "it is the despotic Beijing regime that has chosen to isolate itself . . . . If the PRC ruling gerontocracy behaves like thugs with not a hint of apology, much less contrition, it can be expected to be treated like thugs (except, apparently, by President Bush)."[4]

In the advertisement, the ISC asked what China had done to earn continued U.S. trade benefits: "Gross violations of human rights have intensified. Systematic suppression of dissidents and the rape of Tibet continue unabated." Despite its 1981 announcement that China would conduct a neutral

---

[4] "Global Perspectives, 1990: The 'Open Door' to China Revisited," *The New York Times*, June 5, 1990.

foreign policy, China had persistently sided with the Third World in "Yankee-baiting." It continued to supply terrorist-supporting states with sophisticated high-tech weapons and was selling cruise and ballistic missiles to Syria, Iran, and Libya.

The statement also questioned the proposition, put forward by supporters of the most-favored-nation status, that China had become an economic asset for the United States. China's per capita GNP has been about *five* percent that of Taiwan and even less that of Hong Kong and Singapore, and its economic policies promise little improvement to the Chinese people irrespective of whether or not it enjoys U.S. trade benefits. The advertisement noted that U.S.-Chinese trade amounted in 1989 to $18 billion, just over two percent of the total value of U.S. world trade and scarcely half of U.S. trade with Taiwan.

The ISC argued further that China posed a growing threat to its neighbors and thus to the U.S. interest in a stable, peaceful Asian environment. Beijing had increased defense spending and mobilized its forces along the Fujien coast across the Taiwan Strait. Its claim of sovereignty over the island territories of the South China Sea and exclusive economic rights on the continental shelf and associated waterways put it in conflict with the Philippines, Malaysia, Indonesia, Thailand, and Singapore.

China's regional strength is bound to grow to the degree that the United States reduces its military presence in Japan and Korea, and with the U.S. withdrawal from military facilities in the Philippines. "Against this perspective," the statement said, "questions must be raised as to the coherence of U.S. policy regarding East Asia as a whole, and the PRC in particular. Tiananmen and MFN notwithstanding, the record shows that the PRC is not and never has been a reliable U.S. partner in keeping the peace in Asia."

Since that statement was issued, there has been growing proof of its central thesis: Intelligence circles have reported a buildup of Chinese forces in new style multi-force strike units along the southern coast, apparently to enforce Chinese claims to control of international waters including the China Sea far from China's continental shelf. Chinese "pirates" have attacked Japanese and Russian ships in international and Korean waters. The North Koreans proceeded with their development of a nuclear weapons capability. The Japanese, now in the range of North Korean super-Scud missiles, are for the first time since the Korean War forced fundamentally to reconsider their security arrangements.

The Clinton Administration's initial response was to propose new multilateral security arrangements for the area which would include Communist China and the North Koreans.[5] The approach symptomizes the chronic American predisposition toward "organizational" solutions to deep-seated international problems, or: "When trouble looms, ask for new regional security arrangements." The proposition might be more plausible if the "salesman" were more willing to play a direct role, rather than preach solutions at long-range, across the wide expanse of the Pacific.

---

[5] See "A New Pacific Community; Ten Goals for American Policy," Opening Statement at Confirmation Hearings for Ambassador Winston Lord, Assistant Secretary of State-designate, Bureau of East Asian and Pacific Affairs, March 31, 1993, before the Senate Foreign Relations Committee, Washington, D.C.

15

China Meets China

There is more to the ISC's "China story." One chapter in that story merits separate treatment.

As Chinese tanks smashed into Beijing's Tiananmen Square on the morning of June 4, 1989, an atmosphere of gloom descended upon Tokyo's Akasaka Prince Hotel. The timing, although coincidental, was ironic. The decision in Beijing to crush the pro-democracy demonstrators gathered in the square threatened also to scuttle the first meeting ever between legislators from the People's Republic of China on the mainland and from the Republic of China on Taiwan.

The presence of four Mainland Chinese and five ROC representatives in the Tokyo hotel that morning capped almost a year of intensive lobbying by the ISC. It was another remarkable demonstration of the breakthroughs that can be achieved by independent think tanks outside the corridors of official diplomacy. The two-day symposium, which also hosted observers from the United States, Japan, the Philippines, Korea, Thailand, and Colombia, addressed the future of the two Chinese polities situated on either side of the Taiwan Strait.

As reports of the massacre in Tiananmen Square trickled into the hotel, outrage rose among the ROC delegates at the brutal suppression of dissent under an avalanche of violence that had not been witnessed in China for more than a

Tokyo, Japan, June 4, 1989. (left to right) Lin Yu-Siang of the legislative Yuan in Taiwan, Dr. Joseph Churba, and Zhao Fusan of the People's Republic of China, co-chairmen of the ISC-sponsored reunification talks.

decade. With barely-controlled anger, they charged in impromptu meetings outside the conference hall that the violence threatened to wipe out the gains made by the reforms of the post-Mao era, warning that it threatened the inflow of capital, technology, human skills, and tourism into China's retrograde economy. After some hesitation, however, the delegates from Taiwan decided not to break up the historic meeting.

For their part, the representatives from the People's Republic clearly were confused and disoriented by the news from Beijing. The conference hung in the balance while Chinese delegation leader Zhao Fusan, a member of the National People's Congress' Standing Committee, consulted by telephone with his superiors in Beijing. When Fusan finally led his delegation into the conference room, he struck an accommodating stance, declaring that his delegation intended to join the discussion without apologies or propaganda. (Fusan later defected to the West.)

ISC Symposium on Peace & Security in the Taiwan Strait. Tokyo, Japan, June 4-5, 1989.

IMPULSES TOWARD A CHINESE DIALOGUE

Economic motives gave both groups of Chinese the incentive to engage in the dialogue. Senior Taiwanese military officials had told us a year earlier that the time might be ripe for a meeting of legislators from both Chinas. They had encouraged the ISC to explore the possibility of arranging such a meeting. Yet the hurdles had seemed unsurmountable. The People's Republic insisted that the contacts would have to be staged in such a way as to avoid any connotation of Communist Chinese recognition of Taiwan as an independent entity.

For its part, Taiwan's official policy banned relations with the Mainland. Nevertheless, an "unofficial" body had been created in Taiwan to maintain contact with the brethren on the Mainland, and with the mission of preparing public opinion, particularly among the Overseas Chinese, for a gradual shift in the Taiwanese stance toward the People's Republic. Within Taiwan's ruling Kuomintang Party, the realization was growing that competition with Singapore,

ISC Conference, Seoul, Korea, May 21-24, 1985.

Richard N. Perle, Former Assistant Secretary of Defense For International Security.

Korea, and Japan in the labor-intensive cottage industries was impelling Taiwanese entrepreneurs to seek cheaper labor on the Mainland. Moreover, with the largest foreign exchange reserves in the world, Taiwan needed to satisfy domestic demand for overseas investment outlets. The debate inside the Kuomintang Party therefore centered on the question of how quickly Taiwan should proceed with establishing links to the People's Republic rather than on whether such contacts were desirable.

Preempting the debate was the fact that Mainland China had already become by 1988 the third largest market for textiles fabricated in Taiwan. Bilateral trade between the two Chinas,—indirectly through Hong Kong and involving, among other things, Taiwan's import of coal and its export of rice—exceeded $3 billion that year. More than thirty industrial plants were established in the Chinese provinces of Fujian and Guangdong with Taiwanese investment capital. In the first eleven months of 1988, Taiwan invested more than $250 million in factories on the Mainland, often wholly owned by Taiwanese entrepreneurs, which manufactured toys, textiles, electrical appliances, shoes, umbrellas, and light machinery.

Trade relations were flowering in an extremely uncertain political climate. The Taipei authorities persisted in officially proscribing contact, negotiations, or compromise with the Communist regime in Beijing. By the time the legislators gathered in Tokyo for the ISC meeting, some 400,000 Taiwanese had visited the Mainland in the preceding 18 months, and Taiwanese courts had ruled that investments in the People's Republic were not "subversive."

As trade and communication across the Taiwan Strait expanded rapidly, a large and aggressive constituency evolved in Taiwan in favor of developing relations with the Mainland. Too much was at stake to allow the burgeoning relationship to drift. This constituency—seeking clarification concerning its investments, the repatriation of profit, the legal limits of equity ownership, and the conditions for employment of local labor in the People's Republic—found expression among the 18 independent political parties that emerged in Taiwan's newly-created multiparty system.

Simultaneously, Mainland China's political leadership sought progress toward political reunification of China. Having established the basis for reunification with Hong Kong and Macao, Beijing sought to construct conditions for reunion with Taiwan. Any movement in that direction would constitute a major political victory for the Beijing authorities.

ABIDING BARRIERS IN THE TAIWAN STRAIT

In short, the situation was ripe by the time the ISC decided to sponsor a frank and unconstrained discussion between Chinese equals. Nevertheless, the Mainland Chinese and the Taiwanese came to the Tokyo meeting with very different visions and strategies.

The Beijing Chinese insisted that reunification be achieved immediately, with the People's Republic exercising sovereignty over all of China. "One nation, two systems" was Beijing's formula, indicating China's acceptance of "special administrative districts" in Hong Kong, Macao, and Taiwan with economic systems very different from the Mainland's rigid Communist Party monopoly. The Nationalist government in Taipei was to become part of a provincial administration.

Predictably the Taiwanese were less than enthusiastic about Beijing's proposal. A precondition for surrendering their sovereignty would be China's ability to convince the Taiwanese of their goodwill and sincerity. The Taiwanese delegation countered Beijing's catch-phrase with one of their own: "one nation, two governments." Their proposal called for retaining separate sovereignties on the Mainland and in Taiwan, which would nevertheless recognize the pursuit of ultimate unity of China. The government in Taipei would undertake to create the necessary precondition for a politically and economically viable reunification of China.

The Taiwanese argued that their proposal held out the promise that the material and political gains of their island republic could be extended to the People's Republic through investment and trade as well as social and cultural contacts. Gradually the differences between the two countries would vanish. This would ensure reunification without Taiwan sacrificing the benefits it earned in four decades of hard work, the *per capita* income in Taiwan being at least twelve times that on the Mainland. Thus, the Taiwanese feared the loss not only of political and civil rights but also of their economic achievements. Both sides embraced the idea of an increased flow of information through nongovernmental agencies, economic groups, sporting clubs, academic societies, and cultural associations.

During the discussions, the Mainland Chinese acknowledged the economic advantages and political freedoms enjoyed in Taiwan and conceded that Taiwan's economy was more efficient, more technologically advanced, and in some ways more equitable than theirs. They supported the concept of increased investment and trade as a way to transfer management skills and human capital to their retrograde economy. They also candidly accepted the need to dismantle the Mainland's highly centralized allocative and command economic system to allow for internal political reforms, a freer flow of information, greater communication with the international community, and a willingness to seek resolution and redress through negotiation rather than confrontation and violence.

The Taiwanese insisted that the transfers of capital and skill were dependent on a credible assurance of peace and stability. Such an assurance could be achieved through confidence-building measures like a statement from Beijing formally renouncing the use of force in China's relations with Taiwan, which would allow the island republic to considerably reduce its defense budget. At the same time, Taiwan could then retain sovereign command of a deterrent armed force capable of providing security without having to depend on policy decisions in Beijing.

This issue gained all the greater prominence at the meeting against the background of the news from Beijing. Events in Tiananmen Square, unfolding as the delegation discussed future relations, did little to reassure the Taiwanese about the Chinese leaders' willingness to refrain from employing force when they felt it served their national interest. Moreover, the experience of Tibet, where Beijing violated its pledge to protect the region's "minority way of life," inspired little confidence in Beijing's commitment to its promises.

The delegation from the People's Republic balked at the Taiwanese proposal, arguing that the use of force to defend national interests was a sovereign right which could not be surrendered. Still, they contended, Mainland China showed evidence of its nonbelligerence by redeploying troops away from the Taiwan Strait and by ensuring that its armed forces did not have the sealift capability necessary for an amphibious invasion of areas controlled by the Taipei government.

The Mainland Chinese, however, had little with which to counter Taiwanese assertions that at least 10 Chinese airfields capable of supporting 1,500 tactical and air superiority aircraft were located within combat range of Taiwan. The Taiwanese argued further that naval vessels that would be used in an air and sea blockade across the Strait could be transferred to suitable staging areas with ease and speed. Shipping to Taiwan's major ports could be interdicted by the Chinese navy's fast attack craft armed with ship-to-ship missiles.

THE PROMISES SET IN TOKYO

Agreement on economic issues appeared within easier reach. The Mainland Chinese recognized that increased economic ties would force them to reform their overly centralized and bureaucratized economy. Both delegations agreed that such ties depended on stability, peace and the rule of law, involving a responsible and responsive business and civil code that would protect citizen's rights.

In addition to internationally recognized political and civil rights embodied in conventions and treaties, the Taiwanese suggested that Beijing consider specific legislation protecting corporate and individual property rights. This legislation would have to cover a broad range of issues from the right to own both the real as well as the financial "means of production," to the protection of intellectual property rights, patents and copyrights, and the ability to repatriate profits and secure equity. The Mainland delegation seemed open to the suggestion that Taiwan be allowed to administer a "special economic zone"—such as Hainan Island or parts of Guangdong—where Taiwanese laws and practices would be applied in modified form to conform to local condition. In short, the Mainland Chinese showed a willingness to accommodate the needs of Taiwanese venture capital.

Four principles governing Mainland policy—the commitment to socialism, the leadership of the Communist Party, the dictatorship of the proletariat, and the rule of Marxist-Leninist-Maoist ideology—were in conflict with the economic cooperation anticipated, the Taiwanese argued. The Mainland delegation's failure to object to this Taiwanese assertion was perhaps the most stunning aspect of the Tokyo encounter.

The sincerity of both delegations was underlined in their willingness to issue a public statement committing themselves "to the peaceful reunification of China" and acknowledging that the greatest threat to their goal is "the intrusion of collective violence into the process." In light of the collective violence that had nearly destroyed the conference on the very day it was to begin, this affirmation represented the triumph of new common cause over the suppressive death rattle of the old.

Interestingly, this ISC conference was widely covered by media in Japan, Taiwan, and Mainland China. The Western press chose to ignore it.

16

Campaign 1988: The Affirmative Strategy

The events in Tiananmen Square followed a political divide in the United States: the end of the "Reagan era." As was amply brought out above, we at the International Security Council had been more than skeptical of the vaunted accomplishments of the Reagan Administration in the foreign and defense arenas. For all its rhetoric, the Reagan Administration lacked a comprehensive strategy to pursue its foreign policy and defense objectives. Construction of such a strategy should have been the National Security Council's priority task in 1981. But it was not to be—first, because of Richard Allen's weakness and his failure to assemble the necessary talent, and second because the entrenched forces in the governmental "baronies" dealing with foreign and defense issues successfully resisted any innovative design that might challenge the comfortable ways of bureaucratic business-as-usual.

CONCEPTION OF A STRATEGY

Mindful of that failure, we determined in 1988 to address such a comprehensive strategy before the Presidential campaign of that year. We staged extensive meetings at the ISC in pursuit of that goal—debriefings, consultations and small seminars involving a score of leading scholars, scientists, and authorities. We then synthesized the findings into an "Affirmative Strategy." Through a systematic campaign—featuring ten installments distributed to 2,000 newspapers and hundreds of television stations—we made our final product available to both candidates and their advisors. We published comments from opinion leaders such as Max Lerner and Morton Kondracke in the ISC quarterly *Global Affairs*. All told, $170,000 was expended on the effort.

What we came up with was a comprehensive, logically argued policy document. It was packaged in such a way that either candidate, or his advisors, could easily avail themselves of ready ideas and supporting arguments. As far as direct responses to the document were concerned, there was total silence from the camp of George Bush. Democratic candidate Michael Dukakis at least made the gesture of responding to the Affirmative Strategy in writing:

> It is an impressive document, and one which takes a thoughtful and creative approach to a number of crucial issues. In a world of increasing complexity and interdependence, there is an urgent need to redefine the means by which the U.S. and our allies can work toward a stable and prosperous world. I commend you and your distinguished colleagues for the contributions you are making in this area.

Still, had Dukakis engaged Bush in a debate on U.S. foreign policy, the campaign might have generated a more thoughtful airing of critical issues.

Fortunately for the American people, providence was at work: despite George Bush, the Soviet empire imploded. Bush ranks as perhaps the luckiest President in American history. Until almost the end of the drama in the dissolving Soviet Union, Bush insisted on centering his own favor—and the weight of American policy—on the person of Mikhail

ISC Conference, Geneva Switzerland, September 13-15, 1987.

Gorbachev. At best a transitional leader and ultimately rejected by his own people, Gorbachev tried desperately to save the vestiges of the Soviet Union as an empire and Communism as an ideology while both crumbled around him. And yet the Bush Administration embraced him in implicit opposition to the forces of democracy and human freedom that were surging to displace him. Then, after Gorbachev's ignoble exit from the stage, Bush brazenly claimed credit for the chain of developments.

A PROPHETIC FOCUS ON SOVIET WEAKNESSES

The unfulfilled task before U.S. policymakers is to learn from history and to exploit the momentous opportunities opened in the last decade of the 20th Century. Our 1988 Affirmative Strategy was prescient. Consider the following excerpts that characterized and predicted developments in the Soviet Union:

> The Soviet Union is a fundamentally flawed society—
> a Third World country with a First World army. The
> Soviets rely so much on the power of intimidation and

their claim of historic inevitability precisely because the model of the Soviet state is neither attractive nor empirically persuasive.[1]

Over time, the Soviet leadership will come to see itself not as the avant-garde of historical inevitability but as the harried protectors of a crumbling domain. Soviet 'Grand Strategy' abroad will come to resemble Soviet reality at home: bullying and intermittently violent to be sure, but inherently divided, fearful, conservative, and inadequate to meet the needs of the modern world.[2]

So far, *perestroika* has had no effect on the Soviet arms buildup or on Soviet foreign commitments. Only a permanent, institutional increase in the level of individual rights, pluralism and regime democracy within the Soviet Union will militate against aggression.[3]

Most of these nationalist ideologies as currently constituted are collective and totalitarian philosophies at least as hostile to individual liberty as Marxism-Leninism. Without the implementation of the concept of regime democracy, the facile substitution of Great Russian nationalism, Ukrainian nationalism and Islamic fundamentalism for Soviet nationalism would merely subordinate individual citizens of the Soviet state to regional leadership that is no less totalitarian or chauvinistic.[4]

The primary effect of *perestroika* so far has been a decline in consumer goods and a rise in savings; in other words, a disincentive to work. The Soviet system still is geared to initiating construction, not finishing it, and to producing industrial machines, not using them. Negative growth is affecting every major sector of the Soviet economy without exception. *Perestroika* is woefully underfinanced; the Soviet reliance upon arms, oil, gas, diamonds, and gold for the bulk of its export earnings and its refusal

---

[1] *An Affirmative Strategy for the Free World*, ISC Report, Washington, D.C., June 1988, p. 15.

[2] Ibid., p. 22.

[3] Ibid., p. 24

[4] Ibid., p. 29.

so far to cut back on the allocation of resources to the military are generating enormous demands for capital and technology that the Soviet economy *cannot meet*.[5]

What did we mean by the Affirmative Strategy? Following is the opening paragraph of our proposal, published in June 1988:

> The fundamental conflict between the Free World and the Soviet Union differs from the rivalries that have characterized human history. This conflict is not about primacy or land or power or historical grievances. Fundamentally, it is a struggle over human values. In forces of totalitarianism—Soviet and otherwise—the human population faces a determined, modern and essentially anti-human adversary. The fusion of ideology and technology, embodied in the totalitarian state, threatens to impose a permanent slavery upon humanity. In such a world, the individual would be extinct, save as a servant of the needs of the state, the party and the ruling group. Dictatorships have asserted themselves throughout history, but the reach and capability of modern totalitarianism make the threat qualitatively different today from centuries past. Soviet Marxist-Leninism is by far the most dangerous manifestation of this threat.[6]

Our strategy was steeped in the premise that the great strength of the United States and its democratic allies lies in their commitment to freedom, human dignity and opportunity. Freedom is a singular value that has universal appeal, transcends cultural differences, and is desired by and applicable to every human community. The strategy was therefore designed to be more than just a set of diplomatic and military tactics and to serve long-term rather than short-term political needs. Its goal was to define the battle and the battleground,

---

[5] Ibid., p. 32.
[6] Ibid, p. 1.

and chart the course to success. It was, in short, a strategy for victory.

In 1988, the strategic initiative in the relationship between the two superpowers continued to be enjoyed by the Soviets, if by default. While this was a most dangerous time, *glasnost* and *perestroika* were viewed by the ISC as rare strategic opportunities to be exploited by the Free World. The Soviets expected a passive West to avoid taking advantage of Soviet weaknesses. Yet, the Free World could not hope to prevail unless dealings with the Soviets were conducted with reference to a set of clear goals that unashamedly targeted fundamental Soviet vulnerabilities.

To prevent the Soviets from setting U.S. priorities by forcing the United States to react to their initiatives, the incoming administration was urged to evaluate the shortcomings in past U.S. positions. One area for reappraisal was the pursuit of strategic arms agreements. Such agreements had exerted little effect on worldwide Soviet adventurism. They also adversely affected the strategic arms balance. Moreover, the pursuit of strategic arms limitations threatened to become a highly politicized end in itself.

Another pillar of the Affirmative Strategy was the call for limiting the Soviet Union's ability to batten upon the West's economic and technological prowess. Given that the single greatest Soviet weakness was economic, the United States was urged to capitalize on its advantage in this arena. The Western industrial states had to be made to understand that it was not in their interest to subsidize the survival of a weak yet oppressive Soviet leadership. Minimizing Western financing of the Soviet economy and careful monitoring of technology transfers would also serve to delay and impede the Soviet military buildup, which was based on the acquisition of Western technology and the infusion of Western capital.

A final cornerstone of the Affirmative Strategy was devising an effective counter to the established pattern of Soviet tactics aimed at undermining and destabilizing emergent democracies. The ISC called for the early application of requisite military force against Soviet-backed insurgent movements and full support for the counterinsurgency efforts of fledgling democratic societies. This also entailed

Dr. Joseph Luns, former NATO Secretary-General, addresses ISC Conference on Security of the Northern Flank and the Baltic Approaches." September 21-23. 1986.

General Andrew Goodpaster, Chairman of ISC NATO Conference, Copenhagen, Denmark, September 21-23, 1986.

decisive and timely preemption against and interdiction of external military and financial support to insurgencies by targeting the lifelines that sustained them. At the same time, the Affirmative Strategy called on the United States to address the local causes of unrest by encouraging nation-building programs aimed at increasing individual liberty, local autonomy, and regime democracy.

ENDURING FACETS OF AN AMERICAN STRATEGY

From the ISC's perspective, the fundamental battle between the Free World and the Soviet Union was one of ide-ology—of slavery versus freedom. Of necessity, the battle-ground was political. In this arena, the strengths of the Western system would inevitably be pitted against the weak-nesses of totalitarianism. In this arena, the military advan-tages and ideological adamancy of totalitarian systems could be neutralized and rendered.

A first priority of the Affirmative Strategy was expan-sion of the ideology of freedom. Democracy and liberty are tangible, relevant, and universal concepts. They are embod-ied in a self-evident philosophy. Western democratic ideals have a profoundly humane purpose: the affirmation of human dignity and the pursuit of happiness. This system is nothing less than a civilization—conceivably, the natural civ-ilization of humanity.

As a practical matter, the extension of democratic prac-tices is desirable in the international sphere for two reasons: First, democratic governments are confident about their legitimacy, and are much more likely to resolve their differ-ences peacefully than are nondemocratic governments. Second, democracies share a regard for the rule of law. This provides the basis for a mutual sympathy, something that communicates a sense of national and international responsibility, reinforces international order, and minimizes reckless behavior.

It is entirely consistent for an American government to make the promotion of democracy the core of its foreign policy. It is equally consistent for the United States to make the currency of democratic practice the primary medium of diplomatic exchange for the Free World. The nature of the American experiment is widely understood throughout the world and carries with it moral force. It overwhelms other ideals and models. It has tremendous attractiveness among diverse peoples. It is invariably under attack from those seeking to obscure its nature and fight its appeal.

Most nations expect the United States to give first priority to its democratic ideals; they are disconcerted by an American policy based on pure *realpolitik*. The American people share this appreciation of the American character. They are uncomfortable with foreign policies that are based on transient needs, that are not anspired by larger ideals.

As a result, the ISC's Affirmative Strategy recommended that U. S. diplomacy embody two normative objectives:

(1) The assertion and realization of the primacy of the individual in both theory and practice. Contrary to totalitarian philosophies of both the left and the right, which assert that the rights of an individual can only be defined in terms of the needs of those in power and in purely material terms—food, clothing, shelter, income—the core of U.S. diplomacy is a moral one. The United States must continually articulate and communicate its belief in the irreducible worth of the individual. Therefore, the United States should explicitly affirm the protection of the individual against the power of the state and the responsibility of the state to the individual; the indispensable nature of the freedom of religion, inquiry, discourse, assembly, movement, petition, the freedom from slavery and the

right to privacy; the need for constitutional government as a guarantee against the arbitrary exercise of power; the value of the free market economy and the protection of pluralism, cultural diversity and identity, combined with an unwillingness to defer to cultural differences about the fundamental nature of freedom.[7]

(2) The concept of the democratic regime and regime democracy. A policy that concerns itself with regime democracy must encourage the protection of individual rights and minority rights, the devolution of power from the government to the people, the credibility and independence of the judiciary, the flow of power toward the legislative branch; protections against governance by decree, the denationalization of economic resources, the development of private enterprise and protection against economic confiscation; the promotion of local autonomy and federalism, the establishment and maintenance of institutional checks and balances within the society and the government, and true accountability of national institutions and leaders to the citizenry.[8]

Similarly, a policy that opposes statism must target the economic, political, and intellectual engines of statism within the society: domestic cartels; unproductive, concentrated landholders and centralized economic institutions; governmental and administrative bureaucracies; self-protective political parties; closed elites in the government and the military; and collectivist members of the media. That leads to a third normative objective:

Cooperation among democracies as a reflexive, natural outcome of democratic practice. The Affirmative Strategy emphasized that efforts to promote democratic values cannot succeed if it is merely a province of the United States. Shared democratic values create a sense of com-

---

[7] *An Affirmative Strategy For the Free World*, published in *Global Affairs*, Summer 1988, p. 6.

[8] Ibid., p. 7.

munity and common purpose in the international sphere. A strategy that affirms democratic values must rally the practitioners of those values to action and involve them in a collective effort to build and expand the democratic domain.[9]

As the leader of the Free World, the United States must define the nature of international diplomacy so that the advocacy of democracy is understood to be the core of collective Western policy. And it must establish collective endeavors that actively involve other democracies in the work of establishing liberty and challenging anti-democratic statism. To achieve this the United States should redefine foreign policy to emphasize the primacy of freedom and democratic practices. This would involve making the apparent "meddling" in the internal affairs of other nations a virtue. Because statist regimes try to obscure their own concentration of power under the guise of a prickly nationalism, there exists no point at which the United States can accommodate the putative national sensitivities of governments hostile to regime democracy. Recent history demonstrates that diplomacy aimed at encouraging democratic practices can achieve short-term success. Through its execution, this diplomacy should be presented for what it is: a justifiably activist exercise designed to protect basic human rights, extend world order, promote true self-determination, and strengthen popular regimes.

STRATEGY AND THE WASHINGTON COMPROMISE

I never believed that the failure to create a comprehensive global strategy bespeaks a structural problem in U. S. politics. Pundits in the political science departments of universities tell us that democracies are inherently incapable of

---

[9] Ibid., p. 8.

devising long-range policies because of the discontinuity inherent in mandated, regular changes in political leadership and the inability to mobilize a popular consensus over the long term. I disagree. I believe democracies harbor long-term interests: they can articulate those interests and define an overall policy to go along with them. We continue to suffer from lack of a broad strategic vision attuned to our interests as a nation. As a consequence, not only are our policies reactive—to a Saddam Hussein or Kim il Jung—but we tend to compromise our long term interests. Yet, that is seldom understood in our body politic because, unfortunately, our leaders have failed to distinguish between policies and objectives. Freedom is not a policy; it is an objective. Prosperity is not a policy; it is an objective.

In short, there is no perspective on strategy. That vacuum is filled by the naive who want to intervene for purposes-of-the-moment—"defined"by pundits-of-the-moment—whether it be in Bosnia, Somalia or Haiti. Until such time that true leadership triumphs and the national interest is responsibly defined, the "pragmatists" will rule the day and lead us from tragedy to disaster. That perhaps is the ultimate price of the Washington Compromise.

17

Grappling With the Big Bear

The Affirmative Strategy accurately fastened upon the weaknesses of the Soviet system. Still, by the late 1980s probably only the denizens in the Soviet Politburo (and perhaps not even they) knew how deeply the cancer had penetrated. Aware that the system was approaching the crisis point, Mikhail Gorbachev attempted to save Communism and the Soviet Empire by reforming them. He gambled the achievements of 70 years of tyranny on promoting reform and seducing the West with his buzzwords: *"glasnost* and *perestroika."* Gorbachev's basic strategy was to win massive Western economic transfusions to revitalize the Soviet system, while using sweeping arms control schemes to brake Western military programs—notably NATO's deployment of intermediate-range missiles—and insure the Soviets' continuing military and strategic advantage over the West. In chess terms, the superpower contest between the United States and the USSR was reaching the endgame.

As was brought out earlier, the vaunted "Reagan Revolution" had fizzled out long before George Bush entered the White House. The historical record of this watershed period will show that if the United States and its allies "won the Cold War," they did so largely by default. Gorbachev successfully plied the endgame abroad by garnering Western economic aid and compliance with arms reductions; he lost it at home by underestimating the political-ideological consequences of his reforms.

But at the dawn of the final decade of a momentous century, the endgame was not yet played out. The rumblings of change within the Soviet Empire were growing louder, but no one could confidently predict their outcome. Indeed, the world faced an almost eerie uncertainty. A large variable in that uncertainty applied to the Soviet military establishment. Irrespective of internal convulsions, the Soviet Union was still a nuclear superpower. And military power always becomes a more dangerous factor in periods of instability and uncertainty.

AN HISTORIC MEETING IN MOSCOW

In 1989 I noticed an advertisement for *Kontinent* magazine in *The New York Tribune*, the predecessor publication to *The Washington Times*, financed by the Reverend Moon. The *Kontinent* magazine, edited by Vladimir Maximov in Paris, was a respected journal published by and for Soviet emigres. The advertisement was an appeal for investors. I called the editor of the *New York Tribune*, Robert Morton, who informed me that the conservative Springer publishing house in Germany was withdrawing support from *Kontinent*. It was obvious to me that in the volatile situation inside the Soviet Union, a key question applied to the Soviet military's role in the coming crisis. Glimpsing an opening in the collapsing state system in the USSR, I asked *Kontinent* connections in Moscow to help organize a conference with the Central Committee of the Soviet Communist Party and the General Staff of the Soviet Armed Forces.

In January 1990, the ISC succeeded in cosponsoring a conference in Moscow with the Soviet Academy of Sciences, involving both the Central Committee and the General Staff.

The meeting was organized to assess whether Soviet military doctrine had indeed shifted, as its leaders professed, from an offensive to a defensive cast. While there was broad acceptance of those professions in the Western media, the ISC saw no real evidence of such a shift. A strong supporter of the Soviet line in the United States was Adm. William Crowe, outgoing Chairman of the Joint Chiefs of Staff, (who, ironi-

ISC Conference, Moscow, January 24-26, 1990, co-sponsored by Central Committee of the CPSU and the General Staff of the Armed Forces of the USSR.

Participants, ISC Conference, Moscow, January 24-26, 1990.

Admiral & Mrs. Elmo Zumwalt take time out for Troika Ride, Moscow, 1990.

cally, was to become the principal military supporter of Democratic Presidential Candidate Bill Clinton[1]).

It seemed crucial to put Soviet doctrinal professions, with their immense implications, into the harsh light of probing analysis before they were swallowed whole on the Western side and accelerated the trend toward unilateral disarmament. We in the ISC had long understood that Russian military doctrine was an embracive phenomenon that stretched over the whole panoply of warfare as it was defined in the Marxist lexicon, including political and "national liberation" war. Therefore, we insisted that the conference agenda explicitly include military policies and concepts and their operational implications, force postures and programs, strategic offensive and defensive forces and programs, military expenditures, and regional conflicts.

This conference, which was convened in a resort hotel near Moscow normally reserved for the pleasures of high Soviet officials, marked an historic first time that senior military men from the United States and the Soviet Union met in

---

[1] Admiral Crowe was rewarded by the Clinton Administration with the Ambassadorship to the United Kingdom.

an open discussion. Americans in attendance included: Former Secretary of Defense Donald Rumsfeld; former Chief of Naval Operations, Adm. Elmo R. Zumwalt Jr.; former U. S. Marine Corps Commandant, Gen. Paul X. Kelly; former Commander-in-Chief of the U. S. Atlantic Command, Adm. Harry D. Train II; former Commander-in-Chief, U. S. Army Europe, Gen. Michael S. Davison; Former Commander-in-Chief, Central Command, Marine Gen. George B. Crist, and Major Gen. George J. Keegan, former Chief of Air Force Intelligence. Prominent on the Soviet side were the division head of the Central Committee's International Department, Lt. General Viktor P. Starodubov; former Deputy Chief of the General Staff, Admiral Nikolai N. Amelko; and head of the Military-Philosophical Department of the Voroshilov General Staff Academy, Major General Nikita A. Chaldymov.

It must have been no easy thing for the Soviet political leadership and military high command to accept the unprecedented idea of a meeting with a Western think tank on sensitive military questions. Not surprisingly, the conference stirred disagreement at high Soviet levels. Initial expectations had been that Marshal N. V. Ogarkov, the flamboyant former Soviet Chief of Staff, and Marshal V. G. Kulikov, former Commander-in-Chief of the Warsaw Pact Forces, would attend, but neither appeared. We had reason to believe that Ogarkov, responsible for much of the restructuring of Soviet forces under Gorbachev, had studied the ISC's Affirmative Strategy. Ogarkov believed in applying the lessons of Israel's stunning defeat of the Syrian Air Force during the 1982 Lebanon war to the Soviet Union's concepts of operations. The last-minute removal of Ogarkov and Kulikov from the list of participants seemed a clear indication that the Party had wrested control of the conference from the military.

We had practically guaranteed the presence at the conference of Gen. Mikhail A. Milshtein (Ret.) by stipulating to the Soviets during our dissension of participant lists: "Anyone but Milshtein!" Milshtein had become widely known as one of the Soviet military's foremost spokesmen (or disinformation agents) in the West. Significantly, at the closing press conference Milshtein said, "We have known of the ISC for a long time, but we were so far apart that we didn't do business with them. We now see that it is important to do business with them."

We came well-prepared for an encounter with some of the best military minds in Moscow. As might be expected, our adversaries also were prepared at all levels, and not only military ones. One night at dinner, I refused the plate served to me. The waitress picked it up, looked at me, and said: "Why? It's Kosher!" My religious-culinary requirements obviously were well known to the KGB, and passed down with great efficiency to the waitress level.

The Soviet participants in the conference tended to dismiss Soviet military policies and practices of the previous five decades as largely irrelevant. Some went as far as to acknowledge that Soviet "errors" might have been "provocative." The theme was adduced that the ideology of "class struggle" no longer was the driving force of Soviet foreign policy, and a purely defensive military posture was in line with the overall shift in Soviet perceptions of and dealings with the outside world.

From the outset, the American participants in the Moscow conference struck a skeptical stance, seeking clarifications with respect to key areas of Soviet policies, concepts and programs, including ostensible changes in the ideological underpinnings of Soviet foreign and defense policy. The Americans noted that contrary to the situation in the United States, where defense policies, programs and budgets were a matter of public record, the Soviets traditionally cloaked these issues in secrecy and deception. We therefore looked for clearer evidence on the question of whether the Marxist-Leninist dogma embracing dialectical materialism and class conflict as the dynamic forces in history and international relations had really been dampened, let alone abandoned, as part of the Soviet Union's "new thinking" in foreign affairs and defense under Gorbachev. We also targeted the Soviet concept of the correlation of forces, the issue of strategic stability, the Soviet definition of military sufficiency and defensive doctrine, the role and scale of offensive operations, the future structure of Soviet forces, the Soviet programs of modernization and qualitative improvements of nuclear and conventional systems, strategic defense, and Soviet views of the implication of political changes in Eastern Europe for the Warsaw Pact and Soviet military planning.

The new Soviet rhetoric, the Americans observed, was appealing. Yet, real change demanded changed behavior—not merely declared intentions—and had to be judged on the record. Soviet leaders had long claimed that their foreign policy was benign and their military doctrine inherently defensive. But what was "defensive" in their massive involvement in such places as Afghanistan, Angola, Cuba, and Nicaragua? Dramatic arms control proposals, including "general and complete disarmament," had been staples of Soviet declaratory policy—even as the Soviet Union deployed the world's most awesome strategic nuclear forces, both offensive and defensive, some of them in specific violation of arms control agreements.

As one American participant bluntly put it: "When we listen to Soviet rhetoric about new thinking, reasonable sufficiency and a purely defensive doctrine, in the light of information we have about Soviet force capabilities, continuing production and modernization programs, and the real magnitude of likely Soviet spending, we cannot place confidence in your rhetoric. For our part, it looks very much as if allegedly new policies are matters of declared intent rather than reality. And for that matter, the impact of past practices cannot be changed overnight: weapons produced under 'old thinking,' for example, hardly become defensive-only simply by the declaration of a new defensive doctrine."[2]

Indeed, in three days of comprehensive and searching discussions, the Soviets failed to convince the American delegates that a fundamental Soviet change in military policy had taken place. They appeared confused and contradictory. When pressed to specify tangible applications of their allegedly new defensive military doctrine, they became evasive. At times, Soviet positions revealed far more old thinking than new. At other times, the Soviets impaired the credibility of their argument with an obvious lack of candor, denying known Soviet capabilities and programs, and lapsing into a traditional ideological interpretation of Western policies.

They reverted to old themes: that Soviet strategic offensive modernization programs merely mirror-imaged those of the United States; that only the U.S., and not the Soviet Union, was pursuing a ballistic missile defense capability and militarization of space; and that the Soviets were unambiguously complying with the Anti-Ballistics Missile Treaty, while the United States was not. The Soviet military participants even contradicted their political leaders in continuing to insist that the radar installation in Krasnoyarsk, Siberia, did not violate the ABM Treaty.

The Soviets zig-zagged in their ideological explanations, failing to disavow totally the principle of class struggle. They insisted that Marxism-Leninism and historical materialism remained valid concepts, but needed to be

---

[2] ISC Conference Report on "The Changing U.S.-Soviet Strategic Balance," Moscow, April 1990, p. 3.

purged of some "distortions" introduced by past errors in the building of socialism. These ideological tenets, they explained, were long-term ideals rather than operational or policy guidelines, and, as such, did not constitute a threat to others.

The Soviets argued further that their military-technical doctrine no longer included tactical offensive operations. Counter-offensive operations were now designed simply to reestablish control of borders attacked by an outside aggressor. The Soviet Union, they said, no longer believed in political or military victory. The Soviets took issue with American reliance on Soviet literature, some of it published in the year prior to the conference, asserting that it was obsolete and did not necessarily represent their new thinking. Twenty-two basic documents of the General Staff had been thoroughly revised and had yet to be published as part of the reindoctrination of the military, they claimed. The Soviets evaded all questions regarding their military budget, as well as areas in which they anticipated qualitative improvement in their armed forces.

Major disagreements at the conference also centered on issues of strategic balance, deterrence and stability. As in the past, the Soviets rejected the U.S. concept of strategic sufficiency which would involve settling for nuclear parity, instead of strategic superiority. Soviet arguments that there was a rough parity between the U.S. and the Soviet strategic forces were discounted by the Americans, who noted that the Soviet Union devoted a far larger share of its defense resources to its strategic forces.

Although the Soviets accepted that nuclear war was unwinnable in light of the unacceptable damage it would inflict on both sides, they ruled out force reductions to a minimum deterrence level. That, they said, would leave the Soviet Union and the United States no other option than to target cities, which they deemed an immoral posture. To the Americans, this was further evidence that Soviet capabilities and programs invalidated their words. On the one hand, the Soviets insisted that they ruled out the use of nuclear weapons in warfare; on the other hand, they continued to design, produce and deploy the same kinds of weapons they had when Soviet military writings acknowledged that their aim was to wage nuclear war successfully.

What we learned at the conference was that the Soviets, no less than the Chinese, respected a worthy adversary. We made it clear to them that frankness was the key to under-standing and negotiating our differences, and that dissem-bling and evasion of the issues could invite only the potentially disastrous consequences of miscalculation. We stuck to our guns and did not fall into the traps of flattery and beguilement that had victimized so many American vis-itors to Moscow. And apparently our Soviet counterparts respected that hard honesty. At our second conference with the Soviet General Staff in Washington in October 1991, General Chaldymov confided to me: "It's not for your dovish views that we selected the ISC."

RIPPLING EFFECTS OF THE MOSCOW CONFERENCE

A constructive outgrowth of the 1990 dialogue in Moscow, with possibly enduring implications, is that it yielded what might be regarded as "testing points" with respect to the fundamental nature of Russian military policy. These include: detailed accountability of Russian defense spending; significant cuts in such spending and in arms pro-duction and military-industrial capacity; redeployment and restructuring of armed forces that will demonstrate empha-sis on defense (e.g. elimination of Operational Maneuver Groups, reduction of airborne and *spetsnaz* special forces units, and removal to the rear of other capabilities that are especially offensive in character); thorough reindoctrination of the armed forces and the replacement of military manuals; observable declines in the pace and magnitude of strategic force modernization; an end to chemical weapons production and significant cuts in nuclear weapons production; and conversion of a substantial portion of military industry to the production of consumer goods.

Events in the former Soviet Union after the Moscow seminar in January 1990 bore out many of the reservations expressed by American participants in the meeting. In 1991, speaking at a seminar in Brussels cosponsored by the ISC, Professor William Van Cleave cautioned that contradictory developments in Russia begged the question whether one should emphasize, in the longer view, the signs of change, turmoil, and disintegration or the elements of continuity like the reassertion of power by the KGB and the military.[3] Van Cleave recalled that the International Security Council had argued in a "Global Perspectives" advertisement in *The New York Times* six months after the Moscow conference that the conclusion that the Russian military threat had irreversibly collapsed rested on thin and very uncertain information. It was too early for the West to lower its vigilance.

Moreover, Van Cleave pointed out, Russian military expenditures in real terms in 1988, 1989 and 1990 were probably 25 percent above 1985 levels and, according to some estimates 35, if not 40 percent higher compared to what Gorbachev had predicted in his five-year defense plan that ended in 1990. Van Cleave also noted that the Russians had not fulfilled Gorbachev's promise to reduce military spending and production by 14 to 19 percent, that no major weapons development programs had been halted or

---

[3] ISC Conference Report on NATO and the Changing Geopolitical Environment, Brussels, 1991, p.3.

stretched out, that research and development of follow-on systems for all major weapons continued, that there had been no significant conversion of the industrial military complex to civilian industry, that the modernization of the ground and naval forces as well as the tactical air force continued apace and that, perhaps more ominously, the strategic weapons modernization program seemed to be expanding.

Finally, military journals in the Soviet Union's final days denounced purely defensive doctrines as civilian concepts that were irrelevant. Instead, Van Cleave said, there was a reemphasis on the doctrine of first strike involving offense and initiative.

As in Beijing, the Moscow conference had a totally unintended side-effect: It undoubtedly helped pave the way for a visit by Rev. Moon, in April 1990, to Moscow, where he was personally received by President Gorbachev. I need to iterate in that connection that, while he continued financial support to the ISC's activities, Rev. Moon remained completely aloof from its operations. In the rare encounters at Moon's residence, when we would chat primarily about the parallels in and differences between Judaism and Unificationism, I sensed that behind his own hardline approach to Communism was a worldview essentially similar to that of most U. S. participants in ISC projects. After all, Moon's understanding of Communist totalitarianism was not theoretical: he had spent three years in a North Korean concentration camp.

REWARDS OF CONSISTENCY

The Russians were well aware of both the ISC's and the Reverend's perceptions of the Soviet Union. From the outset, the ISC's viewpoint was conditioned by the philosophy expressed in the Affirmative Strategy. On numerous earlier occasions, the ISC had clearly advocated a wary approach to Moscow.

Already in 1985, in a conference held in Brussels on the Brezhnev Doctrine, the ISC had charged that the Soviet policy of expansion was based on aggression and intimidation. The Soviet Union exploited regional conflicts employing guerrillas, terrorists and sophisticated techniques of subversion, disinformation and propaganda as well as its own military forces and those of proxy states. Soviet aggression was backed by the paralyzing menace of Soviet nuclear superiority and a multifaceted nuclear capability which was growing far more rapidly than that of the United States.

> "The Soviet Union is seeking to profit from the accelerating disintegration of the (global) state system. It is claiming recognition of a unique right to commit aggression at will as the acknowledged overlord of an enlarged empire characterized by Soviet-style repression and the denial of basic human rights. In short, the Soviet Union claims to be above the law."[4]

To stop Soviet expansion and force the Soviet Union to live within its legal boundaries, the declaration called for a recommitment to the policy of alliance solidarity around the world. Such a recommitment would be based on an unchallengeable American nuclear deterrent force capable of preventing Soviet intervention. The declaration urged the United States to insist on the principle of Soviet-American nuclear arms negotiations, and of strict Soviet compliance with agreements.

---

[4] ISC Conference Report on International Security and the Brezhnev Doctrine, Brussels, July 1985, p. 3.

Three years later, in Geneva in 1988, an ISC conference squarely addressed the vulnerabilities of the Soviet empire. The Geneva Declaration portrayed Gorbachev's policy as follows: "That it is the obligation of the Free World, on behalf of 'peace,' to undertake by loans, credits, technology transfers, and unilateral disarmament to save the Soviet Union from its own infirmities." Ever since the 1917 revolution, the Soviets have attempted to buy essential respite to shore up their systemic failings on the backs of Western wealth, productivity, and technology without a fundamental retreat from their global hegemonic ambitions.[5]

An ISC roundtable convened in St. Louis in 1989 noted that "the very fluid and uncertain situation in the Soviet Union, should induce us to remain skeptical regarding Soviet intentions, to remain vigilant, and to uphold the military balance." The consensus statement at the conclusion of the roundtable noted that the West was not dealing with a Soviet Union that had been transformed either internally in the distribution of power or externally in agreeing to assume responsibility for maintenance of a stable international system.[6]

Later in 1989, an ISC study on the Soviet concept of peaceful cooperation warned that the Soviet leadership (i.e. Gorbachev) continued to view peaceful coexistence as an interim—and economically urgent—measure pending the achievement of communism worldwide. "Indeed, the very concept of peaceful coexistence as a form of anti-Western struggle is inseparable from the Soviet system itself," the study said.[7]

---

[5] ISC Conference Report on *Vulnerabilities of the Soviet Empire*, Geneva, June 1988, p. 8.
[6] ISC Conference Report on *Assessing Change in the USSR*, St. Louis, 1989, xvi.
[7] ISC Conference Report on *Peaceful Coexistence, A Study in Soviet Doctrine*, Washington, D.C., 1989, p. 73.

In an advertisement in *The New York Times* in July 1990, the ISC warned that the Bush Administration's assumption that the Soviet military threat had irreversibly collapsed and that the Soviet Union was being transformed into a partner for peace rested on a thin and perilous ledge of knowledge: "In fact, the more chips the Administration places on the Gorbachev card the more it blinds itself to information and interpretations that challenge the official wisdom."[8]

The advertisement noted that in April 1990 the Defense Intelligence Agency had submitted to Congress a report that could support conclusions contradicting those of the Administration. Huge stockpiles of Russian arms remained and were being increasingly updated; there had been no slowdown in naval force modernization; vigorous and broadly-based modernization of both strategic offensive and defensive forces continued at very high rates of production; and the conversion of military plants to civilian industry remained virtually non-existent.

Finally, in November 1990, a number of outstanding scholars, all experts in their respective fields, gathered under ISC auspices in Washington to explore the problem of Soviet nationalities and its threat to the very cohesion of the Soviet Union. No longer marginal players on a Russian-dominated stage, the minority peoples of the USSR were totally transforming the character of the country into an unrecognizably new form. Discussion focused on the process of disintegration in the Soviet empire, the fading of Communist Party control over and within the national republics, the potential "reversibility" of the process of democratization, the emergence of Russia as an independent entity in its own right,

---

[8] Global Perspectives 1990: Bring on the B-Team," *The New York Times*, July 18, 1990.
[9] *ISC Conference Report on The Soviet Nationalities Problem*, Washington, D.C., 1990.

and finally, the outlook for future relations among various Soviet nationalities.[9]

At the Brussels seminar in 1991, there was nearly unanimous agreement that the Soviet empire was dead and could not be resuscitated. It was concluded at the meeting that Russia was emerging as an independent country that may be more intent on establishing its own future and prosperity than attempting to perpetuate a moribund and costly imperial system, internal or external. It was as yet uncertain whether Russia would succeed in the long run in its new course toward democracy and the liberation of former imperial subjects among the nationalities.

THE "HERO IN WASHINGTON"—BUT NOT MOSCOW

We in the ISC thus consistently tried to sustain pressure on the Soviet system, contributing to the external pressure that, arguably, accelerated the collapse of the Soviet Empire—or "pushed that which was falling." That our view of the Soviet Union and its objectives was essentially correct is borne out by the historical record gradually being unveiled by the successors to the Soviet regime in Moscow.

Still, there are certain constraints. The Russians always had a keen grasp of the "correlation of forces," or what we call the balance of power. There were elements in Russia, including Gorbachev, who understood the dangers in the transition of a power balance to a new constellation of forces. The world faces those dangers.

In retrospect, Gorbachev—once described as the "most resourceful Soviet leader since Lenin"—remains something of an enigma. By all rational calculation, Gorbachev should have used his military instrument, in accordance with the Communist dogma, to rescue the economic underpinnings of the Soviet Empire. In the 1980s, the U.S. intelligence community was very fearful that the Soviets would strike south into the Persian Gulf in a bid to acquire the oil wealth of the region in order to resolve the Soviet Union's economic dilemma. Perhaps Gorbachev's predecessors—especially Khrushchev and Brezhnev, who ordered Soviet tanks into Budapest and Prague, respectively—are turning in their graves. As it was, the Soviet Empire fell with nary a shot being fired.

Gorbachev's attempt was to save communism by reforming it.

Nothing better demonstrated the "trendy" moral and political weakness of Washington than the accolades that continued to be heaped upon the "man behind the birth-mark," long after he was totally discredited by his own people. It was yet another sign that the Washington Compromise is alive and well!

18

Wooing the Lion of Damascus

We shift the focus of our narrative from Moscow southward to the Middle East, specifically Syria. Viewed from Damascus, the world at that time was not a friendly place. Relations between Syria and its Arab neighbors were frozen at best. Archenemy Iraq was as bent as ever on installing a more sympathetic regime in Damascus in place of President Hafez al-Assad. Palestine Liberation Organization Chairman Yasser Arafat decided to throw in his lot with Arab moderates such as Egypt and Saudi Arabia. Acting on their advice, Arafat seemed to be moving toward recognition of the state of Israel and a renunciation of terrorism. Prospects for a Middle East peace, in which Israel might return the Golan Heights captured from Syria in the June 1967 Middle East War, were virtually nil. The regional climate was hardly conducive to an imposition of Syrian will on obstinate Christians in Lebanon, viewed by Syria as its soft underbelly.

To add to the gloomy picture seen from Damascus, the Soviets made it clear to Syria that they would not support Assad's efforts to achieve strategic parity with Israel, a cornerstone of Syrian Middle East policy for the previous decade. Syria would no longer get whatever it sought from the Soviet arsenal, nor count on advantageous financial

ISC Conference, Jerusalem, Israel, October 19-21, 1986.

arrangements for its military purchases. The democratic revolution in Eastern Europe, moreover, had led to a severing of
Syria's economic and intelligence ties to the Soviet Union's
former satellites.

At the same time, relations with Western nations
remained strained at best. The United States listed Syria
among those nations that sponsored terrorism because of its
support for various terrorist organizations. Britain had broken off diplomatic relations after foiling an attempt by a
Syrian-trained Palestinian to smuggle a bomb on an Israeli El
Al airliner departing from London's Heathrow Airport.

In 1988, the Syrian regime almost certainly was implicated, along with the Libyans, in the destruction of Pan Am
flight 103 with its 270 victims, as well as the 1983 slaughter in
Beirut of 241 Marines in their barracks and 63 people at the
U. S. Embassy. In 1985, Assad's surrogates raided the Rome
and Vienna airports, gunning down five Americans.

In a persistent and bloody campaign against U.S. interests, the Assad regime had spearheaded the destruction of the pre-civil war government in Lebanon, an American ally to whose aid the United States had come twice with the intervention of troops, and which was now replaced by a puppet government run from Damascus. Less widely known was the fact that senior Syrian officials were running one of the largest international drug operations. Heroin, produced in the Bekaa Valley of Lebanon under Syrian control, was (and continues to be) fed into West European and American veins.

In this shifted environment, Syria lost two key levers in its attempt to shape regional events. It no longer had the option of waging war in a bid to turn the tables and improve its regional and international standing. Its reduced influence also meant that it no longer could stymie regional developments by exercising its veto, as it had done successfully when it thwarted the 1983 agreement between Israel and Lebanon engineered by then Secretary of State George Shultz following the Israeli invasion of Lebanon, and when it also frustrated a bilateral accommodation between Israel and Jordan.

The logical conclusion to be drawn at the time was that Syria's tightening international isolation threatened to undermine the domestic position of the Assad regime, which was already worried that Israel might exploit its weakness by striking preemptively. The time perhaps was ripe, it seemed to me, for Syria to contemplate a more unconventional route in breaking the deadlock and overcoming its problems. Such a route might be the initiation of direct secret contacts between Assad's ruling Baath Party and Israeli Prime Minister Yitzhak Shamir's governing Likud Bloc. The contacts would be directed toward achievement of a Syrian-Israeli agreement on the future of the Golan Heights, West Bank, and the Gaza Strip.

AN INITIATIVE AIMED AT DAMASCUS

Encouraged by our prior success in bridge-building between Mainland China and Taiwan, the ISC looked toward repeating that role between Damascus and Jerusalem. More specifically, we envisioned a Syrian-Israeli agreement in which Israel would recognize their common interests in Lebanon, with the exclusion of the Christian areas that would look to the Jewish state for their protection. In exchange, Syria would acquiesce in Israeli control of the West Bank and Gaza under some arrangement with Jordan, which would preclude the establishment of an independent Palestinian state. The future of the Golan Heights would be determined as part of an Israeli-Syrian peace treaty.

To get the process going, the ISC needed a direct and secure channel to Assad. Retired French General Albert Merglen, who enjoyed close ties to Syrian Defense Minister Mustafa Tlass, qualified for that role. In several meetings with ISC Vice President William J. Mazzocco in Nice, France, in 1989, Merglen agreed to travel to Damascus to present the Syrians with the proposal.

In Damascus, Tlass reportedly deemed the ISC proposal a good approach. Still, nothing happened. In June 1989, I arranged to meet in London with British journalist and Assad biographer Patrick Seale, known for his contacts in the Syrian regime. Seale promised to pass on the proposal to Damascus, but also argued for sending a delegation of prominent Americans to the Syrian capital—something long sought by the Assad regime in order to break out of its isolation. Again, however, there was no response from the Syrians. A third possible conduit emerged in the person of a prominent Lebanese Christian businessman. He, too, was unsuccessful in eliciting a Syrian response. Still, our go-between seemed to make sense in suggesting that Assad feared that a dialogue between the Likud and the Baath could not be kept secret. Perhaps some "arm's length shuttle diplomacy" was in order, with the businessman maintaining contact with the Syrians, and the ISC with the Israelis.

Meanwhile, the rationale for a Syrian-Israeli agreement seemed to grow in the deepening shadow of crisis in the Persian Gulf. Such an agreement would wrest the fulcrum of the power balance away from President Saddam Hussein's regime in Baghdad. It promised more generally to stabilize the Middle East when global uncertainty and strategic changes enhanced the chances for an eruption of violence.

In July 1990, while the Lebanese businessman traveled to Damascus for a meeting with Assad, I sought to gain approval of our proposal from Israeli Prime Minister Yitzhak Shamir. Having read my memorandum and listened to my explanation, Shamir indicated that Israel would be interested, but needed a sign from Assad of his willingness to engage in a serious dialogue. In Damascus, however, Assad was noncommittal, preferring to temporize.

Assad's attitude was not surprising. Lebanese professor Antoine Makdisi, quoted in an article in the *New Yorker*, explained that "to understand Assad, you must see him as a link in the chain of Syrian peasants who lived with Ottoman pressure for centuries. The Syrian peasant is never sponta-neous—he is always calculating, always suspicious... The peasant asks: 'What does he want and how can I use it to my advantage?' He is trying to play the parties he deals with against one another so that in the end he is on the side of the winner."[1]

That was exactly how Assad dealt with the ISC pro-posal. With the Iraqi invasion of Kuwait, he opted for those

---

[1] Cited by Milton Viorst, *Sandcastles, The Arabs in Search of the Modern World*. New York: Alfred A. Knoph, 1994, p. 126.

he believed would be the winners. Syria's immediate problems seemed to resolve themselves. Syria was no longer
shunned; indeed, its radical credentials were needed to
enhance the prestige of the multinational coalition being
arrayed against Iraq. On a visit to Damascus, U. S. Assistant
Secretary of State John Kelly solicited Syrian participation in
the coalition, giving Assad a new lease on life—at a time
when his weakness could have been exploited to push him
closer toward peace with Israel.

In fact, participation in the U.S.-led coalition allowed
Syria to acquire strategic leverage in its relations with Israel.
U. S. accommodation with Syria meant a lost opportunity for
Syrian-Israeli peace. Instead, the United States aligned itself
with Syria against Israel, demanding an Israeli withdrawal
from the Golan Heights. Similarly, an opportunity was
missed to force Syria to account for the thousands of political
prisoners over the previous 20 years of the Assad regime, to
prepare a schedule for Syrian withdrawal from Lebanon, and
to bring an immediate halt to the drug-trafficking out of
Lebanon's Bekaa Valley. Neither the United States nor Israel
mustered the acumen or tenacity to exploit the opportunity.

Assad, however, had both acumen and tenacity. The
U.S. carrot allowed him to gain funds and legitimacy as well
as to establish a firm grip on Lebanon without giving anything in return. The $2-3 billion he obtained from Saudi
Arabia for his participation in Operation Desert Shield were
used for the purchase of Scud missiles from North Korea,
which improved Syria's military posture against Israel,
thereby also elevating the specter of an Israeli preemptive
strike against Syria. "Syria too often and too easily has been
let off the hook by the United States," commented Lebanese
Christian professor Habib Malek at a November 1990 ISC
conference in Washington on Syria's role in the Persian Gulf.

Realizing that only in a personal meeting with Assad

would I be able to salvage the proposal, I went back to Patrick Seale's suggestion. An ISC proposal to send an American delegation to Damascus to discuss the situation in the Gulf following the Iraqi invasion was enthusiastically received by the Syrian ambassador to the United States, Walid Muallim, a confidant of Syrian Foreign Minister Farouk Shara'a. Yet, Muallim's endorsement notwithstanding, there never came a formal response from Damascus.

SYRIA IN THE WAKE OF THE GULF WAR

Assad's troubles were eased as a result of the Gulf crisis, but by no means were they ended. The Syrian president still had to contend with strong opposition to his little-changed policies. In the eyes of many Americans, as well as Europeans and Israelis, nothing much differentiated Assad and Saddam Hussein. Both were ruthless dictators with no regard for human rights. Both were widely viewed as anti-Western and as instigators of some of the most lethal terrorist attacks against U.S. and other western targets.

During the Gulf crisis, many felt that there were only cosmetic differences between Iraq's occupation of Kuwait and the presence of some 40,000 Syrian troops in Lebanon. Taking advantage of the Gulf crisis, Syria ousted Lebanese Christian leader Michel Aoun and slaughtered thousands of his supporters. Syria also collected its profits from the Lebanese-based drug trade. U.S. acquiescence in the ousting of Aoun by Syria two months after the Iraqi invasion of Kuwait threatened to make a mockery of the Bush Administration's rejection of any linkage between the Gulf crisis and efforts to resolve the Arab-Israeli conflict.

Members of Congress, as well as others inside and outside government, wondered whether the United States might not come to regret its newly forged alliance with Syria. Those critics feared that the United States was thus making implicit commitments to a force that was bound to reemerge as a principal contender for dominance in the Middle East, thus replicating the follies of past U.S. support for Iraq against Iran. They also suggested that the credibility of the U.S. fight against terrorism could be severely damaged by the Administration's implied willingness to gloss over past Syrian-sponsored atrocities and to ignore Syria's continuing links with the international terrorist network.

An ISC conference on Syria was held in Washington in November 1990. One observer suggested that Assad had been strongly influenced by the example of Saladin, the Kurdish warrior who defeated the Crusaders and reconquered Jerusalem. He told of reports by visitors of a huge painting in Assad's antechamber depicting the Battle of Hittin near Tiberias in 1187 AD, in which Saladin's triumph paved his way to Jerusalem. "I personally have no reason to believe that Assad has shed this vision for something more constructive," said Israeli Professor Haim Shaked at the conference. Instead, he opined, Assad was making adjustments during the Gulf crisis to changed circumstances without altering his fundamental approach: "He has patience, he moves very slowly."[2]

I remember during an earlier conference in Jerusalem sharing the dinner table with Geoffrey Kemp, a former Middle East analyst in the National Security Council, and former U.S. delegate to the UN Security Council, Ambassador Charles Lichenstein. With a wink to Ambassador Lichenstein, I turned to Kemp: "It seems to me that the one way to make peace is to dismember Syria, since it is an artificial state, as are Jordan, Iraq, Saudi Arabia, and Lebanon. One has the name of a river, the other of a mountain. The word 'Souriya' is not even Arab; it's Greek. Iraq was

---

[2] ISC Conference Report on *Syria's Role in the Gulf Crisis*, Washington D.C., 1990, p. 5.

always Mesopotamia. Dismemberment may be the only
answer for Syria."

Kemp reacted with shocked consternation. As a relative
newcomer to Middle East studies, he was not steeped in the
region's history. I was telling him that there could have been
an alternative policy, but it meant changing the political map
of the region.

THE LONGER LEGACY OF U.S. MISTAKES

More generally, failure to understand the basic nature of
the balance of power in the Arab world and the Middle East
has led to grievous miscalculations of American policy, exacerbating the instability of the area. Not only have we lacked
a political purpose of our own, but we have prevented those
of our allies who mustered such purpose from fulfilling it.
American policy toward Iraq is a salient case in point.

As early as June 10, 1984, *The New York Times* published
my letter to the editor warning against the U.S. tilt toward
Iraq.

> As the escalating war in the Persian Gulf shifts into its
> 45th month, the mindless American tilt toward Iraq sets
> the stage for a reversal of Soviet alliances reminiscent of
> the Soviet-Ethiopian conflict of 1978. In that affair, the
> American courtship of a committed Soviet ally (Somalia)
> resulted in Moscow shifting its focus to Ethiopia—the
> greater prize in East Africa.
>
> Clearly, the strategic prize in the gulf is not Iraq but Iran,
> which historically functioned as the geographic barrier to
> Russian expansion into the gulf and Indian Ocean region.
> At a suitable moment unwittingly prepared by American
> diplomacy, Moscow will abandon its huge investment in
> Iraq for rapprochement with Iran, thereby fundamentally
> altering the configuration of world politics.
>
> After all, from Teheran's perspective, Soviet SS-21s to
> Iraq (scheduled for delivery in August) are far more dan-
> gerous than American Stingers to Saudi Arabia and must

therefore be neutralized. Moreover, Moscow—not Washington—is the power of geographic proximity, demonstrating far greater will and determination. By upping the ante in Iraq, Moscow exploits the self-defeating U.S. tilt toward Iraq in the reasoned expectation that Teheran will accommodate to the necessary.

Teheran radio recently announced that, at the Kremlin's request, a senior Iranian official had flown to Moscow on a mission that informed sources said could be intended to persuade Moscow to curtail its massive arms deliveries to Iraq. The departure of Sayyid Muhammad Sadr marks the first such high-level contact with the Soviets since early 1983.

It therefore appears that the process for a Soviet- Iranian rapprochement may already be under way.

What subsequently became the Iran-Contra affair may well have been at least partially motivated by the belated perception in the Reagan Administration that Iran was the strategic prize in the subregion. The perception, however, was both belated and short-lived. Before and after, the Arabist clique in the State Department prevailed. That clique took its cue primarily from Saudi Arabia, which faced Iran, by far the largest and potentially strongest nation-state in the region, as its principal rival.

I am certain that following the Iraqi attack on the *USS Stark* in 1987, the State Department was divided, with the Arabists siding with Iraq and the more strategically-minded minority with Iran. As usual, the Arabists won out, notwithstanding Iraq's deliberate bombing of a U. S. ship in an effort to get the United States involved in the war. The telling fact in the attack on the *Stark* was that two Exocet missiles were fired, meaning that two Iraqi aircraft were targeting the *Stark*. In other words, it was no accident, but a coordinated operation. Here is how I saw the situation at the time, as described in a UPI story on August 2, 1987.

Joseph Churba, a former chief Middle East intelligence analyst for the U. S. Air Force known to have excellent intelligence sources, said "the attack was deliberate," designed "to embroil the U.S. more deeply in the gulf crisis in order to promote an armistice that would not favor Iran." Churba, president of the Center for International Security, a non-profit think tank in Washington, said the plan was part of a "long-term Arab strategy."[3]

Only several years after the fact did the Defense Intelligence Agency confirm that there had been two Exocets and that it was a deliberate attack.

My argument all along has been that the United States should endeavor to maintain a balance among Iran, Iraq, and Saudi Arabia. The U.S. not only made no move to deter Iraq from attacking Iranian tankers, but in the latter stages of the Iran-Iraqi war, in the late 1980s, set out to prevent Iran from retaliating by "flagging" ships moving through the Gulf—that is, lending them American registry and thus, in effect, U. S. military protection. By so doing, the U.S. aligned itself directly with Iraq in a purely regional conflict, choosing the side of the unprovoked aggressor. But then, Iran and Israel have always been on the low end of the policy scale in the State Department. The Middle East has always been perceived as Arab—and not just Arab, but Sunni Arab.

American Mistakes Repeated

But let us return to Syria. As I noted earlier, when Iraq invaded Kuwait, the U.S. strove to enlist Syria—at the strong urging of Saudi Arabia—as part of the anti-Iraq alliance. The

---

[3] John Chancellor of National Broadcasting Company called saying he was intrigued by the letter and wanted to use it as the basis for a commentary. He asked about the International Security Council. But when he realized we were pro-defense, he cooled and we never heard from him again.

theory was that by having one of the "radical" Arab states in the coalition, we would somewhat dampen the xenophobia aroused even among the populations of the Gulf states by an "invasion" of Western forces into the area.

Whether or not this calculation was valid, by ending Assad's isolation—indeed, welcoming him into the "community"—we killed any incentive as well as opportunity to force Damascus into meaningful talks with Israel. At the very least, the Bush Administration should have demanded that Syria demonstrate its sincerity by the following steps: developing together with the United States a mutually acceptable definition of terrorism; stopping anti-Israeli propaganda that incited violence against civilians; halting its involvement in narcotics traffic and the promotion of narco-terrorism; closing terrorist bases in Lebanon and Syria, including those of the Popular Front for the Liberation of Palestine; arresting and prosecuting terrorist leaders under Syria's jurisdiction; agreeing to extradite to the United States terrorists such as General Command (PFLP-GC)[4] leader Ahmed Jibril; preventing the acquisition and use of weapons of mass destruction by terrorists; and clamping down on the misuse of diplomatic facilities in support of terrorism.

In bringing Syria into the coalition, the United States sought to symbolically align Saddam's archenemy Assad of Syria within a broad Arab coalition in the Gulf—a coalition without military force or political will to oppose the Saddam regime. And when it began to totter, the U. S. was urged by its Arab allies to save the leader we had labeled "another Hitler" for fear that a collapse in Iraq might threaten the *status quo* in the rest of the region.

---

[4] Popular Front for Liberation of Palestine—General Command.

One can only imagine what would have happened if the United States had told Syria, after Iraq's attack on Kuwait, that the best thing Assad could do was to seek peace with Israel. The balance of power *within the region* would have shifted against Iraq and in favor of the West. Syria's tacit alignment with Israel would have posed a serious threat to Saddam. A regional balance would have been constructed against Saddam Hussein under the aegis of the United States.

In fact, what Washington did was repeat the mistakes it committed during the Iraq-Iran War by allying itself with the Syrian regime, one of the bloodiest in the region. The rationalization was that Assad was "becoming more moderate." But the history of the Assad regime showed that he always desired to wage war on Israel. When the Soviet Union denied Assad the strategic parity with Israel that he sought after 1973, and especially after Camp David in 1978, the threat of open hostilities was reduced. By convincing Israel not to intercept shipments of Scud C missiles from North Korea and M-9 international ballistic missiles from China to Syria and Iran, the United States promptly moved into the breech after the Gulf War, allowing Syria to acquire another kind of strategic parity with Israel.

As this is being written, Qaddafi, Saddam Hussein, and Assad are still in power. They are spokesmen for the radical forces that the United States sought to appease and in so doing worsened the situation. Of the three survivors, Assad is the clear winner. He got money—payments from the Saudis for his "participation" in the Gulf War alliance, which he promptly used to buy Scuds from North Korea—hegemony in Lebanon, and an improved military posture vis-a-vis Israel. All this with effective U. S. support.

As has been described above, during the two-year window of opportunity for the Syrian-Israeli deal, the ISC did everything possible within its means to arrange a meeting between Syrian and Israeli leaders. But beyond ambivalence in Damascus, the initiative died as a consequence of Israel's policy of "restraint" in the Gulf War. That policy evoked a great deal of official American rhetoric of gratitude, but the reality of U.S. policy aligned Syria against Israel. Israel's policy of "restraint" was that state's biggest single military-strategic blunder since the 1973 War—and that includes the Lebanon debacle. It indicated a fundamental failure in understanding the character of the American tie to Israel. Furthermore, Israel displayed classic self-delusion in misunderstanding the difference between friend and enemy.

THE LEGACY OF ISRAELI ERRORS

Israel's willingness to accept, without retaliation, a direct attack on its civilian population from an Arab power—Iraq—with which it did not even share a border, was the most damaging decision ever made by that country. The psychological impact on the population was enormous, as evidenced by Israelis reduced to wearing gas-masks and huddling in their bunker-rooms in fear of attacks from a remote enemy. We can conjure up many rationales for this Israeli decision, none of which are adequate in the face of this monumental failure of basic policy. It was the repudiation at the highest level of what Zionism stood for, a betrayal of the supreme obligation of government: defense of its citizens.

By surrendering the inherent right to self-defense for political expedience, Israel set a precedent—i.e., not responding to Scud missile attacks—that immediately sent Assad shopping to North Korea for more and better Scuds. Furthermore, this further eroded the U.S.-Israel alliance by encouraging those in the American bureaucracy who, either because of their misunderstanding of geopolitics or their anti-Israel prejudices, would treat Israel as just another element in the Middle East equation.

I remember visiting Israeli Ambassador Zalman Shoval after Iraq's first Scud attack and asking if the U.S.-Syria rapprochement was in Israel's interest. His answer was vaguely equivocal.

In retrospect, I believe that the historic opportunity for peace with Syria was lost. There is no incentive for Assad to negotiate anything. His purpose is to stay in the twilight zone of no war-no peace, while Israel twists slowly in the wind. Chances are that even were Israel to offer every inch of the Golan, Assad would not sign a peace agreement. He would want Israeli recognition of his absorption of Lebanon—especially Beirut. Moreover, he would insist on controlling the Palestinian Arab course, demanding that Israel concede to the Palestinian "diaspora" the "right of return"—after the territories are handed over.

I would also argue that American diplomacy in the Middle East will continue to fail because it is not attuned to political realities on the ground. In President Bush's "New World Order," there was no room for Israel. There was room for a terrorist state like Syria, a corrupt monarchy like Kuwait, a feudal oligarchy like Saudi Arabia, or a Palestinian state, but not for the lone democracy in the region with the ability and the will to defend itself against enemies who have vowed repeatedly to end its existence.

CHAPTER
19

Iraq:
The Key That Did Not Turn

Ironically, the basic vacuum of U. S. policy in the Middle East was most clearly demonstrated in what, ostensibly, was the greatest success of that policy. Almost immediately, the military victory over Iraq by the U.S.-led coalition in 1991 was negated by its political aftermath—or better said, by the inconclusiveness of a military campaign that, from the outset, had not been waged in behest of clear-cut political objectives, let alone waged with any kind of conception of a postwar regional scenario.

Indeed, "victory" has an ever more hollow ring in retrospect. Hussein, after all, not only sustained himself in power, but outlasted by a long shot his antagonist, George Bush. True, a substantial portion of Saddam's war machine was destroyed. Yet the skill with which Saddam had put together that war machine in the first place—and did so after the deep drainages of a costly conflict with Iran—indicated how quickly the power curves in the Middle East can change, and change again.

THE GULF WAR IN PROSPECT

All this was eminently predictable. On January 17, 1991, just as the air campaign of Desert Storm was being launched, we assembled in Washington a meeting of a number of ISC "regulars" to look to the broader stage on which the drama in the Gulf was being played out. Besides myself, discussants included Major General George J. Keegan, former Assistant Secretary of Defense Frank Gaffney, Jr., Dr. Leon Goure, General Fritz Kroesen, Prof. Eugene Rostow, Admiral Harry Train, II, and Ambassador Charles Lichenstein.

We projected how the war might optionally be conducted militarily and, more important, toward what kind of political settlement. We touched on a wide range of basic considerations:

- Did the fact of the war, as well as Saddam's atrocities, warrant a broadening of U.S. war aims from the limited ones addressed in the UN Security Council resolutions to the elimination of the Saddam Hussein regime? Should there be call for unconditional surrender?
- How should the U.S. respond to Iraqi use of chemical/biological warfare?
- Should Israel be kept out of the war? Or should it, on the contrary, be brought in?
- Could U.S. policy turn the forces unleashed by the Gulf conflict into a framework for peace in the region?
- Should Iraq's military infrastructure be totally destroyed? Or should some consideration be given to a postwar balance among Iraq, Iran and Syria?
- Should an occupation of Iraq be staged to ensure the installation of a regime that would not threaten its neighbors?
- And finally, what should be the Russian role in the region? How could Moscow be made to accept the U.S. as the region's predominant power?

Professor Rostow, for one, addressed the last question with guarded optimism. While he discounted the euphoria surrounding the alleged end to the Cold War and projected reform in Russia, he foresaw that the changes in Russia opened opportunities for some degree of cooperation with the United

States. Rostow took note of the harsh criticism Gorbachev was taking in Russia for seeming to be cooperative with the United States in forcing Iraq to withdraw from Kuwait. This had already been made clear by Soviet participants at an earlier meeting of the ISC in November 1990, who argued that Iraq should *not* be pushed into a corner and that Iraqi troops should *not* be evicted from Kuwait by military force.

Still, Rostow believed that Moscow was now, in fact, limited in its ability to undermine Western interests for years to come. He quoted a young Russian diplomat: "We're not a great power for the moment—but we'll be back." I did not take issue with my friend, Gene Rostow, at the time, but I believed even his guarded optimism to be premature. Russia was still a great power, if only because of its military capabilities, led by its nuclear arsenal, and, as such, had to be taken seriously as a continuing factor in the regional equation. Moreover, while Russian fortunes had fluctuated throughout a long history, a constant of that history had been the southward thrust of Russian external ambitions.

As far as U.S. objectives in the war were concerned, Rostow believed that an occupation of Iraq would be required in order to make sure that any Iraqi capabilities for nuclear, chemical and biological warfare were eradicated. General Kroesen joined the view the U.S. should set as its objective the complete destruction of the Saddam regime, "and we'll do that with a land operation that would not be very costly."

Frank Gaffney expressed strong skepticism of Russian interests and intentions in the embroglio. He pointed out that Moscow had given various alibis for the continued presence of a large number of military and intelligence personnel in Iraq, and that those excuses were downright incredible. Moreover, the Russians were blatantly circumventing the economic and military embargo imposed by the U.S. on Iraq.

There were persistent, credible reports that Cuba, Libya, North Korea and other Russian clients had been smuggling spare parts into Iraq for Soviet-built military equipment. According to Gaffney, it was obvious that the Russians were conducting business in Iraq as usual.

There was also, Gaffney emphasized, the issue of Russian diplomatic and political activity on Saddam's behalf, most notably in the various missions to Baghdad of a leading KGB official, Yevgeny Primakov, a Russian Arabist known for his close ties to the Saddam regime. Such missions were evidently intended to split the U.S.-led anti-Iraqi coalition and serve the long-term joint interests of Iraq and Russia. One of these ideas called for an international Middle East peace conference.

In short, these and many other factors underscored what Gaffney called a Russian "double game" in Iraq. Not only had there been a senior Russian military specialist in Baghdad in the weeks just before the invasion of Kuwait, but it was obvious from the crackdown taking place in the Baltic states at the time against the independence movements there that Moscow might well have been "just as interested in bringing off the crisis as in simply adapting to its existence."

I contented myself, for the time being, in arguing that the fundamental factor of confusion was in the failure of the U.S. to clarify its war aims in the collision with Iraq. I asked a simple question: "Do we want the surrender of the Iraqi government, or do we want no more than the destruction of the Iraqi army?"

Dr. Leon Goure, an eminent Sovietologist, essentially agreed with Gaffney. He thought that the conventional U.S. praise of Moscow for cooperating with the U.S. tended to obscure the actual Soviet objectives and behavior, which were "at odds with U.S. interests." It was the United States, after all, he said, that was carrying the main burden, while the Russians were positioning themselves to become the main beneficiaries of whatever happened. Not only was Moscow attempting to have its cake and eat it, but it was bent on emerging from the crisis with an even larger piece of cake.

Goure quoted a Russian analyst to the effect that, while the U.S. was seeking Saddam's removal and the dismantling of his war machine, the Russians were concerned over the possibility that Saddam might be supplanted by someone less friendly to Moscow. Hence the Russians had been insisting on a peaceful resolution of the crisis that would not include Saddam's replacement. Goure attributed hollowness to the Russian claim that Moscow's support in the Security Council gave "special weight and importance" to its "condemnation" of Iraq. He pointed out that Moscow's role was generally interpreted by many Arabs as "placing restraints on the aims of the military operations" now being prepared by the United States. Goure concluded that Moscow was insistent on finding an "Arab solution" to the crisis.

I reacted favorably to Goure's presentation, but pointed to a larger historical perspective: Moscow's policy had allowed for the fall of regimes, but historically opposed the dismemberment of states and the redrawing of the political map. Also, Moscow had always opposed the exercise of unrestrained U.S. force directly south of its southern borders; hence the Russians were concerned about U.S. activity in the Gulf and about a massive destruction of Moscow-built military equipment.

"That would embarrass the presumed alliance between Iraq and Russia," I contended, "since it would point up the weakness of the Moscow government as an ally for allowing the physical destruction of their equipment and technology." In addition, the Russians did not want to see the U.S. inherit the former British monopoly in the Persian Gulf. I ended on what I thought was a common sense note: "We are going to hear from the Russians soon enough."

A strong contribution to the meeting came from Habib Malek, a Lebanese Christian scholar, who suggested that the Gulf crisis could be used to put "some meat on the skeleton" of the emerging conjuncture in world affairs by focusing attention on the problem of Syria. Malek pointed out that since the Arabs are easily impressed by the display of Western power, this was the time to persuade Assad to accommodate Syria to the new order that was about to prevail. He even suggested adding Syria to the potential pillars of the Pax Americana in the Middle East: Lebanon, after all, in spite of all the horrors of the long-drawn-out civil war, was a natural seedbed for democracy, since strong segments of its society were longing for a free-market economy in a pluralistic democracy.

I then gave a summation: While American credibility had been restored by the awesome display of its airpower in the Iraq war, I warned that this would eventually be checked by Moscow's intrusion into the very process of the settlement itself. I could not believe that the Russians would not, in one way or another, look for a role to counterbalance the United States in the Middle East. Certainly, irrespective of the regime in power, Moscow would do everything within its means to prevent the establishment of a Pax Americana in the region. I still regard that projection as both valid and enduring.

AMERICAN FAILURE AND THE MIDDLE EAST CAROUSEL

The spectacle of "impotent victory" became manifest less than a year after Iraq's August 1990 invasion of Kuwait. By then it was obvious that Saddam, having survived what had seemed as an all-devastating display of American mili-

tary power, and having been ostensibly reduced to a second-
class position in the Gulf, not only had crushed Kurdish and
Shiite dissidents, but was steadily regaining his footing overall. He even seemed to be tempting fate by toying in an
ostentatiously contemptuous manner with the U.S. and the
U.N. with respect to Iraq's nuclear assets. What had, in the
immediate aftermath of American victory, beckoned as an
extraordinary opportunity to vitalize U.S. policy in the
Middle East and cast a framework for security and stability
in one of the world's most explosively volatile regions, had
almost entirely evaporated.

On May 2, 1991, I called another meeting of the ISC to
survey the results of the seeming American victory over Iraq.

Habib Malek propounded a radical thesis: He urged the
deliberate Balkanization of the Middle East as the key to
regional stability in the long run, while assuring minorities of
genuine self-determination. He believed that this would produce a more natural, more "authentic" map of the Middle
East in line with its religious and ethnic divisions, which otherwise could not simply be "wished away."

The proposal predictably generated intense argument
among the regional experts assembled. P.J. Vatikiotis,
Professor of Middle East Studies at the University of London,
believed that ethnic- religious borders no longer could be cat-
egorically drawn. He pointed as an example to the Copts in
Egypt, who had been integrated into the surrounding Islamic
society and had even attained high office in government.

I made the general observation that Islam provides no
theoretical basis for dealing with non-Arab, non-Muslim
societies or, for that matter, for a clear separation of religious
and secular authority in the modern state. I thought nothing
could be accomplished to calm regional turmoil—including
the redrawing of maps—until Muslim theoreticians stopped

rejecting the minority groups in their midst and came to grips with the fundamental problem.

Professor Elie Kedourie of the London School of Economics concurred in his own way, observing that in the Middle East the rule of Muslims over non-Muslims was simply taken for granted, and that in the modern period this had been exacerbated by the decay of the traditional order. Now the very existence of minorities is seen as a danger to the state, especially to the extent that the self-awareness of minorities has sharpened considerably.

Dr. Assad Homayoun, former Minister of the Iranian Embassy in Washington, rejected Malek's idea in toto, cautioning that concepts of multiplied autonomy pose commensurately multiplied dangers to whatever stability could otherwise be mustered. He thought that Malek's proposed break-up of existing states would simply lead to deepened chaos and war. He summed up the sequence of salient phases in the post-World War II development of the Middle East as follows: (1) the transition to nationalism in the 1950s; (2) the discovery of new-found oil wealth; (3) the emergence of religious fundamentalism in the wake of Khomeini's victory in Iran; and (4) the current phase of alliance between nationalism and religious fundamentalism. Homayoun concluded that "time is needed for Arabs, Persians, and Israelis to feel secure enough to discuss the issues that divide them."

Graham Fuller, senior political scientist of the Rand Corporation in California, deprecated the fact that most people tended to "demonize" Islam, which had proved, notably in Turkey, that an Islamic state could become genuinely secular. He expressed optimism that stability could be built in the region on the basis of an "exchange" of land held by Israel in return for peace with the Arabs, contending that many Israelis considered a peace with the PLO to be entirely in the realm of the possible.

Later in the discussion Fuller insisted that the Palestinian Arabs symbolized all Arab grievances against Israel. He predicted that if a "Palestinian Arab state" were established on the West Bank and in Gaza, full and genuine peace would result. (It is noteworthy that Graham Fuller had been the CIA National Intelligence Officer for the Middle East in the Reagan Administration. He has always been the foremost advocate of a "Palestinian" state—a remarkable line of continuity for a government official!)

Dr. Arnold Beichman, a Research Fellow at the Hoover Institution, flatly contradicted Fuller's remarks. He characterized the "land-for-peace" formula for a deal between Israel and the Arabs as "sheer nonsense." Giving up land, Beichman contended, could never, in itself, produce anything but greater peril to Israel's security in view of the goals shared by the Arab states. Beichman also expressed scorn for the idea of an international conference on the Middle East: even if it were to take place, and even if it produced "agreements," it would be an exercise in futility, because such "agreements" would not be worth the paper they were printed on. And the very idea of inviting the Russians into such a conference would be utterly counterproductive.

This line was supported strongly by Admiral James Nance, former Deputy Director of the National Security Council. He argued forcefully for continued Israeli control of Judea and Samaria—the so-called "West Bank." Indeed, Admiral Nance cast doubt on the status of these areas as "occupied" following their conquest by Israel in the 1967 war because their previous status had never been recognized after 1948. When Jordan had attempted to annex these territories, none of the Arab states themselves had recognized its claim, to say nothing of the international community.

Nance went on to emphasize the vital importance to Israel of the Golan Heights. In the initial phase of the 1973 war, Nance reminded us, Syrian troops pushed the Israelis to within 12 miles of the Mediterranean. It must constantly be borne in mind, he argued, that Israel cannot afford to lose *any* war without facing extinction.

The consensus of the conference was that at least for the time being the Arab-Israeli conflict seemed insoluble; hence Israel had a vital interest in retaining control of Samaria, Judea, Gaza, and the Golan Heights.

Meanwhile, the instabilities in the region fed upon each other. At the conference I ventured the prediction that, following the ambiguous outcome of the Gulf War, Saddam Hussein inevitably would give high priority to regenerating Iraq's infrastructure and "wait out" the U.S. and the U.N. with respect to the dismantling of its weapons of mass destruction. It seemed obvious to me that within several years Iraq would once again be in a position to challenge the regional balance of power. The carousel in the Middle East would continue, as if the U.S.-led intervention had never taken place.

Poking the Pariah
of the Pacific

Geopoliticians refer to the periphery of Eurasia as the Rimland, which guards the approaches to the Heartland at the center of the landmass. More modern developments suggest also that traversing the Rimland is a "faultline" of instability and conflict. That faultline extends from the Mahgreb countries in North Africa through Libya, the Middle East, the Indian Subcontinent, Southeast Asia and up into Korea in the northwest quadrant of the Pacific Basin. Not discounting a few peripheral engagements like the Falklands war, the major conflicts in the second half of the 20th Century all have taken place in that belt. They include Korea, Vietnam, Cambodia, the India-Pakistan clashes, Afghanistan and the various Middle East conflicts, up to and including the Gulf war.

Perhaps it is no coincidence that this faultline of instability and conflict cuts through some of the richest natural resources on the planet, notably Middle East oil and the troughs of raw materials in Asia essential to the industrial machines of the more developed nations. And because instability tends to feed upon itself, it is no coincidence also to discern patterns of interaction along the faultline. Thus, there has been a strong nexus between the Middle East and Northeast Asia in the form of a consistent traffic in modern arms from North Korea to Arab countries, notably Iran and

ISC Conference on "Peace and Security in the Pacific Region," co-sponsored by the Beijing Institute for International Strategic Studies.

Syria. That traffic takes on ever more ominous dimensions in a period marked by the thinly-veiled proliferation of weapons of mass destruction and the means of their delivery.

A TREK TO PYONGYANG IN 1991

If anything, the faultline described above has been enhanced by the general uncertainties of an international system in transition and the more central drama in the Heartland of the former Soviet Union. Against that background, I decided that it was worth the gamble to stage a reconnaissance into one of the last "walled nations." Through patient plying of various contacts, the ISC arranged for a meeting with high-level North Korean officials in Pyongyang in late June 1991. General Richard G. Stilwell, a former commander of UN forces in Korea and later Assistant Secretary of Defense in the Reagan Administration, agreed to serve as co-chairman of the conference.

We were probably the first Americans to enter Pyongyang in any kind of formal capacity since the Korean War. We found there a society in the throes of tightening iso-

ISC Conference, Honolulu, Hawaii, December 6-8, 1987.

ISC Conference, Washington, D.C., April 16-18, 1989.

lation. Increasingly cut off from its sole reliable ally, the Soviet Union, North Korea was facing economic deterioration, food and energy shortages, and a huge defense burden on its own. The leadership elite was retreating into deeper paranoia and hardened resistance to change.

Notwithstanding that paranoia, the North Korean regime was trying to reach beyond its uncertain lifelines to Russia and China toward a rapprochement with Japan, with its massive potential for capital investment and economic aid. The regime was also looking for some inroads in Washington. I suppose that was the principal reason for our admittance to Pyongyang—although as the conference unfolded, I had cause to wonder about the North Korean motives, and/or whether those motives had undergone a change after the agreement to hold the conference.

As the meeting got underway on June 20, 1991, it quickly became obvious that this would be anything but a sincere, let alone amicable, dialogue. The North Korean spokesmen did little more than repeat long-standing ideological litany on all major issues. They made concessions neither in their statements nor in their manner. In fact, while pretending to "clarify" some of their positions, ambiguously expressed in the past, they actually hardened them. The unremitting aggressiveness of the North Korean spokesmen made for a curious spectacle, indeed. They were downright insulting at times. The last thing on their mind was to accommodate us.

Furthermore, in spite of the ostensibly firm agreement we had struck with North Korea's Deputy Ambassador at the U.N.—that the conference would be an open, free-flowing discussion with no prepared statements—the North Koreans came prepared with written texts, from which they never deviated. Thus their team of translators from Korean to English worked with ease, while those charged with the opposite translation struggled to keep up with the spontaneous, often heated American responses.

While in private conversations the North Koreans showed somewhat more flexibility—and while they seemed to understand that some moderation of their hard line was needed, if only for the sake of opening locked doors—whenever pressed, they simply retrenched into dogmatic positions.

It was obvious to me that outside the conference halls the North Korean regime was just as unyielding in marshalling its sequestered society. Despite dire economic straits, the regime was in firm totalitarian control. The North Korean delegation reaffirmed its celebrated policy of "Juche," which we were told meant "self-reliance," but which I interpreted as the arrogance of dictatorship.

SHIFTING TIDES IN THE FAR EAST

On the American side we assumed from the beginning that we were to discuss both the global geopolitical environment, as well as the issue of Korean reunification. In fact, the North Koreans harped almost exclusively on reunification.

The North Korean co-chairman of the Conference, Song Ho Gyong, insisted that the United States had never been sincere about improving its relations with North Korea. Nevertheless, Song announced himself in favor of frequent contacts aimed at reunification. Song pointed to the obvious: With United States and North Korean forces arrayed along the demarcation line, there was constant danger of armed confrontation and explosion.

According to Song, it was the United States that, in fact, opposed the global trend to detente. He repeated North Korea's long-standing proposal for a confederation based on the simple principle of one nation and one state, but with two equal, social, economic, and political systems, and two regimes ruling autonomous northern and southern regions. Such a state, he said, would of course be neutral or "nonaligned." He also called for a formal declaration of nonaggression between North and South Korea, with a peace treaty eventually replacing the armistice still in force. He criticized both the United States and South Korea for failing to respond to these proposals.

General Stilwell responded eloquently and clearly: he pointed out that we spoke merely as private American citizens who wished to further a useful dialogue in order to reduce tension and avoid miscalculations in one of the world's few areas of confrontation. Nevertheless, we as citizens supported the basic tenets of U.S. policy in Northeast Asia and the Korean Peninsula. It was high time, while the circumstances were propitious, for a dialogue between the United States and North Korea. Still, the alliance between the United States and South Korea to defend South Korea against an external threat remained a pillar of U. S. policy, whereas it was obviously the North Korean aim to weaken that alliance as best it could.

Stilwell explained the logic behind America's interest in the whole area dating back over some four decades. Korea's geostrategic location gave it primary importance, while the deployment of large forces, mostly North Korean, along the line of the DMZ created a permanent danger of armed conflict that would inevitably spread. In addition, the U.S. was bound to be concerned about the division of the Korean Peninsula, which held more than 70 million people of the same stock and heritage.

This was a natural position for any American spokesman. I followed Stilwell's forceful presentation by stressing one of his major points: that although we were best equipped to discuss military matters, we were more than willing to tackle political issues, since politics, after all, is the essence of relations between states. I explained my own view as supplementing and extending Stilwell's, emphasizing the importance, in spite of everything, of the Pyongyang meeting. I made use of the old cliche that our conference was "an idea whose time had come," in the precise sense that all past attempts to challenge the existing balance of power inevitably led to a crisis—indeed, a war—because American,

Asian, and European diplomacy had never succeeded in managing transitions in that balance of power. That applied, I said, to World Wars I and II, to the war in Korea itself, and of course, to the recent conflict in the Persian Gulf, where both sides had miscalculated each other's intentions.

I went on to explain that ISC's symposia and seminars were aimed at clarifying the global strategic picture, and that should also be the function of diplomacy. The acute element in the Korean equation related to one-and-a-half million men deployed in a confrontation from which hostilities could erupt without warning. A clash in Korea, however remote some believed it to be from the central world stage, would send destabilizing tremors throughout the globe. While it was obviously up to North and South Koreans to lay down the modalities of reunification, the United States had, after all, a broad network of interests in the region, and was bound to regard developments in Korea within a larger East Asian context.

William Van Cleave stressed the new flexibility displayed by the Soviet Union, which had restored diplomatic relations with South Korea despite its alliance with North Korea. More generally, however, Van Cleave pointed out that reforms in the Soviet Union had not yet produced fundamental change, and there could be a regression at any point. Meanwhile, notwithstanding retreat from Eastern Europe, Russian military power obdured—and in fact gained even greater relevance for the Asian theater.

Professor A. James Gregor, of the University of California, stressed the global framework for U.S. policy. The U.S. saw the issues of peace and security on the Korean Peninsula against the background of projected rapid economic growth in Japan, Taiwan, and South Korea. Even though the markets of these last three states might be expected to contribute to international understanding, the Russian presence in Northeast

Asia remained just as vigorous as before. Agreeing with Van Cleave and me, Prof. Gregor pointed out that the Russians were maintaining all their military capabilities in the region, even if they were not, for the moment, increasing them. The abiding Russian military presence in Asia understandably provoked uneasiness in Tokyo: Japanese home islands, after all, were exposed to attack from all points of the compass. Japan was unable to muster a credible self-defense: it absolutely required a proximate U.S. military presence for its own security. Seen in this larger light, U. S. forces in South Korea were not aimed especially at North Korea, but rather were essential for the defense of Japan as well as for deterrence of violence in the region, more generally. Gregor acknowledged that Korean reunification would no doubt contribute to peace and security in the region, but he stressed that U.S. forces had no aggressive intentions. Indeed, to withdraw U.S. forces from the Peninsula might force Japan to embark, finally, on its own massive rearmament, with immensely destabilizing consequences for the region, North Korea included.

PREPARED DIATRIBES

The North Koreans at the conference were energetic in propagating their prepared positions. Li Son Yon Sok, representing North Korea's Committee for Peaceful Reunification of the Fatherland, forcefully stated the case for reunification, dwelling on the theme that Koreans had remained a homogeneous people who had lived on the same land for thousands of years with the same language and culture, despite all political differences. Even now, notwithstanding the artificial division, they were still one people. Only once Korea was reunified could peace and security in Asia be restored. At the same time, however, since the two Koreas do have contradictory economic, social, and political systems which neither side would give up, a confederation of two autonomous entities was the only answer.

Li was thus rehearsing the hopelessly utopian idea of a united nation with two socio-economic systems! It struck me as almost laughable that intelligent people could devote so much time to proposing the impossible. I understood it as a mere modality of intransigence.

There was an amusing outburst of sentimentality about Moscow when Maj. Gen. Kim Yong Chol, one of the two North Korean military officers present, commented on the Gorbachev reforms. Gen. Kim embraced the new reforms wholeheartedly and dogmatically. In an endlessly droning speech, he accepted hook, line, and sinker all the extravagant illusions fostered by the Russian reform movement, by Gorbachev's "new thinking," and simply called for the withdrawal of U.S. forces from the Peninsula if security there were to be achieved together with Korean unification.

The conference was stunned by North Korean Foreign Minister Kim Yong Nam, who assailed our ears with a speech lasting about an hour and a quarter without let-up. He attacked the United States as the source of all the difficulties with North Korea, because of the U.S. refusal to recognize realities and its insistence on blocking peaceful reunification and vilifying North Korea. He reiterated recent history, from 1983, to show how all attempts made to bring about a rapprochement with South Korea failed because the U.S. was so "timid, narrow-minded, and indecisive," as well as "small-hearted and feeble-minded."

Reacting to this harangue with consummate poise and self-control, General Stilwell simply pointed out that the ISC delegation had come to Pyongyang at North Korea's specific invitation, in expectation of a frank dialogue. We Americans had assumed that North Korea's deteriorating economy, the loss of its credit rating, and its heavy defense burden might have prompted the invitation. But, Stilwell noted, there had not been the slightest change in the North Korean attitude, and after a day nothing had been accomplished.

Like North Korea, Stilwell said, the United States also had preconditions for an improvement in bilateral relations: these included the renunciation of terrorism, the signing of a nuclear safeguards agreement, an accelerated program for repatriating the remains of Americans missing-in-action, and a more responsible policy for exporting intermediate-range missiles to the Middle East. He stressed that the constancy of U.S. policy toward the Korean Peninsula did not imply cowardice but a prudent concern for the well-being of 70 million Koreans.

I made a point of asking Kim to comment on reports that during a September 1990 meeting with Soviet Foreign Minister Shevardnadze, Kim had threatened to develop nuclear arms and support Japan's territorial claims against Moscow if the latter established diplomatic relations with South Korea. Kim dismissed this out-of-hand, asserting that if Shevardnadze had quoted him to that effect, he was a "shameful man" and was spreading such falsehoods only because North Korea was refusing to submit to the Russians' wishes. He said he had warned Shevardnadze that Japan intended to become a military power, which naturally worried the Asian nations, and he also told Shevardnadze that North Korea would scrap all its military alliances once Korean reunification was achieved. Kim reemphasized the theme pushed by all the North Koreans—that North Korea's policy was one of self-reliance—and he described relations with Moscow pointedly as a "nominal alliance."

When Stilwell asked for his position on carrying out the North Korean obligation to allow IAEA inspection of North Korean nuclear facilities under the Non-Proliferation Treaty it had signed in 1985, Kim dismissed it out-of-hand: Regardless of whether North Korea had signed the Treaty, he said, it would allow no inspections unless the same inspections took place in South Korea. He was referring, of course, to inspections of U.S. nuclear arms there. Kim claimed that North Korea was under "constant military threat," and that U.S.-North Korean negotiations showed that the United States was poised for action against it.

As a final gesture, Kim curtly dismissed Stilwell's offer of 100 four-year scholarships in the United States for North Korean students to be selected by their government.

A DRY BED FOR ARMS REDUCTIONS

The opening atmosphere of the conference was disheartening. Nor did it improve on the second day. The North Koreans clung to their fixed arguments, particularly in their discussion of arms reductions. When we pointed to the lessons of the U.S.-Soviet arms control record—which, if applied, required reliable military data as the basis for meaningful negotiations and hence would force North Korea to disclose some real information about its military capabilities— the North Koreans made it very clear that this was out of the question.

Kim reviewed the history of North Korean disarmament proposals from 1987 to the present. He claimed that these proposals would have led to a defensive military equilibrium, with both North and South Korea limited to armed forces of 100,000 each, *after* the withdrawal of U.S. forces. North Korea had renewed these proposals the following year, he said, and most recently had called for the cessation of joint U.S.-ROK military exercises. Kim contended that a prerequisite for arms reduction was a declaration of nonaggression between North and South Korea, which had first been proposed by North Korea as early as 1984 and which would have turned the DMZ into a "zone of peace."

Stilwell recounted the long and agonizing process of arms reduction in Europe and its lesson: It was only after the

Soviet Union and the Warsaw Pact countries agreed to provide real data on their armed forces that any progress could be made. Yet North Korea simply refused to disclose any facts about the strength and equipment of its armed forces, and denied the accuracy of all the figures published by a variety of reputable sources, including the International Institute for Strategic Studies and also Jane's Defense Weekly, which estimated the North Korean Army at one million strong.

Stilwell expressed hope, nevertheless, that North Korea would be more forthcoming, because without agreement on the military strength of both sides there could be no good faith in negotiations. A second essential step would be mutual agreement to intrusive inspection to verify the sides' reduction of personnel, equipment, and repositioning of units. The third step would be the demilitarization of the DMZ and the elimination of the tunnels dug by the North Koreans. These steps, Stilwell said, would set the stage for the actual reduction of forces, achieving parity between the two sides and precluding either from threatening the other.

I did my best to generalize the discussion and steer it away from the sacred texts the North Koreans kept using, but without success. I questioned the whole idea of comparison with the European disarmament process. I pointed out the obvious: nations arm themselves because they are insecure; they are not insecure because they arm themselves. Disarmament by itself would not be enough to create a positive climate between North and South Korea: required was a general loosening up, in which ideas and people moved freely, families were united, and commerce flowed. These notions evoked no response.

THE ISSUE OF MIAS IN KOREA

One topic, introduced at our insistence, did generate discussion in Pyongyang: American MIAs—missing-in-action soldiers—from the Korean War. And it was a revealing discussion.

Stilwell led it off. He said an essential step in improving North Korea's relations with the U.S. was to accelerate the search for and return of America's dead from the Korean War. He recalled that both sides had made serious efforts after the signing of the armistice in the Korean War to recover and return the remains of North Korean, Chinese, and United Nations Command soldiers. In 1954, the remains of more than 4,000 U.N. personnel, including almost 2,000 Americans, were returned. But over 8,000 Americans on Korean soil were still missing. Since 1954, North Korea had been asked, repeatedly, to account for over 2,000 U.N. prisoners of war who had not been repatriated immediately after the armistice. Yet, North Korea had not lifted a finger.

In December 1982, in August 1986, and in 1987, North Korean representatives had been given information vitally needed for a search: a map of POW Camp #5 and the adjacent cemetery where many prisoners who had died in captivity were known to have been buried; the locations of various temporary U.N. Command cemeteries in North Korea, where the remains of 288 dead had not been recovered in 1954; the specific locations of 291 air-crash sites where some 300 Air Force personnel had been lost; and finally, the names and locations of the 14 POW camps just south of the Yalu River, where 2,233 unaccounted-for U.N. Command POWs were known to have been buried. The last incident in the long and frustrating story, in 1987, was bizarre: The U.N. Command had recovered the remains of 25 members of the North Korean army, and full documentation was dispatched to the North Koreans. Yet, the regime refused to accept custody of its own people for "procedural" reasons—which gave a new dimension to the word "incredible"—and the 25 were buried *again* in the south pending a resolution of the matter.

All this, Stilwell pointed out, was by no means an issue between North Korea and the U.S. alone. On the contrary, the dead of at least eight nations were involved, all represented in the UN Command forces. True, the reason given by the North Koreans for not having resolved the issue was technically correct: that the issue was not an Armistice Agreement matter, and hence should be pursued in a special channel between the U.S. and North Korea. Plainly, however, the North Koreans were using the legal technicality in order to block any progress toward resolution.

Stilwell insisted that Americans were now looking for a serious commitment from the North Koreans to find the remains of all MIAs. The U.S. would be pleased to provide technical assistance and financing, and suggested that the overall venue be international. Rear Admiral James Nance added a trenchant point: the U.S. Congress was very emotional about the MIAs, and might insist that the United States veto North Korea's membership in the U.N. if the issue was not resolved.

The North Koreans, in general, were grudging in their reaction to this seemingly apolitical issue. They correctly concluded from our insistence on its importance that it was a condition for the improvement of relations with the United States, whereas they—out of pride, it seemed—insisted that relations should be improved without conditions.

EARLY CHALLENGE OF NORTH KOREAN NUCLEAR AMBITIONS

Li, Director of the Institute for Disarmament and Peace, did make a rhetorical effort to guide the meeting to broader ground: He proposed that the United States and North Korea bring about better relations directly through the simple expedient of the U. S. putting an end, without preconditions of any kind, to its "cold war" treatment of North Korea, and replacing the Armistice Agreement with a peace treaty between the U.S. and North Korea. If that were done, the U.S. could withdraw its troops from South Korea under a negotiated timetable.

But this "lofty level" did not last. Kim Byong Hong (Vice-president of the Institute) promptly returned to the question of the stockpiling of nuclear arms—in South Korea, of course. He contended that the U.S. still had 1,000 nuclear weapons there, including some 16 neutron bombs; Koreans were worried about becoming victims of a nuclear war; and since the U.S. and the Soviet Union were already agreeing to nuclear reductions, there seemed to be no longer any reason to leave such weapons anywhere on the Peninsula.

Van Cleave emphasized the seriousness with which the U.S. regarded the issue of proliferation of nuclear weapons. He vigorously denied that the United States opposed only "horizontal" proliferation (the spread of nuclear weapons to new contenders) and not "vertical" proliferation (the intensification of nuclear capabilities in the hands of those who already held them). He mentioned in the latter context the strategic arms treaty with the Soviet Union to reduce strategic offensive weapons and the agreement on intermediate-range nuclear forces in Europe. In addition, he pointed out that since the Non-Proliferation Treaty had been signed, the U.S. had unilaterally removed some 8,000 nuclear weapons from its own arsenal and withdrawn over 2,000 such weapons from Western Europe even before any arms control agreements were concluded.

Van Cleave firmly charged the North Koreans with avoiding their obligations under the NPT (Non-proliferation Treaty) by artificially tying U.S. nuclear weapons policies to the issue of fulfilling their own obligations. There was no connection whatsoever between the NPT and U.S. nuclear arms policies except for one thing—the obligation not to transfer nuclear weapons or technology to non-nuclear states. Thus, if North Korea insisted on continuing a nuclear weapons program of its own and refused inspections, or if it sold nuclear materials, the U.S. would have to take that into account. He characterized the North Koreans' approach to the NPT Treaty as dubious and indefensible.

Van Cleave challenged the North Koreans to take a stand on their intentions and their policy. He noted the effort and resources North Korea was pouring into the construction and improvement of its budding nuclear complex, which included two or three reactors and a probable plutonium reprocessing plant. Then, suddenly, he held up a French satellite picture of the whole complex. Looking at it, he said he could identify a reactor capable of producing plutonium, a probable plutonium separation plant, and possible enrichment plant.

Firmly and emphatically, Van Cleave stated that there was no indication whatsoever that North Korea was using this remarkable complex for the production of electricity or energy; rather, it had all the attributes of a weapons facility. He made a suggestion: Let the Americans simply visit the complex and take a look. Unless there was, in fact, weapons production there, he asked, what was the purpose of separating the fuel from the plutonium and reprocessing it? He observed pointedly that the answers to his questions had a direct bearing on the improvement of U.S.-North Korean relations.

By this time, it was clear that the North Koreans had not been briefed to respond substantively to any serious questions. That was, indeed, the whole reason for their reliance on prepared texts from the very outset of the conference. It was very disappointing for us, but not really surprising.

At the very end of the conference, I reminded the North Koreans that we knew that the North Korean government had signed the Non-Proliferation Treaty only because

Moscow had made that a condition for the sale of a large nuclear reactor, and that they were deliberately disregarding countless private U. S. assurances that the U.S. would never use nuclear arms in a war against a nonnuclear nation unless it was linked to a power that did have such arms. I further reminded them also that North Korea was incontestably selling ballistic missiles to the Middle East, further destabilizing that region. I expressed wonder at how they could deal so blithely with states whose leaders were pursuing irresponsible, reckless and incendiary policies.

I voiced the verdict that the conference had been neither useful nor imaginative, and that our hopes in coming to Pyongyang had been frustrated. We had come to find flexibility as a basis for the development of further relations, but instead had collided with a campaign of malicious slandering of the United States and not the smallest evidence of any real understanding. I told the North Koreans they had offered nothing new, that their disarmament proposals were merely aimed at disarming the South and having the Americans' nuclear arms removed. I challenged them to give us something to take back with us—some flexibility on a key issue on which there could be some negotiations. "Otherwise," I told them, "we've made no progress!"

Song played tit-for-tat. He averred that he, too, had had high hopes for the conference, had expected it to provide a clue—at least—to the improvement of U.S.-North Korean relations, but his hopes had been dashed as well. Still, he observed, perhaps the meeting had been useful for a better understanding of each other's positions.

Stilwell tried to leave the North Koreans with a final note of insistence on the seriousness of the concrete, practical proposals we had in fact made: the offer for the 100 scholarships for North Korean students to come to the United States, the proposal to provide the resources for the search for a repatriation of the MIAs, and the offer to help North Korea prepare its disarmament proposals. Still, however genuine and substantial these initiatives were, Stilwell said in conclusion, there was no hope of any serious progress at this stage in world affairs, with the Soviet Union still an enigmatic actor on the world stage and with the North Korean government in a stance of fundamental ambiguity vis-a-vis not only its southern neighbor, but the world at large.

PROPHETS AT THE WRONG TIME

Against that somewhat dismal background, it is interesting to note that five months later on November 25, 1991, I testified as follows before the U. S. Senate Committee on Foreign Relations.

> Everything we know about the present regime (in North Korea) suggests that a nuclear weapons capability in its hands would destabilize the politics and diplomacy of East Asia. Moreover, this regime is likely to sell not only nuclear technology, but also plutonium to other radical irresponsible regimes which seek to overthrow the existing nation-state system...
>
> Pyongyang's capacity for mischief-making would be used as leverage on the U.S. and the industrial democracies. This is not a scenario we need face or even risk if we are prepared to take courageous steps today...
>
> Preemptive, nonnuclear attack against such sources of threat may seem an extreme course of action, but it is preferable to retaliation only after the fact. The alternative is to leave the United States and its allies open to disaster simply waiting to happen...
>
> Two, three, or four years ago, we had political, diplomatic, and economic sanctions as a lever. That does not exist today. I think the military option which does exist today will not be here three years from now.[1]

---

[1] Hearings before the Subcommittee on East Asian and Pacific Affairs, November 25, 1991.

My warnings obviously fell on deaf ears in the outgoing Bush Administration. It was during the Bush Presidency, in 1989, that North Korea shut down its nuclear reactors for 100 days in order to acquire weapons grade plutonium. It was the same Administration that subsequently canceled planned military exercises with South Korea and removed tactical nuclear weapons from land and sea. As with ISC warnings on Iraq, the evidence was studiously ignored. In the same testimony before Congress, I stated that no diplomatic or economic action by the U.S., even in coordination with other powers, is likely to force North Korea to abandon its nuclear ambitions.

Despite our best efforts, the ISC once again had to bear the onus of being right at the wrong time. Some three years after our meeting in Pyongyang, the implications of a nuclear-armed North Korea finally registered on the U.S. policy agenda. By this time, however, the Clinton Administration seemed to be confronting a *fait accompli* with a sense of help-lessness. On May 5, 1994, *The New York Times* reported that Robert Gallucci, the Clinton Administration's "point man" in the dispute over North Korea's nuclear program, stated he was not confident that a diplomatic solution would be reached, and that the United States had not yet won China's support for economic sanctions. He also expressed the judgment that the alternative options of preemptive military strike on the North Korean nuclear sites—or even a unilateral move by the U.S. to impose economic sanctions—were "dangerous." Gallucci could have made that same statement a year later, in May 1995. In the meantime, a much-publicized U.S.-North Korean "accord" was reached in October 1994. The "Agreed Framework"—if one was truly reached—has unravelled rapidly. Not only does the United States face the same problem in North Korea, but it does so now with a deepened wedge having been pushed into U.S.-South Korean relations.

It is noteworthy that the Clinton Administration, at the same time that it decried its lack of options for dealing with a nuclear-armed North Korea, was determined to eliminate the vestigial remains of the Strategic Defense Initiative, which promised the only viable safeguard against the delivery means of nuclear weapons—especially in the hands of rogue powers that are largely impervious to the kinds of "deterrence" rationale that obtained in the era of superpower confrontations.

Is the world more broadly running out of options—and of time?

21

A "Jerusalem Compromise"

The peripatetic trail of the International Security Council led from Pyongyang in 1991—with a few stops in between—to Jerusalem the following year. There we staged one of our more spectacular undertakings. We sponsored a meeting on June 7–9, 1992, between a group of active duty Russian general officers and members of the Israeli military. The event was a direct spin-off from the ISC roundtables conducted in Moscow and Washington with leaders of the new Russia. We broached to the Russians the idea of sitting down with their counterparts in Israel, and they responded with strong interest.

It is difficult to exaggerate the significance of the encounter. It marked the first time Russian military visited Israel under any auspices. Not only were high-ranking Russian officers paying a friendly visit to a state vilified by Soviet propaganda for five decades, but the meeting also presented military professionals who had been on opposite sides with the unprecedented opportunity to "compare notes" about the strategies and tactics of the Arab-Israeli wars, in which Soviet weaponry and expert advice were liberally provided to the Arabs.

The implications, however, went beyond the Middle East. It was largely the superiority of U.S.-supplied or adapted weaponry in Israeli hands over their Russian coun-

Alexander E. Bovin, Russian Ambassador to Israel, speaks as Foreign Minister Moshe Arens (left) listens. ISC Israel Conference, June 1992.

terparts—especially in electronic warfare—that convinced Moscow it faced a growing technological gap with the West. That recognition, along with the challenge presented by Reagan's Strategic Defense Initiative, was a major propellant behind Gorbachev's effort at a more general "restructuring" of the Soviet industrial base—an effort that led, in turn, to the collapse of the Soviet system.

A tremendous opportunity was thus in the offing. Still, from the beginning I had some doubts about the Israelis' ultimate cooperation in the project. I knew that negotiations to set up the conference would be difficult despite the obvious benefits to be gained by the Israeli military, intelligence and the politicians in Jerusalem. In late 1991, I dispatched the ISC's Advisory Board Chairman, William Van Cleave, to meet with then-Defense Minister Arens in Israel. Arens agreed in January 1992 to the proposed conference. Yet barely weeks before the scheduled event, the Israeli Government began to show cold feet.

In fact, for reasons still unknown to me, just prior to the start of the conference the Israelis unilaterally acted to downgrade the whole affair. First, they requested that reserve and retired generals replace the active-duty officers originally scheduled for the roundtable; members of the active Israeli General Staff, the ISC was assured, would attend as

Col. Gen. Igor N. Rodionov, Chief of the Military Academy of the General Staff (left) and Col. Gen. Vladimir Shkanakin at ISC Jerusalem, June 1992.

General Benny Peled (Ret) co-chairman of Israel's delegation to Jerusalem Conference, June, 1992.

Foreign Minister Moshe Arens addressing Russian and Israeli generals, ISC Conference, June 7–9, 1992.

observers (in the end the observers failed to show up). Second, inasmuch as the Russians' visit was to be "unofficial," the ISC was asked by the Israelis to select and directly invite the Israeli reservist substitutes—and to bear all expenses connected with tours and briefings for the visitors.

That presented us with three basic options. First, we could reject the downgrading of the conference. Second, we could limit the enterprise strictly to several days of no-frills meetings, depriving the Russians of the courtesy and benefit of official tours and briefings. Finally, we could simply postpone the meeting until a more propitious time (presumably after the Israeli elections scheduled for late June 1992).

In deference to the "larger interest," we elected to proceed with a one-week visit, accepting the downgrading of the conference and the Israeli terms. We assumed all expenses, including those associated with courtesies that are customarily extended to visiting dignitaries in Israel. Thus, the ISC paid in full for all costs entailed by Israel Defense Forces (IDF), briefings for the visitors, as well as all transportation and maintenance costs, including electronic equip--

ment, translators, and tour guides. In other words, we rose above the pettiness of our "hosts."

An Historic Israeli-Russian Encounter

The conference commenced on June 7, 1992. Members of the Israeli Defense Forces were thorough in defining for their Russian guests the nature, scope and intricacies of the overall threat to Israel's security. In particular, the meetings with the Israeli Deputy Chief of Staff and other senior military leaders were probably invaluable to the Russian officers, all of whom were still serving in important commands—and some of whom, ironically, had acted in more junior positions as advisers to Syrian and other Arab forces in the earlier Israeli-Arab wars. An extensive helicopter tour covering the length and width of Israel—including some of the most sensitive and important security points—was impressive and convincing.

In contrast to the prickly relations at the government level, the general mood at the symposium was far more relaxed. In my welcoming remarks at the opening banquet, which was attended by all conference participants and some 80 Israeli guests, I tried to put the conference into historical perspective:

> It is perhaps fitting that we meet on the anniversary of both the Six Day War and the Israeli strike on the Osirak nuclear facility in Iraq. Both actions were taken to preserve the regional equilibrium upon which peace depends. Where in the first case, Israel was forced to fight a defensive war, in the second, it wisely chose to deny the acquisition of nuclear weapons by Iraq which then, as today, would threaten the general peace. The consequences flowing from both decisions were fateful indeed for the politics and diplomacy of the region . . . .
>
> The great Russian nation—in the evolution of its democratic character—meets with the lone democracy of the

region to discuss mutual security concerns in the wider perspective of rapprochement and the new configuration of global politics. In peace as in war, Russia as the power of geographic proximity plays a significant role in the region. It is only natural that these two powers join in the elusive search for an environment conducive to peace and prosperity . . .

Tonight, then, is the beginning of a unique Russian-Israeli dialogue aimed primarily at creating the basis for a better understanding. While some might complain that the ISC's timing is just a bit off, none can dispute the logic or necessity of this exchange. In fact, this exercise is the consequence of several American-Russian seminars sponsored by the ISC. These ongoing discussions will continue so long as they are useful. Among the distinguished American participants are the recently retired service chiefs who request that I pass on their sympathies to the Israeli generals whose turn it now is to engage in round-table combat with some of Russia's most able generals.

There is much wisdom in this approach, and so the ISC is honored to facilitate and function as secretariat for these proceedings.[1]

Defense Minister Arens made his remarks off-the-record. In sum, he welcomed this indication of new Russian interests and policies in the region and the promise it carried of improved Russian-Israeli relations. He reviewed recent developments and threats in the region from Israel's perspective. He emphasized Israel's democratic culture, the importance of Israel's "qualitative edge" in personnel and equipment, and Israel's concerns about arms being shipped to its Arab neighbors from Russian and other powers—all themes that were addressed repeatedly by Israeli participants in the conference that followed.

---

[1] ISC Conference Report on The Russian-Israeli Rapprochement: From Confrontation to Cooperation, Jerusalem, June 7–9, 1992, p. 2.

The address given by Alexander E. Bovin, the Russian Ambassador to Israel and a former KGB official, was forthcoming and challenging. He put into focus the whole post-World War II history of Russian strategy in the area and daringly projected a new and dramatic turnabout of events. He observed that "we are gathered to discuss strategies for peace rather than war," but that "the danger of regional and ethnic conflicts" is on the increase, especially in the Middle East. Agreeing with Defense Minister Arens' comments that the Soviet Union's unilateral policy of supporting only Arab nations had harmed peace, he offered: "Thank God this has ended!" With the rebirth of Russia, he hoped, a new strategic approach could be found for the region. "We are overcoming unilateral opposition and coming closer to Israel and [moving] further from the Arab states." He noted that the opposite trend could be seen in United States policy. "We are seeing a new paradigm" with emphasis on the balance of interests rather than power, he said.[2]

Taking note of the large and growing Russian Jewish community in Israel, Ambassador Bovin projected a population of one million such immigrants by the year 2000. These new citizens of Israel would be loyal to their new homeland, he predicted, but would understand Russia, and this bond would result in closer relations between the two nations.

Not coincidentally the contrasting behavior of hosts and visitors continued through the discussions for the next two days of the conference. While the Russians came prepared with notes—i.e., "homework"—to address old and new issues, the Israeli participants seemed to be dealing extemporaneously, and often in a condescending and emotional tone rather than an appropriately professional manner. Absent were the active duty generals who were supposed to

---

[2] Ibid., p. 3.

back up the reservists. This suggested that either the IDF had a diminished interest in the symposium, or had been restrained by its political bosses. With a few exceptions, the Israeli input could have been more forceful and persuasive. An historic opportunity was thus missed to emphasize Israel's continuing geopolitical significance in the larger strategic equation.

There is an ironic footnote to the Jerusalem conference. It had been, after all, Israeli Defense Minister Arens who decreed a downgrading of the meeting. Shortly after the conference, Arens turned up in Moscow in search of Dr. Vitaly Shlykov, the Russian contact point for our working sessions in Jerusalem. Arens apparently was seeking better access to important Russian sources.

But there is a much larger, transcending irony. The Jerusalem meeting offered the opportunity at the very least to wean the Russian military away from the old Soviet client relationships in the Arab world, particularly in arms transfers. It is worth noting that one of the Russian participants at the meeting was Lt. Gen. Viktor L. Samoilov, who was later to be placed in charge of Russian arms sales. One might speculate that, had the opportunity been more effectively exploited, Israel might not be facing, for example, the sinister problem of Russian nuclear reactor exports to Iran.

AMERICAN MISPERCEPTIONS IN THE MIDDLE EAST

After the Jerusalem Conference, the ISC decided to strike a lower profile vis-a-vis the Israeli-Arab problem. I felt profoundly that both Israeli political blocs, the Likud and Labor, were pursuing policies that could only lead to disaster. Israeli failures were becoming ensnarled with—and compounded by—American failures in the region. For fuller explication, I must go back in time.

In 1988, a tumult of events—including the Soviet troop withdrawal from Afghanistan, the ceasefire between Iran and Iraq in their bloody eight-year-long war, the Palestinian uprising in the West Bank and Gaza, and the abandonment of his claim to the West Bank by Jordan's King Hussein in favor of the Palestine Liberation Organization—prompted 100 retired U. S. generals and admirals to join in signing a full-page statement in *The Washington Times* on October 12, 1988, sponsored by the ISC. It contained the following key formulation:

> An Israeli withdrawal from the (Jordan River) would, in the present political reality, lead to the establishment of a irredentist Soviet-oriented PLO state in the 2,000 square miles of the West Bank. A dwarfed Israel would then be an irresistible target for Arab adventurism and terrorism and ultimately for an all-out military assault which could end Israel's existence.

The statement went on to make the case that the hills of Judea and Samaria could not be effectively demilitarized or adequately inspected, yet they dominate the coastal plain of Israel. Since Israel's capture of the West Bank "the natural barrier and the short border provided by the Jordan River have enabled Israel to control raids and infiltration and to prevent the country from turning into another Lebanon."

The retired military officers dismissed the notion that territory could now be sacrificed because the introduction of missiles into the Middle East had rendered Israel's need for strategic depth irrelevant: "Missiles, artillery and aircraft can cause devastation. They cannot occupy. Only infantry and armor can overrun a country—and those are still vulnerable to natural barriers." The statement concluded:

> A strong Israel has served America's interests. To remain strong it must retain the Jordan River line as its eastern security border. Pressing Israel to withdraw from this line will neither bring peace nor serve America's interests.

Notwithstanding the strength of the pro-Arab forces in the U.S. Government, described in previous chapters, statements like the one above still found a basically receptive audience in Washington in the late 1980s. After all, from a vantage point of U.S. global interests, Israel was still identified as a partner of the U.S. in the larger context of Soviet-American rivalry. It was perceived then not only as a barrier to Arab radical hegemony in the Middle East, but also as an important counter to the extension of Soviet influence through its client Arab states in the region. Another ISC statement published in *The Washington Times* on December 11, 1990 listed some of the other attributes of U.S.-Israeli partnership:

> As the only democracy in the vast region between the Pacific Ocean and Western Europe, with the capability to project military power as far as the Indian subcontinent and the heart of Africa, Israel would serve as a multipurpose access point, a land route for supplies and a refueling base. Its innovative military technology and renowned intelligence capabilities faithfully served U.S. interests.

Yet even then—in 1990—the progressive collapse of the Soviet Empire in Eastern Europe, along with the intensification of problems internal to the Soviet Union, prompted some policymakers and analysts to begin to argue that, given the decline of the Soviet threat, the U.S. special relationship with Israel was becoming a relic of the past. Indeed, the systematic devaluation of Israel became a hallmark of the Bush Administration's Middle East policy. The trend, unfortunately, extended into the Clinton Administration.

It was predictable that with the downgrading of Israel's strategic value to the U.S. would come stronger pressures from Washington to the effect that Israel should trade conquered territory for peace. In this, U. S. policymakers have continued their confusion of symptoms with cause. They have insisted on Israeli withdrawal from areas to which it has an historical claim, without addressing the root causes of the Israeli-Arab conflict, and in the process, overlooking the abiding importance to the United States of the U.S.-Israeli strategic relationship.

Washington's priority should all along have been on the importance of Israel as a strategic U.S. ally, not on some quick fix for the West Bank that may threaten Israel's security. There are wider strategic considerations at work. As the prospect increases for deep slashes in the U.S. force presence in Europe, NATO's southern flank becomes increasingly vulnerable. At the same time, even with the temporary eclipse of Iraq, the warmaking potential of Arab states assumes more menacing dimensions with proliferating missile and chemical warfare capabilities.

Cooperation with "allies" during the Gulf crisis demonstrated the intrinsic shallowness of such alliances. Saudi Arabia, the "linchpin" of the Persian Gulf, required an immense U.S. military deployment for its survival—despite its expenditures of over $100 billion for arms in the previous decade. Egypt, an overpopulated, impoverished nation, dares not commit itself too far in regional affairs, lest the regime risk the escalating wrath of its domestic enemies led by Muslim fundamentalists. Syria, which differs little from Iraq, is a police state forever on the brink of a violent coup. Jordan's King Hussein initially aligned himself with Iraq in the Gulf crisis in order to appease his often alienated Palestinian population. His "peace agreement" with Israel in 1994 may prove as durable as was his alliance with Saddam.

Each of these regimes suffers from lack of political legitimacy. All are inherently unstable, reliable neither for defense of the region's oil resources nor for long-term diplomatic and strategic support of the West.

Efforts to develop a viable security policy for the Middle East and the Gulf are complicated by the lack of shared values between the United States and the majority of Arab states. A viable security policy cannot be built on the shifting sands of constantly changing autocratic regimes.

Partly at the root of the U.S. failure to correctly perceive Israel's value and repeated U.S. miscalculation in the Middle East has been an apparent inability to comprehend the inherently volatile character of Arab politics. Unless that failure in outlook is redressed, the United States is likely to have to contend with at least two related phenomena that could once again seriously threaten Western interests in the region:

- the convergence of Islamic fundamentalism and Arab nationalism, two potent anti-Western forces which enjoy considerable grass-roots support in Arab countries;
- the danger of sophisticated U.S. arms provided to Saudi Arabia and other conservative Arab Gulf states falling into hostile hands should the regimes of those countries give way to more fundamentalist-nationalist constellations.

The pillars of American regional policy also should be cohesive nations rather than the fragments of artificial post-World War I colonial divisions. Such nations should have no compunction about declaring their alliance with the United States, be willing to pay the price and reap the benefits of associations with the United States, be at peace with each other, and be democratic or have demonstrated serious movement toward democratization. Such states include Turkey, Israel and Egypt and, potentially, Iran.

Inclusion of Iran in the above list may be surprising. Yet already in 1989, following the election of Hojatoleslam Ali Akbar Hashemi Rafsanjani as president of Iran, an ISC conference concluded that "Rafsanjani, despite his strengths, has also built a significant array of enemies, and it is more than likely that a new leader of Iran will emerge in the coming few years, almost certainly someone who is both unknown and untainted at this stage."

The conference called on the Bush Administration:

- to entertain contacts, discussions and negotiations with Iran.
- not to allow itself to be manipulated or paralyzed in its relations with Iran by the issue of Americans held hostage in Lebanon and Iranian links to terror-ism;
- to undertake a program of research and analysis of Iran so that better informed and appropriate policies can be adopted;
- to be prepared to work with European allies and Japan, and through international monetary and eco-nomic institutions, to assist in the re-construction of Iran;
- to recognize the strategic advantages of a Western presence in Iran.

Those recommendations retain validity despite the con-tinuing cloud over developments in Tehran.

THE INFECTION OF APPEASEMENT

What is unfolding in the Middle East, meanwhile, is a compounded Israeli-American tragedy. Let us go back to the immediate aftermath of the ISC's Jerusalem conference in June 1992. The election of the Rabin government meant that Israel would be more reliant than ever on American decision-making. There also would be no basic departure from the direction taken immediately before, under Likud. Rabin's and Peres' policies were bound to lead to capitulation to the sirens of "peaceful settlement."

In fact, the Rabin-Peres "settlement" with Yassir Arafat's Palestine Liberation Organization is creating the basis for a withdrawal to the 1967 lines. There is a misbegotten idea that this will defuse the regional crisis; in fact, for all the reasons that have been elaborated, it will do just the reverse. It will reignite Arab opposition to Israel's very existence. At the same time, because of the sacrifice of natural lines of defense, that existence is destined to become inherently fragile.

But the Labor Government in Jerusalem is not acting strictly according to its own predilections; it is also responding to perceived opinion trends in Israel. Basic to a prevailing view in Israel is the belief that Israel can survive in the region in splendid isolation—and can do so even in the face of the grave dangers lurking in the "peace process." The Israelis have disdained an active role in the regional balance of power game; their policy remains largely inactive. Great powers, such as the United Kingdom in its heyday, always understood that their survival depended on adroit manipulation of a regional balance of power. But Israelis want sovereignty and security without having to shape the power environment in which they live. Basically and increasingly they want America to do it.

For all these reasons, the longer-term prognosis for Israel is ominous. Moreover, once the present qualitative edge in Israeli military power is blunted, the quantitative superiority of the Arab armies will come decisively into play. Not to prepare for that contingency with a strategic view is simply to wait for another holocaust.

How soon the Israelis have forgotten what survival was all about! In 1948, they knew the meaning of survival. The memory of that miraculous victory over all their Arab neighbors should have been the underpinning of their policy goal: never to allow the conditions that loomed in 1948 to be repeated—that is, when one war could spell the difference between survival and extinction. Instead, Israeli intellectuals have said: "Why should we continue to sully our hands with such distasteful things as commando raids, covert operations, and assassinations, let alone outright warfare? What we want is freedom, democracy, and prosperity." And the general Israeli population bought consumerism and wishful thinking of "peaceful accommodation."

Perhaps more than policy has radiated from America to Israel. Perhaps appeasement, as a more embracive societal phenomenon, is an infectious disease. Is there now a "Jerusalem Compromise" to go along with its Washington counterpart?

22

An Intense Dialogue With The Russians

After our initial conference with Russian defense officials in Moscow in 1990, it became increasingly clear to me and my colleagues in the ISC that: an opportunity of potentially transcendent importance was arising in the turbulent wake of the reform movement pressed by Gorbachev: a rapprochement, at least on professional-technical levels, between the military authorities of the former Soviet Union and the United States. Irrespective of the abiding political uncertainties, after all, no one now believed that a U.S.-Soviet conflict was still a serious possibility—except for an accidental detonation, which was all the more reason for a closer dialogue. In two memorable conferences held in Washington in 1992—on July 19–20 and November 16–17—strong strides were taken in the direction of cooperative understandings.

FOCUS ON STRATEGIC DEFENSE

Clearly at the center of any U.S.-Russian agenda on military issues was (and remains) the contentious issue of nuclear arms, with two particular and interrelated focal points of urgency: proliferation of nuclear weapons and a defense against such weapons. The Russians, at a meeting in October 1991, agreed to support the exploration of coopera-

Ambassador Henry Cooper, Director of the Strategic Defense Initiative (SDI).

tive ventures in this general arena.[1] They enhanced that support in a February 1992 roundtable in Moscow, when it was agreed that the ABM Treaty should not be allowed to impede the development of early warning and defense systems, space-based as well as ground-based.

In May 1992 a working session took place in Washington. Its main purpose was to pave the way for a conference scheduled for July. In the process, however, the working group itself commenced substantive discussion of potential areas and means of U.S.-Russian cooperation in ballistic missile defense—with specific reference to a defense system then being promoted in the U.S. defense establishment: a system for "global protection against limited attacks" (GPALS).

The ISC conference in July was thus well prepared. It featured distinguished arrays of experts on both sides. The selection process had centered on an appropriate blend of military professionals with broad philosophical grasp, as well as scholars with practical familiarity with military data and problems.

---

[1] ISC Report, "Change and Continuity in Soviet-Military Policy," October 1991.

The American delegation included, in addition to William Van Cleave and myself, the following: General Michael Dugan, a recently retired Chief of Staff of the Air Force; Dr. Lowell Wood of the Livermore National Laboratory, known particularly for his work in strategic defense against missiles; Dr. William Graham, Science Advisor in the White House during the Reagan Administration; Dr. Frank

Lt. Gen. Viktor I. Samoilov, Counsellor for Military Affairs

Col. Gen. Mikhail Kolesnikov, currently Chief of the Russian General Staff (left), and Air Force Col. Gen. Igor Kaluain, Chief, Strategic Air Force Command, at ISC Conference on "Change and Continuity in Soviet Military Policy, Washington, D.C., October 6-8, 1991.

Army General Konstantin I. Kobets, Chairman of the Committee for the Preparation and Implementation of Military Reform, speaking at ISC Conference in Washington, D.C., October, 1991. To his right, Major General Nikita Chaldymov (Ret.).

Alexander Belkin, Consultant to the Russian Ministry of Defense (left) and Dr. Stepan S. Sulakshin, Chairman of the Industrial Committee of the State Duma.

Gaffney, Jr., Director of the Center for Security Policy; and Dr. Leon Goure, a well-known specialist on Russian military affairs. The Russian delegation was headed by Dr. Vitaly Shlykov, Deputy Chairman of the State Committee on Defense; Lt. General Viktor I. Samoilov, Yeltsin's Counsellor for Military Affairs; and Dr. Alexander Savelyev, scientist and Vice-President of the newly formed Moscow Institute for National Security and Strategic Studies.

The free-wheeling discussion touched on a wide range of subjects, but targeted more squarely possible ways of cooperation between the two powers in ballistic missile defense deployment, global protection systems (both ground-and space-based), and the issue of the ABM Treaty. Specifically, a joint resolution agreed that the ABM Treaty should not be allowed to inhibit the development of strategic defense on both sides.

I made a strong effort to steer the discussion toward what I deemed the more urgent problem, connected though it was to missile defense: namely, nuclear arms proliferation. The problem was taking on more ominous dimensions with the apparent diffusion of authority in the Soviet Union. I mentioned reports to the effect that Iran had obtained several nuclear weapons of Soviet origin. That would make Iran a nuclear power. I asked our Russian visitors pointblank: "What is your vision of this problem and how would you deal with it? Is the answer a concert of powers, starting with American-Russian cooperation on the Strategic Defense Initiative (SDI) that would be extended to other nations? Does the real answer lie, beyond defensive systems, in the coercive disarmament of 'nuclear rogues'? Or, are we just talking, biding our time until the inevitable disaster hits? If we cannot cooperate in this arena, what *can* we cooperate on?"

Unfortunately, no clear answers were forthcoming to those questions. Nor have they been really answered since that time.

There was lively discussion at the conference of relative U.S. and Russian efforts with respect to the modernization of their strategic offensive forces. Dr. Wood of the Livermore National Laboratory pointed out that the United States halted all efforts to modernize its strategic forces and was no longer building strategic offensive platforms of any type. It had stopped missile production; the Midgetman and Minuteman modernization programs had been greatly slowed down; and a successor generation to the Trident sea-launched missiles was not being developed. He asked the Russians about their continuing activities and plans in the modernization space realm, which would become even more important as both Russia and the United States sharply reduced their quantitative inventories in strategic weapons in accordance with the START agreement.

General Ghely Batenin, Chief of the Personal Staff of then-Vice President Rutskoi of Russia, warmly endorsed the concept of applying the brakes to strategic force modernization. He averred that Russia was acting in just the same spirit. But then he gave some illustrative figures that prompted Dr. Wood to question whether, notwithstanding the apparent scaling down of Russian strategic forces, the cutbacks in both production and modernization matched the pace and magnitude being pursued by the United States. He asked specifically about the famous "Fat Boy," a new and larger type of mobile Intercontinental Ballistics Missile (ICBM). General Batenin conceded that a "modest" upgrading necessary to maintaining a modernized Russian strategic force was bound to continue.

In general, I was satisfied with the conference. It had been, at the very least, an open and apparently sincere meeting of minds, which pointed to the utility of a continuing and intensifying dialogue. Regrettably, it subsequently emerged that neither the Bush nor Clinton Administrations were interested in any consensus in support of practical, ground-based and space-based defenses or early warning systems. Indeed, the Clinton Administration scuttled the effort in its Washington Compromise on strategic defense. After first gutting the U.S. investment in strategic defenses in May

Ambassador Lichenstein making a point to Former US Marine Commandant Gen. Alfred Gray. Dr. Vitaly Shlykov in background.

1993, President Clinton in the following year negotiated away America's right to effective theater missile defenses— and did so in the context of the obsolete ABM Treaty whose provisions were never intended to limit theater defenses. At the May 1995 summit in Moscow, Clinton consummated the strategic defense surrender by agreeing on the sanctity of the 1973 ABM Treaty as an abiding barrier to the creation of strategic defenses. The opportunities opened by the ISC-sponsored dialogue were thus hopelessly squandered.

OBSTACLES TO ECONOMIC REFORM

Meanwhile in 1992 the auguries were good for the next U.S.-Russian conference sponsored by the ISC, which took place in Washington on November 16 and 17, of that year. That meeting was focussed on the critical topic of Russian economic reforms, with emphasis on their implications for the defense realm. It became clear during the two-day conclave that while there was little question about the sincerity and impetus behind the reforms being pushed by Yeltsin, their implementation was another matter. In particular, the Russian participants at the conference confirmed the difficulty of separating the military sector of the economy—which was based inevitably on a continuing command structure—from the civilian economy, which had not taken on a distinguishable shape and function.

The very idea of "privatizing" the Russian economy as a whole—a step toward the establishment of a free market system—was mitigated by the circumstance that privatization was supposed to come about not as a free confluence of market forces, but as a consequence of privatization programs imposed by the government itself. This confusion regarding the very conceptual genesis of creating a free-market economy through the privatization of the civilian economy seemed compounded by the difficulty in rationalizing the command structure of the military within that conception.

In principle, after all, the military establishment of a great power exists apart from—and to one extent or another insulated against—the overall economy. A defense budget is created in accordance with perceived military requirements. As long as those requirements are generally embraced by the civilian government, military priorities tend to transcend others. It is true that in relaxed times, when the danger of war dwindles, there is more room for debate about relative civilian and military priorities, and commensurate leeway for slashing the military budget. But separating those priorities becomes all the more difficult for a society emerging from a "command economy"—a society, moreover, in which the military traditionally has enjoyed a privileged and protected military-industrial economy of its own.

This major problem hung over the conference. More broadly, developments in Russia seemed in a state of pervasive confusion. Our Russian guests were distinguished: the aforementioned Vitaly Shlykov, Advisor to the Russian Ministry of Defense, Lt. Gen. Samoilov, Advisor to the First Deputy Prime Minister, Yuri Yaremenko, of the Russian Academy of Sciences; and Yevgeny Saburov, Director of the Center for Information and Social Technologies of the Russian Federation. These four specialists, from their somewhat different vantage points, seemed in agreement on a major point: that the whole movement for the introduction of free markets in Russia had run aground on the shoals of fundamental confusion regarding the construction of a free enterprise system from the ground up. The verity was that the government could not simply "install" such a system. Rather, all it could do was adopt plans cast at the top strata of the state bureaucracy—still functioning despite the last eight years of reform—and implementing them piecemeal as it saw fit. Yet, such implementation in and of itself implied state constraints—i.e., the very opposite of the free interplay of market forces.

At the very opening of the conference, both Saburov and Samoilov evinced in different ways their personal confusion and ignorance about the privatization scenario taking place. They admitted openly, and sadly, that they could not begin to grasp the factors involved in the generation of a military budget, and still less the prospects for a new free market based on the bureaucratically-induced privatization of the economy. Saburov's simple verdict was that the reforms were in extreme trouble, and he personally did not have the slightest idea of what would happen. Vitaly Shlykov, known for an eccentric sense of humor, poked fun at his colleagues for overreacting. Meanwhile, Yaremenko, a high-level planning specialist, contented himself with praising the remarkable zeal of the analysts who were trying to solve the problems.

A telling point was raised by an American participant— Dr. Steven Rosefielde, Professor of Economics at the

University of North Carolina—about a fundamental weakness in the civilian economy as that was envisaged by the Russian leadership. Rosefielde observed that what had hamstrung the civilian economy was a simple fact: The managers of the economy, who had been appointed from above, owed nothing to anyone and had no accountability whatsoever. Since attempts were being made from the top to unshackle the civilian economy without managerial freedom, without managerial responsibility, and without ownership, there was simply no way to make the would-be economy competitive. Hence, privatization could not possibly be more than partial at best—i.e., a pseudo-privatization. But, if one took seriously the unique viability of a free-enterprise economy, the very idea of a program was inherently futile, and counterproductive to boot.

With respect to the interrelationship of the Russian civilian and military economic sectors, Dr. Rosefielde said a new type of conversion to civilian economy had to be conceptualized: What was needed was to harness Russian military expertise by transferring to the civilian economy technological elements of engineering design for new products and the technology for mass production of consumer goods. That could enable a marriage between technology that was now restricted to the military economy and the free economic functioning that was expected from the civilian economy. At present, however, Russian leaders willy-nilly were leading the civilian economy back to the archaic Soviet institution of the Gosplan—the all-encompassing state plan for the economy.

It seemed to me that the discussion, although interesting in its theoretical aspects, could lead to no solid ground so long as our Russian visitors were genuinely uncertain about both the meaning of developments in Russia and the plans of the leadership. Quite likely, the Russian leaders themselves were not sure of their objectives—whether they wanted to construct a genuine free-enterprise economy, modeled on the advanced industrial countries of the West, or whether they were simply "muddling through" with half-hearted new starts and a readiness for all forms of improvisation.

What was clear to us all—on both sides—was that the reform programs had not yet brought the Russian military-industrial complex under control. The latter continued to generate armaments at substantial levels while draining away huge economic resources, including high technology, human skills and reserves accumulated over the past half-century. The export of armaments as a stop-gap economic measure was, of course, particularly dangerous—not only for its incendiary implications abroad, but also because it would serve to deepen the domestic crisis, while reducing the prospects for genuine reform.

Arms reduction was essential, we all agreed, if not disarmament—an unthinkable idea for a great state. It was in the Russian military's best interest to see how it could serve the cause of stabilizing the economy as a whole, while in the process, keeping the military-industrial workforce engaged in constructive enterprises, and maintaining the technical base for modernization. It was agreed that the transfer of these resources from the military-industrial complex to the civilian economy offered the only prospect for implementing genuine, radical, structural reform that would avoid the pitfalls of hyperinflation and unemployment. Vitaly Shlykov, the strongest Russian advocate of this point of view, proposed that the expertise already available at all layers of the military-industrial complex be harnessed in a coordinated attempt to develop new goods and technologies for the civilian sector. These proposals would have incentives to sustain aggregate production while shifting it toward peaceful ends. The concept, while plainly requiring elaboration, seemed to provide a promising path to surmounting a crisis that had otherwise defied resolution.

ECONOMIC AND MILITARY-INDUSTRIAL CONTRADICTIONS

Both the July and November 1992 ISC-sponsored conferences generated intense and meaningful U.S.-Russian dialogue, and even drove that dialogue toward limited areas of agreement, or at least understanding, far in advance of anything comparable attempted (if, indeed, it could be attempted) at the government-to-government level. It showed what a non-governmental institution can accomplish in a fluid situation in sharp contrast to the results typically achieved by the lethargy, unwieldiness and timidity of governmental bureaucracies.

Nowhere was the role of the ISC in addressing basic issues in the Russian conundrum more important than in the results typically achieved by the economic arena, into which so much American attention had been directed with so little in the way of results. What concerned us particularly was a seemingly dangerous paradox in the Russian situation. As the economy spiraled down, not only was the defense sector of the economy ostensibly immune to the general trend, but military production was continuing at a high level.

On March 15, 1994, William Van Cleave opened the tenth ISC-sponsored U.S.-Russian roundtable discussion by summarizing the meeting of November 1992, which had focused specifically on the relationship between economic reform and the military in Russia.

Van Cleave reminded the participants of the conclusion strongly voiced by both Drs. Shlykov and Yaremenko—that true economic reform depended heavily on a successful structural demilitarization of the Russian economy.

Yet, Van Cleave contended, a "Catch-22" had emerged. Radical demilitarization in Russia depended on the ability to coerce or cajole the Russian military into supporting this policy. But why would the military voluntarily accept its own diminution? As far as coercion was concerned, in the months since the last conference, the Russian military had grown much stronger politically—in fact, made itself potentially the decisive force in Russian politics. Certainly President Yeltsin owed his continued stay in power mainly to the military. Moreover, the Russian military was beginning to show revanchist symptoms vis-a-vis the so-called "near- abroad" states that once made up the former Soviet Union. Given this situation, Dr. Van Cleave posed two questions for discussion: Was the priority on structural demilitarization for economic reform still valid? If so, how can it be implemented, particularly in light of the political-military problem that he had described?

Professor Yaremenko responded to Van Cleave by summarizing a paper he distributed. In his view, the two-year experiment with the "Gaidar reforms," entailing radical price liberalization, had failed. The results were high inflation, a drastic decline in production, and a decrease in investment. The threat of mass unemployment loomed large. While the Gaidar approach had proved inadequate to the task, it had not yet run its full course.

According to Yaremenko, a major reason for economic decline lay in the destruction of the price system that caused major changes in the relative prices of goods in Russian markets. Thus large increases in some areas, e.g. for oil and petroleum products, could not be absorbed by consumers, as was possible in the agricultural sector. Another cause was the reduction in incentives for added value to products resulting in a breakdown of production. Finally there was the appearance of "non-payments of debts" by enterprises. They provided goods, but no payment for products. As a result, an intra-regional bartering system has grown. This has led to the government's printing money to handle these debts, including the mammoth military industrial complex's needs. Subsidization of the huge military industrial complex had continued at the expense of economic reform and the economy as a whole.

Yaremenko expressed the startling conviction that "normalization" could come about only by recentralizing economic management. What was needed was a less revolutionary approach, he maintained. Foreign trade could help, but was no panacea because trade is such a small percentage of a large country's industrial output. The newly centralized system proposed by him would temporarily adjust and control prices on certain goods, adjust or freeze wages, especially in the energy sector, and move the current military economy into consumer production, ending the military economy's present autonomy.

Dr. Shlykov followed with an analysis of the then-current budget debate in Russia. What he recounted was as revealing as it was frightening.

There was intense competition among the energy, agriculture and military-industrial sectors for funding, according to Shlykov. The Ministry of Defense was to have received 37 trillion rubles, or 24%, of the total government budget (compared with 15–16% in the peak spending year of 1989, and 17% the previous year). The Ministry, however, suddenly demanded a budget of 83 trillion rubles, primarily to purchase new armaments. This figure—which did not include the costs of nuclear weapons, intelligence, civil defense, the KGB or ministry of interior troops, or subsidies to the military-industrial complex—represented some 80% of total government resources. The increase in authorized arms purchases was more than four-fold, from 5.5 trillion rubles to 24.3 trillion rubles in one year! Without this overall increase, the MOD warned that it would have to cancel the purchase of all arms and cut an additional 400,000 men from the armed forces. Military leaders, including General Grachev, had spoken publicly, in threatening terms, of a complete loss of control of the military and of a social catastrophe if the budget demands were not met.

This, according to Shlykov, was tantamount to blackmail of the government. The Finance Ministry had responded to the Defense Ministry initiatives by arguing, unsuccessfully, that the privileged position of military forces—i.e., demanding and receiving the best the economy had to offer—was no longer justified and must be reduced, if not eliminated.

In his response to the internal debate, Prime Minister Chernomyrdin had concluded that the Ministry of Finance's attack on the system of privilege for the military was tantamount to blackmailing the military. He announced that he would guarantee arms production at the 1993 level. For his part, President Yeltsin apparently had told Minister of Defense Grachev that the military allocations for 1994 were not enough and argued for working out "a balance" of the differences that would not jeopardize in any way the Ministry of Defense.

Should the government acquiesce in the Defense Ministry demands, said Shlykov, 80% of projected state revenue would go to the military. If the budgets for nuclear weapons, border guards, interior troops, civil defense, KGB, and military conversion were added, the military-industrial complex in its entirety could require more money than the country expected to earn in 1994! No money could be spent on anything but the military-industrial complex. With inflation, the cost of arms production alone might be more than 150 trillion rubles by the end of the year. This would spell economic chaos. Shlykov said that while the whole nature of this debt seemed fantastic, there were those in the Russian leadership who regarded this situation as "normal".

How could this situation be explained? What will be the outcome? Collapse? Return to a wartime economy? How could it be resolved? The answer lies in an understanding of why it came about, Shlykov argued. In the pricing structure of the former Soviet Union, military arms were always state-subsidized. For example, in 1992 prices, the C-300 (or SA-12) SAM/ATBM system has been offered for sale abroad at $300 million per unit. It was sold to the Russian military for 1.5 million rubles. Similarly, the $24 million dollar Mig-29 was purchased for the military for only 7 million rubles. The T-72 tank that was sold abroad for $1.5 million dollars cost the Red Army only 200,000 rubles. So weapons, essentially, have been provided to the military for free.

Sharing a lack of understanding of this key issue by senior leaders in the government, Gaidar believed that a two-thirds reduction in the state budget for military production in 1992 would provide great savings. He was proven wrong, Shlykov argued, because, ultimately, the state paid all the costs of the military industrial complex. In August 1992, prices for military hardware (and many other goods) began to rise. For 1993, the government's military procurement spending was 500 billion rubles, despite a much lower budget allocation. By January 1994, the MOD needed 2.4 trillion rubles to pay for its purchases. Yeltsin intervened and provided an additional 1.5 trillion rubles. Now (at the time of the conference) almost 30 trillion more was being demanded. In fact, it turned out that the MOD did not pay a single ruble for production in 1993: it simply ran up debts and expected the government to pay them "off budget."

This chronology reflected, Shlykov contended, both the enormity and the power of the military-industrial complex.

Another part of the problem was the fact that the true costs of weapon systems was not understood in Russia, and there was no one in the Ministry of Defense capable of providing them. This prevented economic reform, and resulted in runaway inflation and disastrous government planning. The Ministry had recently handed this problem over to Deputy Defense Minister Kokoshin, and in a panic he had bowed to the military, demanding that the government provide a fourfold increase in the Ministry budget. Grachev has accepted this estimate and made the same demands public, warning of dire consequences if the demands are not met.[2]

However, also involved was a conflict between the military and the military-industrial complex over military priorities and industrial production. In 1992, the military complained that it was receiving new strategic and conventional forces when what was needed above all was money for social services, maintenance, readiness, and spare parts for sustaining the military. The Economics Ministry argued that continued production of new weapons was necessary to feed the military-industrial complex's workforce, some 5–10 million workers plus their 10–20 million dependents. As a result of that plan, and the continuation of old production plans, new strategic weapons, including a new nuclear-powered submarine, soon would enter service.

The military, Shlykov argued, did not participate in the creation of the plan for military production. A distinction should be drawn between the professional military and the military industrial complex. The military has existed apart

---

While the demand had formally been refused by Chernomyrdin, there was a general expectation in Moscow that the demand would be met "off budget"—or simply by printing money to cover the deficits of the military-industrial enterprises. This, in fact, happened, thereby further destabilizing the ruble.

from the military-industrial complex, and was not involved in decisions on what would be produced and at what cost.

MILITARY RULE AS THE LESSER EVIL?

According to Shlykov, the military today is potentially the most powerful force in Russian politics. If the military took the side of the military-industrial complex, with the support of the KGB and Interior Ministry forces, and decided to change the government, nothing could stop them. Fortunately today, he told the conferees, the Army did not side politically with the military-industrial complex. In fact, contrary to the latter, Shlykov argued, the military could be a force for stability. The military was not anxious to assume political leadership, he maintained, but if it did make the decision to take over, that might not necessarily be bad: it could offer at least a barrier to catastrophe. In any event, the military needed to become involved in the reform process, and not just as a passive recipient of resources. According to Shlykov, at the moment the military leadership was hesitant to take over, but in the future it might feel compelled to do so.

Shlykov seemed to suggest that a benevolent and efficient military could manage the government and effect economic reform while maintaining order better than any other leadership. On the other hand, he acknowledged that a military coup might produce a very troublesome dictatorship.

Dr. Stepan S. Sulakshin followed Shlykov's analysis with a somewhat different perspective. He believed that many of the changes in Moscow were the result of what was happening in the regions. For example, the closed city of Tomsk-7, with 30,000 workers and 80,000 dependents, was on the verge of economic and environmental disaster. Ninety percent of the enterprises were not paying workers, even in areas—e.g. nuclear energy—that posed significant danger to the population.

In the beginning, the Gaidar reforms (and the military budget cuts) were possible because they had the broad support of the people, Sulakshin said. But this consensus was changing. New political pressures were developing for increasing the military budget, lobbying groups had formed, and the people were stirred by appeals to nationalism and patriotism, as well as for order and economic security.

All of this was putting significant pressure on the Duma to maintain or even increase the military-industrial complex's share of national resources. Specific measures being considered included: adopting the 1994 military budget indexed to inflation; reducing expenditures for research and development in the economy as a whole; and returning to procurement of weapon systems and enhancement of incentives for arms sales abroad.

The Duma was also considering legislative proposals affecting the military in the areas of arms purchases, military-industrial enterprises, and defense conversion. Dr. Sulakshin argued that the reformers, themselves, were responsible for the fact that the population was rejecting reform. While the Russian economy must demilitarize, it must do so in a conservative, controlled way, over five to ten years, and in a manner that preserved the potential of the military-industrial complex. The key to this, he believed, was economic decentralization. Political centrism in Russia must yield to economic decentralization.

Future reform laws to be passed will be characterized as conservative, not radical, Sulakshin said. They will be guided by a gradual rather than revolutionary restructuring of the economy. Underlying this would be foreign policy goals of self-sufficiency for Russia, and new, more negative attitudes toward NATO and the United States.

Van Cleave noted that the Russian participants described the military as responsible, progressive, and a source of order, while the military-industrial complex was irresponsible, conservative and a source of disorder. He questioned whether this distinction was carried too far, while ignoring elements of a longstanding and continuing partnership. If the military was so eminently responsible and at odds with the military-industrial complex, why was the military not exercising a positive influence for military-economic reform? And given the resurgent nationalism in Russia and political influence of the military, would not any effort to curtail the military-industrial complex be viewed by the military as a downgrading of its political power?

Dr. Shlykov noted that his comments, along with the situation in Russia, contained many contradictions. In particular, he wished to emphasize that he harbored no animosity toward the military-industrial complex. While the military-industrial complex had been unable to convert to the production of civilian goods, competitive in quality or price, nevertheless it is that same complex which houses the huge wealth of Russia, especially its human potential. And, Shlykov added, the salvation of Russia as a developed country must come from the military-industrial complex.

Shlykov argued persuasively that what he called "structural demilitarization" would have to take place if the Russian economic situation were to be fundamentally reformed. A way must be found to make an ally of the military-industrial complex, the potential engine of Russian economic growth and prosperity. To do that it should be divided into two parts: one for controlled military production within the military budget, and one removed from military production but kept for civilian production. Voluntary demilitarization is the necessary, but difficult part in getting there.

The Russian delegation's chief was very forthright in predicting what lay ahead: In the coming period Russia faced increasing destabilization. The prospects for a military take-over were ripening. Either Yeltsin would dismiss military leaders making outrageous demands, or he would lose all authority and be pushed aside for a more authoritarian government, probably created by the military itself. That military government could take the form of a benevolent and efficient military dictatorship—a transitional bridge toward a more stable and effective elected government—or it could be of a more reactionary and threatening nature. Shlykov went further out on a limb by mentioning the charismatic General Lebed, 14th Russian Army commander in Moldova, as a possible candidate to lead a Pinochet-type, benevolent authoritarian government. There is no ground for a return to a totalitarian regime, Shlykov contended, only an authoritarian one.

Shlykov warned of ominous changes taking place in Russia, inducing him toward temporary preference of a military leadership. The outright nationalist candidate, Zhirinovsky, wanted to stop conversion to a civilian economy, export arms, maintain a strong military and KGB, and even dream of Russian forces on the warm waters of the Indian Ocean. Bonapartism in the army was on the rise. Shlykov stressed again that either Yeltsin would face down the military or he would lose his authority.

I believe that Shlykov was fundamentally correct when he said that many Western observers were simply not looking at the realities of what the former Soviet system had left behind. The following statement by him merits fuller citation:

> In a Western country possessed of a strong defense industry, for example, the United States, the defense technology and industry are a part of a much larger and usually more efficient civilian economy. In Russia, which inherited its defense industry from the Soviet Union, it is the core and substance of the economy. The civilian part of it is an adjunct and economically totally inefficient. The

consumer value of civilian goods produced by Russian enterprises is so low that if they were priced correctly they would not earn enough to cover raw materials for their manufacture.

This kind of economy can exchange its products only on a compulsory or non-commercial basis, that is through direct distribution of resources at artificially fixed prices. In other words, an economy such as this can function only if it defies the laws governing market systems. If such an economy switches prices corresponding to world prices, it would inevitably collapse. And this is exactly what has been happening during the past two years in Russia.

Structural militarization is what I call the distortion of an economy that does not respond to such monetary measures as cutting defense expenditures or defense purchases. It is an economy that doesn't allow an overflow of resources from the defense to the civilian sectors—as opposed to the usual militarization measured by shares of defense spending, production in national budgets and GNP. You could halt all defense procurement in a structurally militarized economy and this drastic measure still would not show in a corresponding increase in the effectiveness of the civilian sector.

Shlykov contended, and I agree, that delusions about "convertability" account for an excessive optimism in the West about the prospect of market reforms, and democracy in general, in Russia. As a result, opportunities have been lost, perhaps irretrievably.

ABIDING DANGER SIGNALS FROM MOSCOW

Our dialogue with our Russian counterparts left us with the strong conviction that Russia will continue to be paramount in U.S. foreign policy concerns. The "post-Cold War" optimism notwithstanding, surely we will enter the 21st century still preoccupied with developments in Moscow and the former Soviet Union.

The dialogue with our Russian friends also convinced us that the only successful road to democratic reform is via structural change of Russia's military economy. Democratic rule of Russia is doomed to fail without demilitarization. That reality was not recognized by the Clinton Administration, which blindly threw its support behind Yeltsin. Clinton thus replicated the mistake committed by George Bush in his support of Gorbachev, who turned out to be a transitional phenomenon. Neither Gorbachev nor Yeltsin had a plan for reform of the military economy. Yeltsin's vaunted economic advisor, Gaidar, only addressed the civilian sector of the economy. Thus, the alleged conflict between reformist and reactionary forces is a false image. Unless and until someone in Russia comes to grips with the military economy, no real movement toward reform is possible.

Shlykov's warning of a military dictatorship in Moscow—"benign" or not—must be taken seriously. In the meantime, Western commentators, while focussing on the bloody fighting in Chechnya, generally fail to assay the growing role of the Russian military in the domestic affairs of the Russian Federation, not to speak of the ever more conspicuous presence of Russian armies in Moldova, Central Asia, the Caucasus, and the Baltics—ostensibly in behest of the safety of ethnic Russians living in these areas. We may have left the "Cold War" behind—in the sense of a "de-ideologization" of the conflict after the collapse of the Communist edifice erected by Lenin and Stalin. But has the potential for conflict itself been left behind? Or do not the instabilities in the wake of the fragmentation of the erstwhile "bipolar world" augur new and as yet even unfathomable dangers?

The End of the Cold War:
A Final Accounting

As I have argued, the United States "won" the Cold War largely by default. Both the Reagan and Bush Administrations have laid claim to the historic laurels of victory. Yet, if Reagan and Bush had succeeded in their chosen policies, Mikhail Gorbachev not only would still be the ruler of the Soviet Union today, but, with massive Western assistance, might be revitalizing the Communist system—and probably planning a revitalization of the Soviet Empire as well.

More generally, as I pointed out earlier, from an historical perspective, the Reagan policies in office bore little resemblance to the planks of his campaign platform in 1980. The Reagan Administration was never serious in pursuing an activist, coherent strategy toward victory. That applied even to the much-vaunted—and tremendously expensive—effort to redress the strategic nuclear balance that was tilting dangerously in favor of the Soviet Union. That objective was not achieved by the Reagan Administration: When it left office, Soviet offensive forces continued to outnumber their American counterparts by a large margin. If the nuclear danger to the U.S. has dwindled, this is the consequence of change within the former Soviet Union, not of U.S. policies.

After nearly a decade in power, the Reagan foreign policy proved itself a more general failure largely because it was captivated by Gorbachev, arms control and detente. Instead of being a catalyst for fundamental change, the Reagan Administration actually inhibited the historic processes by embracing the Gorbachev regime, failing to recognize the opportunities for fundamental change inside the Soviet Union, and adapting its policies accordingly.

In the end, Reagan caved in on arms control and the Middle East. It was a sad day when he appeared in Red Square and intoned that the Soviet Union was not the evil empire that he had described in previous years. Ironically, this Presidential apology came at a time when most Soviet citizens recognized how close to the truth he and other "virulent anti-Communists" had been. In the Middle East, Reagan failed to exploit the chance to redraw the political map in the Levant despite the U.S. military intervention in 1983 and the bloody price paid for that adventure; in the end, he spared the PLO by allowing its militants to leave Lebanon in 1983 with their weapons. Bush merely carried that Reagan policy to its logical conclusion. Like Reagan in Lebanon, Bush squandered the opportunity to redraw the political map in the Persian Gulf.

On the economic front Reagan was more fortunate. The OPEC cartel collapsed during his tenure and this decisively fueled the unprecedented prosperity during his Administration. Reagan had another great asset: The "Great Communicator" was liked by the populace.

While Bush lacked the Reagan charisma, he, too, was lucky—at least in foreign policy. He presided over a zero-growth economy, and the economic and social problems in the United States deepened during his tenure. But in global affairs the Bush Administration reaped a harvest not of its own sowing. In fact, it did its best to bungle even the acceptance of that gratuity.

ILLUSORY BACKING OF GORBACHEV

The Soviet Union collapsed under the weight of its "internal contradictions," as the Marxists are wont to say, not because of, but despite, the Bush policies. This has permanently changed the structure of world politics as it emerged in the past half-century, but not the fundamental forces that have shaped the world scene throughout modern history and will continue to do so. The tragedy is not only that U.S. policymakers failed to cast a formula or framework for exploiting the historic opportunity for the industrial democracies and civilization as a whole, but that they have not even discerned the basic forces shaping the world of the future.

In his State of the Union Address on January 28, 1992, President Bush claimed credit for "winning the Cold War." Had there been any verisimilitude to that statement, our economy would have been booming and Bush could have played golf straight through his campaign for reelection. For all his vaunted expertise in foreign policy, George Bush could claim no credit for the downfall of Communism. Neither could the U.S. State Department or any or all of the stalwarts in the American foreign policy establishment, so many of whom had constantly preached about the necessity for acknowledging the Soviets' "legitimate concerns," or talked of "convergence" of the two systems, or even prated about the desirability of a U.S.-Soviet "global condominium"—a kind of "pax Americana-Sovietica" that would underwrite world peace and stability. That certainly was a strong rationale behind the formulations of the powerful "arms control lobby" in Washington. Global "stability" was elevated over all other considerations, even moral ones.

It is fashionable now for some of these same people to engage in a form of "revisionism" in order to rationalize their past failures of analysis. Seizing upon the collapse of the

Communist system, they argue retroactively that this proves somehow that the Soviet threat was always a figment of the propaganda of the U.S. military-industrial complex. The argument is hardly worth responding to. In more genteel circles, it has become fashionable to assert that we anti-Communists overestimated Soviet military power. Yet, whatever arguments may be mounted *ex post facto* about the workings of the Communist system, there can be no controversy about the Soviet military machine. In fact, recent Russian admissions confirm that we *underestimated* Soviet military strength, particularly in the nuclear realm.

It can only be by the grace of God or by blind luck that the United States finds itself in an advantageous, if uncertain and dangerous, geopolitical position 75 years after the launching of the Bolshevik Revolution in St. Petersburg. And if the Cold War is over, it is not yet completely won.

As I have described, we at the ISC foresaw the possibility of an eventual Soviet breakdown and formulated an "Affirmative Strategy" in 1988 with the principal aim of stimulating a policy debate during that year's presidential election.[1] Indeed, our purpose was to focus the thinking of U.S. policymakers on the need for a coherent strategy designed both to exploit the weaknesses and contradictions in the Soviet system and to have a policy in place for dealing with their consequence. We did not anticipate that the collapse would come so soon; we feared, in fact, that in some last-minute thrust of madness, a nuclear-armed state might try to "break out" of its rapidly deteriorating "convergence of forces," as the Marxist ideologues termed it. But we did see the coming crisis and warned that without a thoughtful response, the U. S. might lose the historic opportunity.

---

[1] See Chapter 18.

I also noted earlier that the response to the strategy from both the Bush and Dukakis camps was almost negligible. Among those who did respond, the popular Washington journalist, Morton Kondracke, seemed to express the conventional wisdom of the time. In a critique of the Affirmative Strategy, published in the ISC's quarterly journal, *Global Affairs*, Kondracke found much to support in the strategy statement. But he faulted the idea of the United States departing from the containment strategy and aggressively exercising leadership at the moment in history when the collapse of the Soviet agricultural and industrial infrastructure and the rise of tensions among the nationalities could lead to a Soviet "breakout" as easily as to its dissolution:

> At the moment, much of the world and the U.S. population is rooting for Gorbachev, believing that the success of his policies will liberate his people, make his society more 'Western,' and inevitably make it less aggressive. If the United States were to set about actively trying to undermine this process, we would be seen as cynics and would lose support politically.[2]

Perhaps it was true that much of the world outside the Soviet Union, including many—like Margaret Thatcher, who should have known better—was rooting for Gorbachev. But these were not the people instrumental in Gorbachev's effort to "remodel" the Soviet system, let alone the democratization he professed to be carrying forward. Yeltsin and the forces of Russian populism swept Gorbachev out of office with such swiftness that Western intelligence and policymakers appeared thoroughly stumped by the exploding political realities inside the former Soviet Union.

---

[2] "A Critique of 'An Affirmative Strategy For The Free World,'" by Morton Kondracke. *Global Affairs*, Fall, 1988, Vol. III, No. 4, page 174.

The Bush Administration to the end sought to uphold Gorbachev in power—to the point where the Administration in effect simply refused to deal with any other option. (We may remember how Yeltsin was treated during his first visit to Washington.) In this, it followed policy lines that were as out-of-touch with reality as those of its Democratic opposition. More importantly, in the process, the Bush Administration forfeited the chance to give the democratic movement in Russia the momentum that could have made it unstoppable. We may still have to pay a price for that missed opportunity as the forces of real reform in the former Soviet Union fight for survival against great odds. From this perspective, the Affirmative Strategy looks very good indeed.

In my 1988 book *Soviet Breakout*[3], I argued that the Soviet Union was in a state of disintegration and could not master its agricultural and technological problems short of staging a military and strategic breakout.[4] I thought that Gorbachev would resort in the end to the one instrument at his disposal—the military—to restructure the basis for a "reformed" empire. But if Gorbachev did flirt with that option—and his ambiguous actions during the aborted coup of 1990 leave some questions on this score—he did so too late.

Gorbachev's dilemma was that to restructure the Soviet system he needed massive outside aid. If he used the military stick, he risked losing that aid. Moreover, Gorbachev did not have "the teeth of steel" of his predecessors. He was indecisive. He equivocated. And even he obviously failed to fore-

---

[3] Joseph Churba, *Soviet Breakout, Strategies to Meet It*, Pergamon-Brassey's International Defense Publishers, Inc., 1988.

[4] Defined on page 39 of *Soviet Breakout* as: "the perceived physical and psychological ability and willingness on the part of the Soviets to counter any Western initiative or counterstrategy and, in so doing, to raise the perceived cost to the United States and its allies for continuing to challenge the Soviet Union."

see the consequences once he opened the Pandora's box of "reform".

But Gorbachev's indecision was, in effect, exacerbated by President Bush's refusal to adopt a clear strategy aimed at the substance of democratic reform in Russia, rather than at the man who was trying to rescue the Communist system. In fact, Bush adopted precisely the opposite strategy by attempting to shore up wherever possible Gorbachev's faltering policies. Until the bitter end, neither Bush nor Gorbachev were in control of the process that resulted in the dissolution of the Soviet Union; neither will emerge as historical figures in that process.

A MISSION UNFULFILLED

On a personal level, the temptation to retire from the ISC and the Washington scene as a whole became stronger as the collapse of the Soviet Empire grew more manifest. However, it soon became apparent that the Bush Administration had no idea of how to cope with the new challenge any more than it had with the dissolution of the Soviet Empire. Indeed, the same politics of defeat that had underscored the chronic failures of the past soon began to spill into the new scenario. Exaggerated emphasis was placed on "peace dividends" and disarmament as though peace had been permanently secured. The situation called for the farsightedness of a Churchill to forge a new balance of power in Eurasia, but fate offered the mediocrity of George Bush. And then Saddam Hussein of Iraq decided to take advantage of the confusion and to preempt a new regional balance of power by invading Kuwait.

Recognizing a threat to U.S. commercial interests in the Gulf, President Bush forged history's greatest concentration of military force in the region under the guise of thwarting aggression. Lost in the din of patriotic drum-beating were the policies that allowed the massive arming of Iraq in the first place. Kuwait's independence was, of course, restored and the Gulf was made safe for feudalism.

But the "New World Order" that was to emerge soon degenerated into the nightmares of the Bosnian and Somalian crises, the North Korean nuclear threat in East Asia, and the no less disquieting possibility of a disintegration of the Russian Federation. In the face of all these developments and more, I recognized that personal retirement would be as elusive as securing the uncertain peace. So in early 1992, I took the initiative within the ISC's Advisory Board for a redefinition of the mission of our organization.

The geostrategic picture, of course, has always been fundamental to our *raison d'etre*. We had combatted the Communist threat for decades. Although we had survived its destruction and dismantlement, we did not deem our purpose fulfilled. It certainly would have been easier for all of us—myself above all—to disband and look for other pursuits. Instead we took the view that we had, at the very least, a moral obligation to do what our Government had failed to do: namely, work for a satisfactory alternative to Communism in the former Soviet Union. We had that obligation because we had worked for the destruction of Communism.

The question had come up in early 1987 when we deliberated on our Affirmative Strategy. Professor Richard Pipes of Harvard University raised it: "What do you put in the place of central authority in Russia?" Pipes had always stressed in his historical writings the continuity of Russian imperialism as the major problem in Russia's relations with the world-at-large but, had begun more lately to focus on ideology as the principal cause of the friction between the U.S. and Russia. He had no answer to his own question. I did: "Democratic government!"

The conventional argument in American conservative circles has been that Western-style democracy is not relevant to the USSR because Russia has no democratic tradition. I disagreed bitterly with this thinking during the discussions surrounding the Affirmative Strategy. I believe that my view has been sustained by events.[5]

In any event, in our self-redefinition in 1992, we took the existentialist position that some sort of participatory democracy had to be made to work in the former Soviet Union—at least in Russia—for a solution to its problems. And without at least a partial solution to its problems, there could be no world peace. That was based on a fundamental view of the world that I and others among our colleagues took as our lodestone in international politics. In the ISC's restatement of its purpose, unprecedented among Washington think tanks, the geopolitical argument is uppermost. It was agreed that we could never reconcile the maintenance of international peace and stability with anarchy in the heart of Eurasia. The stability of the entire Eurasian landmass turns on the viability of the Russian Federation.

That is why closer relations with Poland, the Ukraine, and the Muslim Republics can never effectively replace a stable U.S.-Russia relationship.

---

[5] Nicolai Petro, "Russian-American Relations: Looking for a New Agenda," *Global Affairs*, Summer, 1992, Vol. VII, No. 3.

CHAPTER

24

A Longer Geostrategic View

Abraham Lincoln once said: "As our times are new, so must we think anew." He was reflecting on the profound changes that gripped a "world in transition" in mid-19th Century—including the United States, which was undergoing a critical and bloody "transition" of its own to mature nationhood.

Lincoln's imperative applies to another "world in transition" at the turn of the Twenty-first Century—albeit to a globe interlocked to an extent that even the farsighted 19th Century statesman could scarcely have envisaged. Nor could Lincoln foresee that his advice would squarely befit a modern institution like the "think-tank," created to generate thought as a guide to policy and action in an ever more complex world.

The demise of the Cold War clearly marked the end of an era. But it marked neither the "end of history"—as some pundits pretended—nor a total revamping of intellectual tool-kits relevant to the analysis of international affairs. Indeed, the collapse of the Soviet Empire was a validation of the ISC's "Affirmative Strategy," which had been based on a fundamentally geopolitical framework of analysis. We realized early on that this basic framework would be more relevant than ever to the post-Cold War world.

This framework of analysis provided the ISC with a unique advantage, but there were others as well. "Freedom of pursuit" was an ISC attribute. Unlike other institutions beholden to contracts, grants and/or partisan political causes—all of which tend to foster in one measure or another a preoccupation with the fashionable issues-of-the-day—the ISC always enjoyed the freedom to set its agenda in accordance with perceived priorities, rather than high "pay-off." This flexibility, enhanced by the "small cadre" mode of operations, allowed the targeting of fundamental issues. The ISC, moreover, has always embraced as its priority mission not merely the analysis of existing trends, but the anticipation of developments and their portents. This intellectual effort becomes all the more important in the "regearing" process that confronts statesmen and policymakers in the post-Cold War environment.

What has distinguished the ISC as well from comparable institutions is a "broad strategic view." In this perspective, the geopolitical framework of analysis was compatible with the ISC's stated purpose "to advance the cause of democracy, freedom, and human rights within the community of nations." During the Cold War the geopolitical and ideological boundaries of the world largely coincided.

GEOPOLITICAL SALIENTS

The ISC's coverage, with its implicit geographical priorities and emphasis on strategic considerations, in a broad sense, retraced the geopolitical map of the geopolitical thinker Halford Mackinder and his disciples. It has featured the following: A focus on Eurasia—in Mackinder terms, the "Greater Heartland"—and its major power factors, the Soviet Empire, the NATO Alliance (with emphasis on extended U.S. power and the German variable), and East Asia (with emphasis on China, Japan, Taiwan and Korea).

Consistent in all of ISC's conferences and studies addressed to this latter region has been the explicit effort to relate the given subject under analysis to the larger picture of trans-Eurasian trends.

There has been corollary attention to the "Eurasian Rimlands." The focal areas of analysis here have been: (1) what might be called a "southern rimland region" (or "extended zone of instability") encompassing the Mediterranean, the Middle East, the Horn of Africa, and South Asia, and (2) an "eastern rimland region" in the Pacific Basin. It is noteworthy in retrospect that rarely had ISC efforts ventured beyond those Rimland regions (e.g., in pursuit of such fashionable subject areas as sub-Saharan Africa on one side, and Southeast Asia on the other). Occasional attention has been given in the past to problems in the Western Hemisphere, notably Central America and the Caribbean Basin. Even those "digressions," however, were staged primarily with an eye toward the larger geopolitical arena rather than in a strictly regional context.

The ISC put an emphasis on military power but again in a primarily geopolitical context. That is to say that the stress was on those elements of military power that could enable the United States, as an insular maritime power, to counter the endemic strategic advantages enjoyed by an aggressive "Heartland power" (i.e., Russia) by dint of geography and interior lines of communication. These "redressive" means of U.S. military power included primarily long-range nuclear weaponry (and strategic defenses), naval power, as well as forward-deployed land forces backed by the needed sinews of alliances and global logistics.

The broad question to be considered is whether this geopolitical framework of overall analysis (and its priorities) continues to be valid for the emerging post-Cold War era. The answer is a strong affirmative. Traditional geopolitical theory, as evolved by Mackinder and his successors, may be flawed by the "single causal factor" approach; moreover, modern technological advances may have modified the purely geographical elements of power since Mackinder's day. Still, the history of the past five decades reconfirms the salient points of geopolitics:

- Eurasia continues at the center of the world system and at the vortex of global trends despite vast changes that have swept other areas of the world.
- Abetted by deeply rooted historical forces, power in its ultimate military expression remains the principal arbiter of events.

Therefore, an equilibrium of power in Eurasia continues to be the key to peaceful evolution of the international system.

If those premises are accepted, several broad questions dominate the agenda for continuing analysis:

1. What are the overall power trends in Eurasia, and their interplay, particularly in the power vacuum created by the collapse of the Soviet Union?
2. How does increasing instability in the "rimlands"— with its ever increasing inflammatory potential for broader conflict—relate to the larger Eurasian balance?
3. What role can and should the United States exert in this unfolding scenario?

IMPERATIVES FOR A NEW BALANCE IN EURASIA

It is undeniable that an American rapprochement with Russia is of incalculable value both to America and to global stability. Although the reunification of Germany in 1990 was the final act in the dismantling of the partition of Europe— and thus the end of the Cold War—nevertheless, the fuller reemergence of Germany as an economic, and potential military power casts a large shadow over global evolution in the wake of the Cold War.

It is now clearer than ever that only Russia can counterbalance both Germany in Europe and China in Asia. Literally at the center of the Eurasian landmass, the Russians are the only power in the position to exert leverage over its geographically disparate peripheries. That is all the more important since both extremities of the Eurasian landmass are caught in the splintering process that marks the end of the largely (if never completely) bipolar world of the Cold War.

While Western Europe still aspires to the ideal of political unification, the European Community already is being torn by the centrifuge of competing interests, especially between Germany and France. France would like Germany to remain "harnessed" within a collective Western Europe (preferably one led from Paris). Germany, in accordance with its historical traditions and its geopolitical interests, is showing ambivalence between its more recent center of gravity in the European Community and the Western Alliance and its "community of destiny" with Russian power to the east.

In East Asia, on the other hand, China grows as a problem during the very period that America's alliances with Japan, Korea, and the Philippines are eroding in the absence of the more visible security imperatives that obtained in the Cold War. Japan, with its vast economic power, might well be drawn into the vortex of world politics more or less involuntarily, and en route find itself returning to the kind of virulent nationalism that impelled it into disastrous adventures half a century ago.

Twice before in this century, diplomacy—which is, after all, merely applied intelligence—failed because of lack of alignment with military realities: The two wars that permanently transfigured the world were the devastating consequences of that failure. Today that same explosive potential exists. The European balance of power is once again being challenged by the reemergence of a united Germany, twice the size of any of its neighbors.

There may, indeed, be a "new Germany" conditioned by its immersion into the West during the past five decades. But there is also the "old Germany" that traditionally has looked eastward for sphere of influence and power. That "old" face was displayed during the break-up of Yugoslavia, when Bonn took advantage of the explosive forces that tore that state apart in order to support the creation of a Croatian sovereignty, thereby exacerbating the process of violent disintegration in favor of a longer-range German interest. If the explosion of long-suppressed nationalist, ethnic, and sovereignty claims in central and eastern Europe is viewed against the growing threat from the "Radical Entente"—North Korea, Cuba, Iran, Syria, Iraq, and Libya—the prospects for stability throughout the Eurasian landmass particularly become dim indeed, especially if Germany continues as a source of weapons—including those of mass destruction—for clients in the radical states.

America's fundamental interests are clear and simple: peace, prosperity, and "making the world safe for democracy." Those interests hinge sensitively on stability in the Western European and East Asian rimlands. Unless America turns isolationist, this goal is achievable. It was in order to safeguard these fundamental interests, after all, that America entered two World Wars and that presidents from Truman to Reagan sustained the basic policy of containment of the Soviet Union, while playing their own—if sporadic—version of the balance-of- power game. Truman, for instance, aligned America against China in the face of what seemed a unified Communist offensive in the Far East, while Nixon reversed that policy, turning China into a geopolitical asset to counter expanding Soviet military power in Asia and more generally enhance the deterrent fear in Moscow of a "two-front war."

Now, with the configuration of Eurasia transformed, Russia may once again become an American ally—this time a durable democratic ally in contrast with the sheer expedience and long-range ambitions that motivated Stalin's pact with Roosevelt during World War II. At the same time, Germany and China—indeed, perhaps Japan—may revert to policy directions that will make them into major threats to fundamental American interests.

Previously fearful of the former Soviet Union, Mainland China had helped the United States in the containment of Soviet power. There was absolutely no altruism in Beijing's willingness to "play along" with Washington: China faced Soviet encirclement by dint of a preponderance of Soviet military power in the Indian Ocean and the Western Pacific. With the collapse of the Soviet Union, China's leaders now feel freer to return to imperial ambitions of their own. Thus Beijing is in the process of cementing relations with North Korea and Vietnam. Moreover, China is emerging as the world's major wellspring of nuclear and ballistic missile proliferation.

At the other end of the Eurasian landmass, the French are still trying to hold onto a Franco-German Alliance—more desperately as an ever more powerful Germany emerges from the throes of reunification. Predictably, however, the focus of the Germany policy outlook is shifting eastward to the traditional "hunting grounds" of *Ostpolitik*, now also impelled by the economic search for a vast and secure market for German industrial goods, particularly in the intensifying competition with Japan. And notwithstanding the profound experience of Western-style democratization during the past forty years, symptoms of past syndromes are surfacing once again in Germany. The very least that can be said is that Germany is becoming a less predictable factor in the power equation of Eurasia.

It is this simple perception of the Russians' unique capability to counterbalance both Germany and China that is the basis for the rapprochement with Russia that I have been striving for over the past few years. A new Russia, having cast aside the corrupting debilitations of ideology and the bankrupt legacy of imperial designs, will be able to function as an effective counterweight to Germany and China and play a crucial role in a stabilizing balance of power in Eurasia.

DANGEROUS MIRAGES IN THE MIDDLE EAST

Like Eurasia, the Middle East also cries out for a new indigenous balance of power. The problems of the Middle East have proved insoluble for both insiders and outsiders. Looking from within, it would seem clear that it is the disintegration of traditional institutions in Arab countries that is among the region's most fundamental problems.

The theorists of Islam have yet to determine the appropriate balance between Western materialism and economic growth and the spiritual content of Islamic civilization. At issue is the source of legitimate power. This has been a festering problem since the collapse of the Ottoman Empire, and the principal reason for continued unrest in the Arabic-speaking world.

If anything, U.S. intervention in defense of Kuwait, the Gulf status quo in general, and the restoration of the Sabah ruling dynasty have sharpened this issue. The search for political legitimacy, I have always argued, transcends the peace processes in the Middle East and the Gulf region. The war demonstrated anew that the Arab quest for sources of legitimacy, along with inter-Arab and Arab-Iranian tensions, pose greater threats to regional and world peace than the Arab-Israel conflict. Neither the arbitrary rule of Arab monarchs nor the region's military dictators can claim support from Islamic political theory. The West has consistently failed to recognize the disparity between Islamic values and Western standards of political behavior or terminology such as "left" and "right." The inappropriateness of such labels is seen in the Western press's portrayal of the parties to the Lebanese conflict as "leftist Muslims" and "rightist Christians." Because Western politicians and media insist on reducing the complexities of Middle Eastern reality to their own simplistic, ethnocentric formulas, it is relatively easy for Arab ideologists to manipulate public opinion in the West.

The evidence belies the bizarre notion that Saudi Arabia acts in the strategic interest of the United States. To believe that is to believe that fires are best put out by dousing them with gasoline. In fact, the Gulf crisis showed that Saudi behavior has more to do with preserving the House of Saud (not surprisingly) than with acting as America's ally. Tribal unrest against the royal house, the disaffection of the Shia minority in the oil-producing provinces, PLO subversion and the abiding Iraqi threat—all these factors combine to heighten the danger.

Understandably frightened by the radical gains in Iran and Afghanistan, and riddled with internal weakness, the Saudis believe they must bow to radical pressures. They doubtless are more fearful of an open rupture with the encircling radical countries than they are of a cooling in their relationship with the United States. Indeed, the "safety-valve" is the Saudi estimate that the U.S. will come to the rescue should appeasement of the radicals backfire. It may be a plausible projection but a dangerous one: appeasement is often the prelude to self-destruction.

The chronic inability of the U.S., and the West generally, to grasp the weakness of the Saudis and other "moderate" Arab regimes enables the latter to manipulate Western publics and political elites. The rationale—and it is seductive to Western ears—is that "of course we really support you (the West, the U.S., such icons as the Israel-Egyptian peace treaty), but we cannot appear to do so lest the radicals 'polarize' the Arab masses." Saudi-sponsored consensus as opposed to polarization allegedly increases Arab "moderation." Saudi payoffs to the radicals allegedly prompt the Arab war coalition to forego its aim of destroying Israel and to accept peace on terms "very close" to those of the U.N. Security Council resolution.

No less fictitious, but equally seductive, is the presumption that no settlement of the Arab-Israel conflict is possible without concessions to the Palestinian Arabs—that unless this "core issue" is settled, U.S. interests remain vulnerable. It is in this context that the U.S. State Department has asserted that Israeli settlements in the territories are "the greatest obstacle to peace." Peace, progress, and prosperity all are contingent on the fulfillment of Palestinian Arab aspirations. So the argument runs.

It may be of some interest to note the evolution of the phrases applied to the territories held by Israel into "an obstacle to peace." The word "illegal," if energetically embraced, obviously left no way out. The Reagan Administration depended on a legal opinion which it had first accepted as authoritative, but then simply abandoned, since as a legal opinion it was demonstrably incorrect.

Politically, however, the problem remained: Arab states were adamant against Israeli retention of the territories. They were also, of course, adamant on the question of Israel's existence, although here they yielded to the diplomatic necessity for carrying on a semblance of negotiations as opposed to

Defense Minister Yitzhak Rabin addressing Jerusalem ISC Conference.

On the lighter side, Prime Minister Yitzhak Shamir and former Undersecretary of State Joseph Sisco, share a joke. Looking on is Jerusalem Post *editor David Bar-Illan.*

war. But it was useful for the Reagan-Bush Administrations to yield to Arab intransigence by focusing on the territories, since the Bush Administration, at least, hoped to reap some political gain by enabling Bush to claim the mantle of "peacemaker" in the Middle East in 1991 and 1992.

The abandonment of the charge of "illegality" against the territories was supposed to make it easier for Israel to come to the negotiations. By concentrating on the "obstacle to peace" formula, Bush and his Secretary of State James Baker were able to indicate a possible solution by giving the Israelis a chance to remove this particular "obstacle."

Yet it is obvious that the issue of Palestinian nationhood is fundamental neither to the Arab-Israel conflict nor to its resolution. It serves only to becloud and to preclude resolution of the main issue: Israel's right to exist. Not one of the several Arab-Israeli wars can be ascribed to the Palestinian Arab problem. The 1948 war began when Arab armies invaded the former Mandate territory to prevent the establishment of either a Jewish or another Arab state. Their intent was to enjoy the spoils of the end of British rule. Had they succeeded in destroying the fledgling Israel, neither Egypt nor Syria nor the Hashemite monarchs of Jordan and (at that time) Iraq would have tolerated the creation in western Palestine of an independent Arab state whose loyalties in inter-Arab rivalries would have been uncertain. More than one observer could state that it is no accident that during Jordan's 19-year occupation of the West Bank, there was no talk whatsoever of separate statehood for its Arab inhabitants.

The 1956 imbroglio resulted from Abdel Nasser's dreams of glory through the nationalization of the Suez Canal and the Soviet arming of Egypt. The 1967 war was caused by Egypt's blockade of Israel's eastern outlet to Africa and Asia. The 1973 war broke out over Egyptian and Syrian claims to, respectively, the Sinai and the Golan Heights. To perceive the "Palestinian problem"—or even the overall Arab-Israel conflict, for that matter—as the vortex of regional tension and turmoil is to ignore the basic unstable nature of Middle Eastern society and to misread the play of fundamental regional forces.

The quintessence of the problem was when, ironically, Saddam Hussein tried to play both the Kuwaiti and Palestinian cards simultaneously, and failed miserably. His essential challenge was to the established order; and now the murderous inter-Arab rivalries remain free to proceed, even if temporarily moving in a different channel. On the one hand, Israel has been of value to the United States (and indeed to the whole West) because of its strategic reach and power projection capabilities; on the other hand, some say that Israel cannot be factored into our strategic calculations unless and until it has been reduced to such vulnerability that it cannot be an asset at all.

Fortunately for the U.S., Israel refused until recently, after the breakup of the Soviet Union, to accept this scenario. It was bound to act assertively as a stabilizing power in the region. Its preemption of the Iraqi nuclear threat in 1981, and its policy of active defense in southern Lebanon, reflected a determination to preserve both itself and the regional equilibrium. Unfortunately for the Israelis, and the United States, the Washington Compromise broke through the gates of Jerusalem . . .

On September 13, 1993, the Israeli Labor government signed a so-called "peace agreement" with Yasser Arafat and his PLO. They proceeded as if the other compromises with Arabs had worked. All of the previous land for peace compromises—the 1922 partition, the 1947 partition, the 1948 armistice agreements, the 1956 withdrawal from Sinai, and the 1977 Camp David Accords—have failed. More recently, in Lebanon, countless agreements were signed and always broken among the factions. Similar agreements by Syria, Iraq, Sudan, and Somalia have met the same fate. Between Israel and Egypt there is a cold peace which in no way reflects the documents signed in the Camp David peace accords. For example, Egyptian government newspapers continue to publish anti-Semitic cartoons and articles.

Predictably, what has transpired since the September handshakes exposes the irrelevance of PLO commitments. Arafat has completely disregarded his promise to stop terrorism as well as his pledge to change the PLO covenant which calls for the destruction of Israel. Indeed, the fact that the "Gaza and Jericho First" negotiations continued, despite PLO violation of the "Declaration of Principles," led Arafat to believe that he does not have to live up to his side of the agreement. Incredibly, the Israel government continues to try to sell the public on the notion that an Israel-PLO alliance will provide cooperative security.

Nevertheless, the labor government's agreement with the PLO is also an astonishing effort to maintain a monopoly of power for itself. This is *deja vu* for Labor party leaders who, as students of Israel's first Prime Minister David Ben Gurion, believed in the sanctity of their political power. To understand this, one must look at the situation from Labor's perspective since the founding of the State of Israel in 1948. Labor always enjoyed a monopoly of power sustained through ownership of state industries and its labor movement, Histadrut, in which the majority of Israeli workers were members. When Labor lost power to Menachem Begin and the Likud Party in 1977, what it expected to be only a temporary hiatus turned into a traumatic 15 year ordeal! During that time, many of Labor's industries and statist affiliates went bankrupt, and the Labor party came close to being wiped out. Withdrawal from territories, Labor reasons, might offer the possibility of preferential access to Arab oil money. The expectation is to shore up their enterprises in Israel and hence Labor's hold on political power.

Thus, shortly after signing the 1993 Israel-PLO accord on the White House lawn, Labor's representatives requested

Saudi investments and the lifting of the Arab economic boy-cott. They hoped the elimination of the boycott would resur-rect their socialist economy and ensure money for party political activity for years to come. To their consternation, the Saudis turned them down. However, the Saudi entrance fee—peace on Arab terms—was paid. In betraying their long term security interest for partisan gain, Labor showed not only an abysmal ignorance of Saudi intentions, but forgot that the Saudis could not even protect Mecca. The Saudis, being no one's fools, said: "No deal with the Bolsheviks!"

For years, successive governments of Israel have rejected peace on Arab terms (e.g., a Palestinian state and total withdrawal from the territories, including East Jerusalem), recognizing those terms as only a ruse to return Israel to the more vulnerable defense lines of 1967. Even the dovish Moshe Dayan admitted that Israel's choice was between security without peace, or peace without security. Until now, every Israeli government has opted for the secu-rity imperative. The Rabin rationale for the shift is that only through peace can security be achieved.

To be sure, such was the logic promoted by Washington in its unremitting pressure for Israeli withdrawal. In sub-mitting to this deceptive rationale, Israel will have neither peace nor security, nor will the U.S. have the independent, strong ally in the region that proved its mettle throughout the Cold War.

And the United States is dangerously deluding itself if it believes that it can dispense with such allies in the post-Cold War world. As previously noted, America's return to isolation—in its fully historical meaning—is effectively barred by the interlocked nature of the world at the turn of the Century, as well as by the depth of the stakes that the United States has implanted in the world. The Gulf war rep-resented ample proof of the durability of those stakes.

What the United States does confront, however, is a relentless retraction in "exertable military power"—a phenomenon dictated, if by nothing else, by an inevitable primacy of domestic demands on the national treasury. The United States may well remain the "world's only superpower," but that becomes a misleading title when the effective reach of that power is progressively curtailed.

The United States, in other words, confronts the challenge of transforming itself from a leader of power into a manager of power. That shifts the premium from muscle (military strength) to intellect and statecraft. And it places a greater emphasis than ever on reliable partners in the creation of a new and stable world order.

CONCLUSION

To some readers, many of the events, arguments, and failures in U.S. policy described in this book will appear to be part of a rapidly aging past. The Soviet Union is dead with its plan for domination of the world. Gone is the Communist "religion," to all intents and purposes, as a credo for world organization and power—though there will be the small but powerful clique around the world that talks of how the Kremlin perverted "real socialism." But that does not mean we have arrived at the millennium. In fact, it is already clear we are at one of those moments in history when the world is chaotic, when new and important alliances and interests are being formed. It reminds one of that old Chinese curse: "May you live in interesting times!"

History has taught us, if it has taught us anything, that the world will always be a dangerous place and that national security—as America's founding fathers so often repeated in their public pronouncements, even in those days of relative isolation from European battles—is a continuing and constant concern. Precisely because we now live in a world of new and unknown perils, we must learn from our past mistakes. A world in which the threat is no longer focused on one enemy superpower, in which old alliances are shifting rapidly if perhaps sometimes imperceptively, in which American resources may be more heavily taxed than ever—is a world all the more in need of sophisticated statecraft.

While our concerns focus on the logic of geopolitics and strategy, my personal belief acknowledges the limits of human reason. As the humble partner in creation, we must also make room for Divine Providence. It is the pursuit of a false idolatry that posits a world without values which has led Western civilization to the brink of annihilation in two wars and which now sponsors an elusive search for an uncertain peace, "a new world order."

A moral order must precede and form the basis of any kind of personal, national, or international stability. That is why as president of the International Security Council I took the view that the righteousness of the liberation of Malta was of no less importance than the state of freedom in Russia or China. It is why I do not see responsibility for formulating an effective American foreign policy toward our former enemies ending with the demise of Communism. Indeed, it is only the beginning.

Despite my long-drawn-out involvement in the intrigues and entanglements of world politics, all my activities seem to me ultimately to stem from two simple convictions: that the image of America, at its best, like that of Israel, should be a "light unto the nations," and that it is significant that that simple phrase itself comes from the Hebrew Bible.

From my earliest consciousness I saw myself as a son of Syrian Jewry, and hence, in the simplest possible sense, an heir to Jewish tradition and learning as a whole. I believe that enabled me to absorb and project, almost instinctively, the vision of a moral America at its best. The ideals of the Hebrew Prophets, of a world recast through the realization of their grand vision, sustained me throughout the often disheartening course of argument, negotiation, organization, exhortation, and grinding labor of international politics. Despite all appearances, and the lament I have expressed here, I believe it was worthwhile because of the luminous goal in the far distance.

To define that goal, I return to the Hebrew Prophets, whom I see, as much as our Greek and Roman inheritance, as the direct inspiration of the very notion of democracy—which is rooted, after all, in the utterly simple feeling that we are, all of us, children of God. On that basis, I could discuss almost anything with anyone—even with people with whom I might deeply disagree. I could, at the very core of my being, cherish the deep belief that I could project our common humanity into the vision of a regenerated world. The primary test of this deep conviction was the Soviet Union, a deeply flawed society, in the view of freedom-loving people. Yet even the Soviet Union started out as a vision—a vision soon corroded by reality.

Hence, in all of our most complicated discussions, with "positions" seemingly calcified beyond compromise, there was always the possibility of a coming together through a belief in common humanity—an unchallengeable ideal. Thus, my own starting-point, properly understood, is merely the view of a world uncorrupted by partisan fervor or ideology. It is a view simple enough to be of value precisely in the era now looming at the end of the twentieth century, with the rapidly increasing formation of multinational conglomerates and the coagulation of vast politico-economic blocs (North America, the European Community, plus the various element states of the ex-Soviet Union, East Asia).

These changes are incalculable. A real effort is needed to recall their momentary reality, since events are moving at such an intensified pace. After a seeming lull in the wake of the Second World War, the next quarter-century witnessed a contest between the Free World and the embattled Soviet bloc. In 1985, at last, the rulers of the Soviet bloc, while clinging to their dominion, changed course, and from then on the world underwent restructuring on the basis of regional changes in which the abstract pliability of the United Nations acquired a new function, beginning with the negotiations terminating the U.S.-Iraq War. The intricate networks of interdependent politico-economic regions and kaleidoscope of international interests cannot be grasped in detail. Only a simple, clear-sighted approach can even begin to cope with these complexities.

I think it fair to say, without immodesty, that my somewhat strange career could legitimately be called a reflection of the upheavals in the modern world.

If I have stressed Israel's survival and expended great effort attempting to define its position among the nations, it is not because of a parochial interpretation of history. After all, the people who gave monotheism to the world also introduced the universality of man and preached the ultimate triumph of good over evil at the end of human history. One of the great ironies of my life is that I have been stigmatized as being pro-Israel, as if any true American could be otherwise.

Instead, I fall back upon the less hallowed grounds of humanism and biological survival, not to mention American national interests, in order to explain my emphasis on Israel. It is all too facile to demonize the German people for their "crime that has no name" when, in truth, no nation—including America—would accept an additional presence of Jews in the face of their imminent annihilation. The decision for the "final solution of the Jewish problem" took place late in 1942 in the Berlin suburb of Wannsee. Even then the combined democracies would not drop a single bomb on the railways leading to Auschwitz or, indeed, sanction any step at all to save groups of Jews—that could be saved—from the crematoria. In truth, through indifference and callousness, the civilized nations acquiesced in the greatest slaughter of a single people in the history of man. It can be argued that this failure of Western humanism remains an inherent element of the Washington Compromise. Its hallmark is not only the lack of moral courage in identifying a vision for the American people, but also a warped judgment on the nature of the threat to civilization.

With few notable exceptions, Jewish leaders also fatally misread the state of play in global politics, underestimating their enemies while overestimating their friends. An ominous repetition of this scenario is currently playing itself out as Israel is surrendering territory to the PLO. As leaders, secular and religious, they, too, share responsibility for the consequences of their behavior.

In any event, Israel's long term survival—like that of many other nations—depends on the ability of the United States to maintain a global balance of power that assures its *own* survival as a genuine, functioning democracy. By no means can this be taken for granted. As an intelligence analyst, I continue to perceive the shape of socio-politico forces in the world threatening the general peace. To offset this threat, the U.S. must develop a forward strategy built on principles and objectives which are comprehensive and clear to friend and foe alike. Such a strategy must constitute the basis for what we actually do if we are to recapture our credibility, the current loss of which makes the world an even more dangerous place than it need be. If enlightened statesmen are to be equal to that challenge, they must also summon the fortitude necessary to resist the seductive embrace of the Washington Compromise.

INDEX

(Page numbers in boldface refer to photographs)

Adelphi University, 12
Affirmative Strategy, 167-178,
    286-287, 293-294
Afghanistan, 301
Agres, Ted, 111
Air Force
Air University, 14, 19
national intelligence estimates,
    20, 25
Aleppo Codex, 2
Allen, Richard V., 60-61, 62, 64,
    70-72, 73-76, **75**, 80-81, 167
Amelko, Nikolai N., 183
American Federation of Labor
    and Congress of Industrial
Organizations (AFL/CIO), 13
American-Israel Public Affairs
    Committee, 48
American Jewish community
    Cold War concepts, 54-57
    experience of Syrian Jews,
    4-7, 9, 10
    Israel and, 16, 45, 94-95
    leadership structure, 47
    participation in U.S. Middle
    East policymaking, 45, 57
    Persian Gulf War and, 50-52
    political representation, 47
    in Reagan Administration
    policymaking, 76
    support for Center for
    International Security,
    109-110
    U.S.-Israeli relations and,
    47-50, 51-52
    See also Jewish culture and
    history
American Retreat, The, 90, 91
Anderson, Jack, 97

Angleton, James, 26
Aoun, Michel, 203
Arafat, Yassir, 52, 197, 255, 305,
    306
Arens, Moshe, 34, 109, **244**, 244,
    246, 248, 250
Arms Control and
    Disarmament Agency, 87-92
Assad, Hafez al-, 142, 197,
    200-202, 203, 208, 209, 211
Atlantic Monthly, 80

Baker, James, 45, 75, **75**, 304
Bakush, Abdel Hamid, 131
Baltimore Sun, 59, 60
Bar-Illan, David, **303**
Batenin, Ghely, 264
Bechtel, Stephen D., Jr., 98
Bechtel Corporation, 81-82,
    98-99
Begin, Menachem, 48, 53, 306
Beichman, Arnold, 221
Beijing Institute for
    International Strategic
    Studies, 148
Belkin, Alexander, **262**
Ben Gurion, David, 306
Beth Joseph Theological
    Seminary, 10, 11
Billiere, Peter de la, 36
Board of National Estimates,
    24, 67
Bonnici, Carmelo Mifsud, 132
Bovin, Alexander E., **244**, 249
Brandt, Willy, 38
Brooklyn College, 10, 11
Brown, George S., 41-45, 57, 59
Brown, Irving, 13
Burns, John F., 68

Bush, George, 24, 25, 52, 65, **66,**
    66-68, 82, 101-102, 124, 152,
    154, 208, 213, 241
    demise of Soviet Union and,
    168-169, 284-289
    Gulf War, 289-290
    Israeli policy, 303-304
    1988 election, 168

Cambodia, 154
Camp David Accords, 33-35,
    34, 48, 305
Carlucci, Frank, 79
Carpenter, Ted Galen, 154
Carter, Jimmy, 33, 34, 35, 60, 61
Cartier, Bruno, 134
Casey, William, 61, 65, 71
Castro, Fidel, 125
Center for International
    Security, 59-60, 92, 93
    support for, 109
Central America
    Soviet threat in, 122-124
    strategic importance, 119-
    121, 122
    See also specific country
Central Intelligence Agency, 44,
    67, 84
    Churba and, 81
    domination of intelligence
    community by, 20-21, 25
    industry relationships, 20-21,
    128
    Kissinger and, 26-27
    Middle East intelligence,
    22-23
    on Soviet capabilities, 22, 25,
    27
Cerny, Howard, 71

Chaldymov, Nikita A., 183, 188,
    262
Chamorro, Violetta, 124
Chancellor, John, 207n
Cherne, Leo, 22
China, 84, 298-299
    as arms supplier to terrorists,
    155
    European highway project,
    145-146
    ISC conferences in Asia and,
    147, 148-153
    ISC position on, 154-156
    perception of Korea in,
    151-152
    perception of Soviet Union
    in, 149-151
    prospects for, 297, 299
    as regional military threat,
    155-156
    relations with Taiwan,
    156-166
    as Soviet deterrent, 153-154
    Soviet Union and, 12, 20
    Tiananmen Square uprising,
    152-156
    U.S. economy and, 155
    U.S. military sales to, 152
    Vietnam conflict and, 12
Chinese Association for
    International Friendly
    Contact, 146
Christian Science Monitor, 59, 60
Churba, Aaron (brother), 7
Churba, Adele (mother), 4, 9
Churba, Albert (brother), 7
Churba, David (brother), 4, 7
Churba, Isaac (brother), 7
Churba, Jack (brother), 7

Churba, Joseph, **132, 158**
  Air Force career, 14, 15, 19, 20
  on American Jewish political interests, 49, 57
  with Arms Control and Disarmament Agency, 87-92
  attempts to defame, 17-18
  AWACS sale to Saudi Arabia and, 81-82
  Congressional campaign, 105-107
  departure from military, 41-43, 44
  early life, 1, 6-10, 15-16
  education, 10-11
  in first Reagan presidential campaign, 60-65
  on future of Russia, 215
  George Brown and, 41-42, 43-44, 57, 59
  on George Bush, 66-68
  on Gorbachev, 288-289
  on Iraq attack on *USS Stark*, 206-207
  Kahane and, 12-13, 15-18
  on Kissinger, 26-27, 29-30, 37-38
  Marcos and, 88-90
  moral philosophy, 309-311
  in National War College, 35-37, 38-39
  opening remarks at ISC Jerusalem conference, 247-248
  on Qaddafi, 128-130
  rebuffed by Reagan Administration, 73-74, 80, 81-82
  relations with U.S. intelligence community, 23-25
  Senate testimony on North Korea, 240-241
  South Africa trip, 65, 68-70
  on Soviet Cold war goals, 54-55
  on U.S. involvement in Lebanon, 95-96, 98-101, 102-103
  during Vietnam conflict, 12-15
  writing career, 59, 91
  Yom Kippur War and, 30, 32, 34, 35
Churba, Moe (brother), **7**
Churba, Rachel (sister), **4**
Churba, Rahamim (father), 1, **2**, 3, 5, 6-10, 7
Churba, Sam (brother), **4, 7**
Clinton Administration, 45, 125, 182
  China policy, 156
  Israeli policy, 252
  North Korean policy, 241-242
  strategic defense policy, 264-265
Cohn, Roy, 106
Colby, William, 27
Columbia University, 11-12
Communist expansionism
  in current Central America, 125
  development of U.S. policy, 298-299
  goals of, 54-55
  ISC counter strategy, 173-177
  opposition of Sun Myung Moon to, 111

role of Israel in demise of, 55
Vietnam conflict and, 12, 13
Conference of Presidents of
Major American Jewish
Organizations, 47
Congressional campaign of
Joseph Churba, 105-107
Connally, John, 65
Cooper, Henry, **260**
Crist, George B., 183
Crocker, Chester, 70
Crowe, William, 181-182
Cuba, 118, 121, 125-126, 298
Current geopolitical challenges,
309-310, 311-313

Davison, Michael S., 119, 122,
183
Dayan, Moshe, 19, 20, 307
Deaver, Michael, **75**, 75
Defense Intelligence Agency,
20, 38, 193
Democratic government
Affirmative Strategy for
global expansion of, 174-177
in Israel, 16-17
long term focus in, 177-178
in Russia, 276-280, 281,
290-291
Desert Storm, 36, 50
Duberstein, Waldo, 38, 127
Dugan, Michael J., 112, **119**, 261
Dukakis, Michael, 168, 287

Eagleburger, Lawrence, 52, 91
Egypt, 254, 304
Camp David Accords, 33-35,
48, 305-306

Soviet policy, 27, 29, 30
as U.S. ally, 253
Yom Kippur War, 30-33
El Salvador, 121
Energy crisis, 20-21
Esposito, Mead, 106
Evans, Rowland, 79

FBI, 81
Federal Bureau of
Investigation, 24
Focus on Libya, 129, 130
Ford, Gerald, 22, 41, 66, **66**
France, 297, 299
Fuller, Graham, 220-221

Gaffney, Frank, Jr., 214,
215-216, 261-262
Galluci, Robert, 241
Gemayel, Bashir, 99
Germany, 38, 296-297, 298,
299-300
Global Affairs, 168, 287
Goodpaster, Andrew, **173**
Gorbachev, Mikhail, 168-169,
179-180, 190, 192-193, 194-
195, 215, 231, 244, 283-284,
287-288
Goure, Leon, 112, 214, 216-217,
262
Graham, Daniel, 61, 62
Graham, William, 261
Gray, Alfred M., 112, **265**
Gray, Robert, 87
Great Britain, 198
Gregor, A. James, 112, 146, 151,
229-230
Gwertzman, Bernard, 41

Habib, Philip, 96
Hahn, Walter, 112
Haig, Alexander, 91, 96, 97
Heflin, Woodford, 14-15
Homayoun, Assad, 220
Hoskinson, Samuel M., 98
Hurewitz, J. C., 19
Hussein, Saddam, 36, 201, 203, 222, 289, 305. *See also* Iraq; Persian Gulf War

Ickle, Fred, 62
Information, Inc., 13
Intelligence community
    Churba responsibilities in, 20
    cooperation with Israel in Reagan Administration, 83
    politicization of, 25-27
    relations with Churba, 23-25
    shortcomings of, 21-22, 25-26
International Security Council, 310
    advisors, 111-112
    Affirmative Strategy, 167-178, 286-287, 293-294
    analysis of China, 154-156
    Asian conferences, 147-153
    Caribbean/Central American analyses, 118-121, 122-124, 126
    China-Taiwan meetings, 156, 159, 162
    conference on Brezhnev Doctrine, 190-191
    conference on Soviet minorities, 193-194
    conferences on Gorbachev government, 192-193
    conferences with Russian leaders in Washington, 259-281
    conferences with Soviet military leadership, 180-190
    on Eurasian balance of power, 296-300
    founding of, 110
    geopolitical perspective, 294-296
    Gulf War analyses, 213-218, 219-222
    intellectual style, 294
    Libya and, 130, 137-142
    mission, 112-116
    in North Korea, 224, 226-240
    on occupied territories in Israel, 251-252
    post-Cold War mission, 290-291
    Russian-Israeli military conference, 243-250
    Syrian conference, 200-203, 204-205, 209-210
    Unification Church and, 110, 111
Iran, 84, 206, 222-223, 301
    U.S. relations, 207, 254-255
Iraq, 50-51, 84, 197, 289, 298, 305
    attack on *USS Stark*, 206-207
    missile attacks on Israel, 210-211
    prospects for, 222
    Russia and, 215-216
    United States policy, 205-206, 207
ISC. *See* International Security Council

Islamic fundamentalism, 220, 254, 300
Israel, 9
  advantages of, as U.S. ally, 63-64, 95, 252, 305
  American Jews and, 16, 47-50, 57
  bias against, in U.S. military, 43-45
  bias against, in U.S. policy-making, 45
  Camp David Accords, 33-35, 48, 305-306
  Carter Administration policy, 60
  Cold War conceptualizations, 54-57
  current challenges for, 312-313
  democratic government in, 16-17
  ISC Russian-Israeli military conference, 243-250
  Kissinger policy, 29-30, 37
  Labor Party, 306-307
  Lebanon and, 95-102, 104
  Likud Party, 48
  missile attacks on, 210-211
  occupied territories, 251-252, 302-304
  "peace agreement" with PLO, 305-307
  Persian Gulf War and, 50-51, 210-211
  prospects for peace, 52-54, 220-222, 255-257, 304
  Reagan Administration policy, 63-65, 79, 82-84
  significance of, 312
  Syria and, 199, 202, 209-210, 211
  U.S. policy, 35
  weapons technology, 104-105
  Weinberger policy, 79, 82-84
  Yom Kippur War, 30-33
Italy, 132

Jalloud, Abdessalaam, 130
Japan, 152, 156, 297
  North Korea and, 232
Jewish culture and history, 1-6, 9-10, 11
  democratic tradition and, 16-17, 310
  modern application, 310-311
  See also American Jewish community
Jewish Defense League, 16, 17
Jewish Stake in Vietnam, The, 13
Jibril, Ahmed, 208
Jordan, 51, 253, 304
Jordan, David G., 112
July 4th Movement, 12-13

Kahane, Meir, 12-13, 15-18, 53, 81
Kaluain, Igor, 261
Kedouri, Elie, 19, 32, 220
Keegan, George J., 20, 21, 23, 24, 25, 26-27, 30, 34, 38, 42, 60, 67, 183, 214
Kelly, John, 202
Kelly, Paul X., 36, 183
Kemp, Geoffrey, 204
Kemp, Jack, 65
Kim Byong Hong, 237
Kim Yong Chol, 231
Kim Yong Nam, 231, 232-233

Kintner, William R., 112
Kissinger, Henry, 31, 61, 62, 66
  capacity for leadership, 37-38
  conceptual basis of policy, 37
  detente policy, 25, 26, 37
  politicization of intelligence
    estimates, 25, 26-26
  relations with intelligence
    community, 26-27
  on Soviet role in Middle
    East, 27, 29
  Yom Kippur War, 30, 33
Kobets, Konstantin I., 262
Kolesnikov, Mikhail, 261
Kondracke, Morton, 62, 168,
  287
Kontinent magazine, 180
Kroesen, Fritz, 214, 215
Kulikov, V. G., 183
Kurtzer, Daniel, 45

Lebanon, 95-105, 197, 305
  Syria and, 203
Lehman, John, 120
Lehman, Joseph, 91
Lerner, Max, 168
Levitt, William J., 34
Lewis, Bernard, 19, 32
Li Son Yon Sok, 230, 236
Libya, 38-39, 298
  current challenges for,
    142-143
  International Security
    Council discussions, 137-142
  plot against Qaddafi, 127-128
  See also Qadaffi, Muammar el-
Licari, Joseph, 130, 137
Lichtenstein, Charles, 132, 204,
  214, 265

Lin Yu-Sian, 158
Lincoln, Abraham, 293
Lord, Winston, 148-149
Lovestone, Jay, 13
Luns, Joseph, 112, 173

Mackinder, Halford, 294-295,
  296
MacNeil-Lehrer Report, 95, 96
Maduff, Sidney, 59, 76
Maimonides, 2, 9
Makdisi, Antoine, 201
Malek, Habib, 202
Malek, Habib, 218, 219
Malta, 130-137, 310
Marcos, Ferdinand, 88-90
Marcos, Imelda, 88
Marxist thought, 11
Maximov, Vladimir, 180
Mazzocco, William J., 15, 112,
  200
Meese, Ed, 65
Meir, Golda, 30
Merglen, Albert, 200
Metzler, John J., 131
Mexico, 120, 121, 122, 125
Middle East
  American misperceptions in,
    250-255
  Arabist orientation of U.S.
    policy, 43-45, 93-95, 98-99,
    206, 211
  failures of Reagan
    Administration, 284
  on fault line of global insta-
    bility, 222
  flaws of U.S. policy, 23-254
  Kissinger policy, 29-30

North Korean arms sales,
222-223
prospects for peace in, 51-54,
220-222, 300-308
Reagan policy, 62-65, 102-105
Soviet Union action and pol-
icy in, 22-23, 27, 29
United States policy, 205-207,
211, 213
U.S. intelligence estimates,
22-23
U.S. policymaking, 45
Weinberger policy, 82-84
Yom Kippur War, 30-33
See also specific countries
Mifsud, Paul C., 134
Miller, Aaron, 45
Milshtein, Mikhail A., 183-184
Moon, Sun Myung, 110-112,
145, 180, 190
Moore, John Norton, 112
Moral order, 308-309
Morgenthau, Hans, 19
Morton, Robert, 180
Mother Jones magazine, 70-71
Muallim, Walid, 203

Nance, James, 221, 236
Nasser, Abdel, 304
National intelligence estimates,
20, 128
on Middle East, 22-23
politicization of, 26
process, 24
shortcomings in production
of, 21-22, 25-26
National Security Agency, 20,
24

National Security Council,
73-75
National War College, 35-37,
38-39
NATO. See North Atlantic
Treaty Organization
New York Times, The, 41-43, 60,
68, 69, 70, 104, 124, 127,
189, 193, 205-206, 241
Nicaragua, 117, 121
current state, 124-125
European perception, 118
Nixon, Richard, 71, 298
North Atlantic Treaty
Organization (NATO), 38
American hemispheric
interests and, 118-119
North Korea, 202, 209, 298, 299
Bush administration policy,
241
China and, 151-152, 156
domestic challenges, 224-226,
231-232
intransigence of, 226-227
ISC conferences, 224, 226-240
MIA issue, 234-236
Middle East arms sales,
222-223
military strength, 233-234
nuclear program, 232-233,
236-239, 241-242
reunification proposals from,
227, 230-231
Russia and, 229-230, 232
United States policy, 228-230
Novak, Robert, 79

Ogarkov, N. V., 183
Ogarkov, Nikolai, 105

Oil industry, 20-21, 128
OPEC, 85
Organization for American
   States, 123

Pak, Bo Hi, 111, 146
Palestine Liberation
   Organization, 96, 99, 100,
   101-102, 197, 220, 255-256,
   305, 306
Palestinian state, 51, 304
Panama, 120, 121
Peled, Benny, 30, **245**
Perle, Richard N., 160
Persian Gulf War, 35, 36,
   289-290
   ISC analyses, 213-218,
   219-222
   Israel and, 50-51, 210-211
   outcomes, 213, 218-222
   policies of Arab states in, 253
   Saudi Arabia in, 301
   Soviet Union and, 214-218
   Syria and, 201-202, 203-204,
   207-210, 218
   United States' goals, 216-217
Petroleum Institute, 21
Pfalzgraff, Robert, 65
Philadelphia Daily News, The,
   129
Philippines, 88-90, 297
Pipes, Richard, 19, 61, 64, 75,
   290
Politics of Defeat, The, 49, 59, 63,
   91
Polmar, Norman, **119**
Powell, Colin, 36
Powell, Jody, 71

President's Foreign Intelligence
   Review Board, 22

Qadaffi, Muammar el-, 127
   Churba campaign against,
   128-129
   Malta and, 130-137

Rabbis of Aleppo, 1, 10
Rabin, Yitzhak, 45, 255, **303**
Rafsanjani, Hojatoleslam Ali
   Akbar Hashemi, 254-255
Reagan Administration, 55, 56,
   66, 75
   accomplishments and fail-
   ures of, 167, 283-284
   Central American policy, 117
   fall of Soviet Union and,
   84-85
   first presidential campaign,
   60-65, 68-72
   George Bush and, 65-68, 82
   Iran-Contra affair, 206
   Israeli policy, 79, 96-97,
   302-303
   Lebanon policy, 96, 98,
   99-102
   Middle East policy, 82-84,
   102-105
   personal qualities of presi-
   dent, 65
   Van Cleave and, 77-81
Retreat from Freedom, 91
Rimlands, 294-295
Rodionov, Igor N., **245**
Rosefielde, Steven, 267-268
Ross, Dennis, 45
Rostow, Eugene, 87-88, 95, 150,
   214-215

Rumsfeld, Donald, 183
Russia, 215, 216-218
    economic reforms, 265-270
    future prospects, 280-281
    ISC Russian-Israeli military
        conference, 243-250
    ISC Washington conferences,
        259-281
    military budget, 272-275, 277
    military issues in economic
        reforms, 269-276
    in new Eurasian balance of
        power, 296-297, 299, 300
    North Korea and, 229-230,
        232
    nuclear policy, 259-265
    prospects for democracy in,
        290-291
    prospects for military rule in,
        276-280
    See also Soviet Union

Saburov, Yevgeny, 267
Sadat, Anwar, 31
Salinas de Gortari, 125
SALT agreements, 25, 67
Samoilov, Viktor L., 250, 261,
    262, 267
Saudi Arabia, 31, 78, 84, 202,
    906
    AWACS sale in Reagan
        Administration, 81-82
    boycott of Israel, 307
    future of, 301-302
    as U.S. ally, 253, 301
Savelyev, Alexander, 262-263
Schumer, Charles, 107
Schwarzkopf, H. Norman, 36
Seale, Patrick, 200

Shaked, Haim, 204
Shamir, Yitzhak, 52, 199, 201,
    303
Shara'a, Farouk, 203
Shkanakin, Vladimir, 245
Shlykov, Vitaly, 78, 250, 265,
    267, 269, 270, 272-274, 276,
    278-280, 281
Shoval, Zalman, 211
Shultz, George, 77, 88, 96-99,
    199
Sisco, Joseph, 303
Smith, William French, 75
Sola, Richard, 134
Solarz, Stephen, 105-106, 107
Somalia, 305
Song Ho Gyong, 227, 239
South Africa, 65, 68-70
South Korea, 297
Soviet Breakout, 288
Soviet Union
    American Jewish conceptual-
        izations of Cold War, 54-57
    Backfire Bomber, 25, 67
    Central American opera-
        tions, 117
    Chinese perspective, 149-151
    Cold War intentions and
        strategies, 19-20, 54-55
    demise of, 179-180, 311
    glasnost and perestroika, 170,
        172, 179
    Gulf War and, 214-215
    ISC Affirmative Strategy,
        169-174
    ISC conference on Brezhnev
        Doctrine, 190-191
    ISC conference on Soviet
        minorities, 193-194

ISC conference with military leaders of, 180-190
ISC conferences on Gorbachev government, 192-193
ISC policy, 112-116
Israeli policy, 56-57
Kissinger policy, 37
Malta and, 130-131, 132-134
Middle East action and strategy, 22-23, 27, 29, 31, 60
operations in Central America, 122-124
Reagan policy, 61
relations with Syria, 197-198
strategic concepts in, 113-115
U.S. intelligence assessments, 22, 24-27
U.S.-Israeli relationship and, 252
U.S. response to collapse of, 68, 168-169, 283-289
Vietnam conflict and, 12
in Yom Kippur war, 31
See also Russia
Stark, USS, 206-207
Starodubov, Viktor P., 183
State, U.S. Department of, 23, 81
Churba's Philippines visit and, 89-90
Reagan Administration, 76-77
Stillwell, Richard G., 224, 228, 231-232, 233-234, 235, 236, 239-240
Stoesel, Walter, 91
Strategic Defense Initiative, 84, 151, 242, 244

Strausz-Hupe, Robert, 141
Sudan, 305
Sulakshin, Stepan S., **262**, 276-277
Syria, 51, 56, 84, 98, 223, 253, 298, 305
in drug trade, 199
Gulf War and, 21, 201-202, 203-205, 207-210
in international terrorism, 198, 208
ISC conference, 200-203, 204-205, 209-210
Israel and, 199, 202, 209-210, 211
Jewish life in, 1-3
Lebanon and, 95-96
in Middle East political landscape, 197
Soviet Union and, 31, 197-198
United States and, 198-199, 203-205, 207-210

Taiwan, 156-166
Tel Aviv University, 19
Terrorism, 18
Thatcher, Margaret, 287
Thompson, D. A., 60
Time magazine, 98
Tlass, Mustafa, 200
Train, Harry D., II, 183, 214
Truman, Harry S, 298
Turkey, 220, 254

Unification Church, 110, 111

Van Cleave, William, 61, 62, 65, 77-81, **78**, 87, 112, 189-190, 229, 237-238, 244, 261, 270-271, 277
Vatikiotis, P. J., 19, 32, 219
Vesco, Robert, 71
Vietnam conflict
    Chinese view, 150
    implications of, for Middle East, 12, 13
    outcomes, 12, 15
Vuono, Carl E., 112

Warhaftig, Mr., 34-35
Washington Post, The, 63, 71, 92, 97
, 251, 252
Weinberger, Caspar, 72, **77**, 78-80, 82-84, 95, 96
Winnipeg, University of, 12, 14
Wood, Lowell, 261, 263-264

Xu Yimin, 149

Yaremenko, Yuri, 267, 270, 271-272
Yariv, Aharon, 32
Yeltsin, Boris, 266, 271, 273, 274, 279, 281
Yom Kippur War, 30-33, 34, 35, 43, 48
Yosef, Ovadia, 1

Zhao Fusan, **158**
Zhi-yuan Ding, 146
Zumwalt, E. R., Jr., 60, 112, **182**, 183